Educational and Vocational Guidance and Counselling

Educational and Vocational Guidance and Counselling

Navendu Pratap

RANDOM PUBLICATIONS
NEW DELHI (INDIA)

Educational and Vocational Guidance and Counselling

ISBN 978-93-5111-437-6

Published in 2014 in India by
RANDOM PUBLICATIONS
4376-A/4B, Gali Murari Lal, Ansari Road
New Delhi-110 002
Phone : +91-11-43580356, +91-11-23289044
e-mail: randomexports@gmail.com, sales@randompublications.com, info@randompublications.com
Reprint 2021

Type Setting by: Friends Media, Delhi-110089
Printed at : Replika Press Pvt. Ltd.

Preface

Some ministries of education are in the process of major educational reform because the emergence of a more 'learning-intensive' economy poses new challenges. Employment is becoming increasingly fluid, work is increasingly complex, occupational boundaries are changing or dissolving, and more jobs are temporary. For these reasons, continual learning is a more important part of work. Students who prematurely discontinue their studies represent a major potential loss to themselves, the economy and the society. In some countries there is considerable pressure on students to quit school and help with the farm-work or otherwise bring supplemental income into their parents' household. Recently some countries have become increasingly active in attempting to lessen the number of dropouts - and this is quite feasible because dropping out is seldom done without prior notice on the part of the student's behaviour. A number of mechanisms have been put in place: guidance curriculum; diagnostic surveys intended to help identify students likely to drop out so that remedial steps may be taken; remedial programmes for students falling behind in their studies; teaching of study skills; the implementation of peer helping programmes to make use of positive peer pressure and to combat negative peer pressure; combined work and study programmes; and changes in school management practices to give students the same rights of grievance and appeal that is common in the workplace. Guidance counsellors are often at the heart of these programmes.

The articulation of school-based learning and work-based learning follows significantly different patterns from country to country. In some jurisdictions there is an almost seamless transition from the school to apprenticeship programmes. In other jurisdictions there is a complete separation between school and work. The role of guidance varies significantly according to the system. In the former it is the task of counsellors to assist students to select the appropriate types of work-based training programme and to prepare them for entry. In jurisdictions without this articulation, the school guidance programme has often been more geared to preparing the most academically inclined students for university than to help students who will go immediately into the labour force. Frequently in cultures that separate secondary education and apprenticeship programmes parents want their children to go to university and not to prepare for the trades even though the children have indicated a preference for a trade. Counsellors have a particular responsibility to explain to parents the many favourable aspects of a career in the trades. Increasingly in jurisdictions that do not articulate school and work-based learning, schools integrate work experience assignments as an integral part of the curriculum and seek the co-operation of local employers, unions and professional associations. According to Stasz (1998) "the power of the work based learning is that authentic work experiences give learners opportunities to apply knowledge in useful contexts. They thereby can gain a deeper understanding of both their abilities and the opportunities they can create for themselves through experience and/or education. In the end, learning is a personal, developmental transformation, so it is crucial to pay attention to whether that transformation occurs, as well as to the context that will enable such a transformation. It is this context that teachers and counsellors, in and out of school, have the most ability to shape".

This book has been designed as an introductory text which undertakes a through exploration the concepts and practices which define the subject. The book will prove very useful for students and teachers.

I thank all members of my team who have helped in the preparation of the book. My special thanks go to "Random Publications" who have published the book.

—Navendu Pratap

Contents

1

Introduction

Counselling Psychology

Counselling psychology is a psychological speciality that encompasses research and applied work in several broad domains: counselling process and outcome; supervision and training; career development and counselling; and prevention and health. Some unifying themes among counselling psychologists include a focus on assets and strengths, person–environment interactions, educational and career development, brief interactions, and a focus on intact personalities. In the United States, the premier scholarly journals of the profession are the *Journal of Counselling Psychology* and *The Counselling Psychologist*.

In Europe, the scholarly journals of the profession include the *European Journal of Counselling Psychology* (under the auspices of the European Association of Counselling Psychology) and the *Counselling Psychology Review* (under the auspices of the British Psychological Society). *Counselling Psychology Quarterly* is an international interdisciplinary publication of Routledge (part of the Taylor & Francis Group).

In the U.S., counselling psychology programmes are accredited by the American Psychological Association (APA), while counselling programmes are accredited through the Counsel for Accreditation of Counselling and Related Educational Programmes (CACREP). To become licensed as a counselling psychologist, one must meet the criteria for licensure as a psychologist (4-7 year doctoral degree post-bachelors, 1 year full-time internship, including 3,000 hours of supervised experience and exams). Both doctoral level counselling psychologists and doctoral level counsellors can perform both applied work, as well as research and teaching.

History

Counselling psychology, like many modern psychology specialities, started as a result of World War II. During the war, the U.S. military had a strong need for vocational placement and training. In the 1940s and 1950s the Veterans Administration created a speciality called "counselling psychology," and Division 17 (now known as the Society for Counselling Psychology) of the APA was formed. This fostered interest in counsellor training, and the creation of the first few counselling psychology PhD programmes. The first counselling psychology PhD programmes were at the University of Minnesota; Ohio State University, University of Maryland, College Park; University of Missouri; Teachers College, Columbia University; and University of Texas at Austin.

Employment and Salary

Counselling psychologists are employed in a variety of settings depending on the services they provide and the client populations they serve. Some are employed in colleges and universities as teachers, supervisors, researchers, and service providers. Others are employed in independent practice providing counselling, psychotherapy; assessment; and consultation services to individuals, couples/families, groups, and organizations. Additional settings in which counselling psychologists practice include community mental health centres, Veterans Administration Medical Centres and other facilities, family services, health maintenance organizations, rehabilitation agencies, business and industrial organizations and consulting within firms.

Median salary for US counselling psychologists is US$64,000

Process and Outcome

Counselling psychologists are interested in answering a variety of research questions about the counselling process and outcome. Counselling process might be thought of as how or why counselling happens and progresses. Counselling outcome addresses whether or not counselling is effective, under what conditions it is effective, and what outcomes are considered effective—such as symptom reduction, behaviour change, or quality of life improvement. Topics commonly explored in the study of counselling process and outcome include therapist variables, client variables, the counselling or therapeutic relationship, cultural variables, process and outcome measurement, mechanisms of change, and process and outcome research methods.

Therapist Variables

Therapist variables include characteristics of a counsellor or psychotherapist, as well as therapist technique, behaviour, theoretical orientation and training. In terms of therapist behaviour, technique and theoretical orientation, research on adherence to therapy models has found that adherence to a particular model of therapy can be helpful, detrimental, or neutral in terms of impact on outcome (Imel & Wampold, 2008).

Research on the impact of training and experience is still somewhat contradictory and even counter-intuitive. For example, a recent study found that age-related training and experience, but not amount or quality of contact with older people, is related to older clients. However, a recent meta-analysis of research on training and experience suggests that experience level is only slightly related to accuracy in clinical judgement. Higher therapist experience has been found to be related to less anxiety, but also less focus. This suggests that there is still work to be done in terms of training clinicians and measuring successful training.

Client Variables

Client characteristics such as help-seeking attitudes and attachment style have been found to be related to client use of counselling, as well as expectations and outcome. Stigma against mental illness can keep people from acknowledging problems and seeking help. Public stigma has been found to be related to self-stigma, attitudes towards counselling, and willingness to seek help.

In terms of attachment style, clients with avoidant styles have been found to perceive greater risks and fewer benefits to counselling, and are less likely to seek professional help, than securely attached clients. Those with anxious attachment styles perceive greater benefits as well as risks to counselling. Educating clients about expectations of counselling can improve client satisfaction, treatment duration and outcomes, and is an efficient and cost-effective intervention.

Counselling Relationship

The relationship between a counsellor and client is the feelings and attitudes that a client and therapist have towards one another, and the manner in which those feelings and attitudes are expressed. The relationship may be thought of in three parts: transference/ countertransference, working alliance, and the real- or personal-relationship.

Transference can be described as the client's distorted perceptions of the therapist. This can have a great affect on the therapeutic relationship. For instance, the therapist may have a facial feature that reminds the client of their parent. Because of this association, if the client has significant negative/positive feelings toward their parent, they may project these feelings onto the therapist. This can affect the therapeutic relationship in a few ways. For example, if the client has a very strong bond with their parent, they may see the therapist as a father/mother figure and have a strong connection with their therapist.

This can be problematic because as a therapist, it is not ethical to have a more than "professional" relationship with a client. It can also be a good thing, because the client may open up greatly to the therapist. In another way, if the client has a very negative relationship with their parent, the client may feel negative feelings toward the therapist. This can then affect the therapeutic relationship as well. For example, the client may have trouble opening up to the therapist because he/she lacks trust in their parent (projecting these feelings of distrust onto the therapist).

Another theory about the function of the counselling relationship is known as the secure-base hypothesis, which is related to attachment theory. This hypothesis proposes that the counsellor acts as a secure-base from which clients can explore and then check in with. Secure attachment to one's counsellor and secure attachment in general have been found to be related to client exploration. Insecure attachment styles have been found to be related to less session depth than securely attached clients.

Cultural Variables

Counselling psychologists are interested in how culture relates to help-seeking and counselling process and outcome. Helms' racial identity model can be useful for understanding how the relationship and counselling process might be affected by the client's and counsellor's racial identity. Recent research suggests that clients who are Black are at risk for experiencing racial micro-aggressions from counsellors who are White.

Efficacy for working with clients who are lesbians, gay men, or bisexual might be related to therapist demographics, gender, sexual identity development, sexual orientation, and professional experience. Clients who have multiple oppressed identities might be especially at-risk for experiencing unhelpful situations with counsellors, so counsellors might need help with gaining expertise for working with clients who are transgender, lesbian, gay, bisexual, or transgender people of colour, and other oppressed populations.

Gender role socialization can also present issues for clients and counsellors. Implications for practice include being aware of stereotypes and biases about male and female identity, roles and behaviour such as emotional expression. The APA guidelines for multicultural competence outline expectations for taking culture into account in practice and research.

Counselling Ethics

Perceptions on ethical behaviours vary depending upon geographical location. Although, ethical mandates are similar throughout our global community. The standard ethical behaviours are centred on "doing no harm" and preventing harm. As counsellors, it is standard that a counsellor should take appropriate action to prevent harm.

Ethical standards are similar in that you should shall not share information that is obtained through the counselling process without specific written consent by the client or legal guardian except to prevent clear, imminent danger to the client or others or when required to do so by a court order.

Counsellors are held to a higher standard that most professionals because of the intimacy of their therapeutic delivery. Counsellors are not only to avoid fraternizing with their clients. They should avoid dual relationships, and never engage in sexual relationships.

Counsellors are to avoid receiving gifts, favours, or trade for therapy. In some communities, it may be avoidable given the economic standing of that community. In cases of children, children and the mentally handicap may feel personally rejected "if" an offering is something such as a "cookie." As counsellors, a judgement call must be made, but in a majority of cases, avoiding gifts, favours, and trade can be maintained. The National Board for Certified Counsellors states that "...important considerations to avoid exploitation before entering into a non-counselling relationship with a former client.

Important considerations to be discussed include amount of time since counselling service termination, duration of counselling, nature and circumstances of client's counselling, the likelihood that the client will want to resume counselling at some time in the future; circumstances of service termination and possible negative effects or outcomes."

Ethical standards are created to help practitioners, clients and the community avoid any possible harm or potential for harm. Ethical standards are a guideline, but for specific standards they are mandates. Recognizing the differences is clear in a majority of organizational codes of ethics.

Outcome Measurement

Counselling outcome measures might look at a general overview of symptoms, symptoms of specific disorders, or positive outcomes, such as subjective well-being or quality of life. The Outcome Questionnaire-45 is a 45-item self-report measure of psychological distress. An example of disorder-specific measure is the Beck Depression Inventory. The Quality of Life Inventory is a 17-item self-report life satisfaction measure.

Process and outcome research methods

Research about the counselling process and outcome uses a variety of research methodologies to answer questions about if, how, and why counselling works. Quantitative methods include randomly controlled clinical trials, correlational studies over the course of counselling, or laboratory studies about specific counselling process and outcome variables. Qualitative research methods can involve conducting, transcribing and coding interviews; transcribing and/or coding therapy sessions; or fine-grain analysis of single counselling sessions or counselling cases.

Training and Supervision

Professional Training Process: Counselling psychologists are trained in graduate programmes. Almost all programmes grant a PhD, but a few grant a MCouns, M.Ed, MA, PsyD or EdD. Most doctoral programmes take 5–6 years to complete. Graduate work in counselling psychology includes coursework in general psychology and statistics, counselling practice, and research. Students must complete an original dissertation at the end of their graduate training. Students must also complete a one-year full-time internship at an accredited site before earning their doctorate. In order to be licensed to practice, counselling psychologists must gain clinical experience under supervision, and pass a standardized exam.

Training Models and Research

Counselling psychology includes the study and practice of counsellor training and counsellor supervision. As researchers, counselling psychologists may investigate what makes training and supervision effective. As practitioners, counselling psychologists may supervise and train a variety of clinicians. Counsellor training tends to occur in formal classes and training programmes. Part of counsellor training may involve counselling clients under the supervision of a licensed clinician. Supervision can also occur between licensed clinicians, as a way to improve clinicians' quality of work and competence with various types of counselling clients.

As the field of counselling psychology formed in the mid-20th century, initial training models included Human Relations Training by Carkuff, Interpersonal Process Recall by Kagan, and Microcounselling Skills by Ivey. Modern training models include Egan's Skilled Helper model, and Hill's three stage (exploration, insight, and action) model. A recent analysis of studies on counsellor training found that modelling, instruction, and feedback are common to most training models, and seem to have medium to large effects on trainees.

Supervision Models and Research

Like the models of how clients and therapists interact, there are also models of the interactions between therapists and their supervisors. Bordin proposed a model of supervision working alliance similar to his model of therapeutic working alliance. The Integrated Development Model considers the level of a supervisee's motivation/anxiety, autonomy, and self and other awareness. The Systems Approach to Supervision views the relationship between supervisor and supervisee as most important, in addition to characteristics of the supervisee's personal characteristics, counselling clients, training setting, as well as the tasks and functions of supervision. The Critical Events in Supervision model focuses on important moments that occur between the supervisor and supervisee.

Problems can arise in supervision and training. First, supervisors are liable for malpractice of their supervisee. Also, questions have arisen as far as a supervisor's need for formal training to be a competent supervisor. Recent research suggests that conflicting, multiple relationships can occur between supervisors and supervisees, such as that of evaluator, instructor, and clinical supervisor. The occurrence of racial micro-aggressions against Black supervisees suggests potential problems with racial bias in supervision. In general, conflicts between a counsellor and his or her supervisor can arise when supervisors demonstrate disrespect, lack of support, and blaming (Ladany & Inman, 2008).

Vocational Development and Career Counselling

Vocational Theories: There are several types of theories of vocational choice and development. These types include trait and factor theories, social cognitive theories, and developmental theories. Two examples of trait and factor theories, also known as person–environment fit, are Holland's Theory and Theory of Work Adjustment. Holland hypothesized six vocational personality/interest types and six work environment types: realistic, investigative, artistic, social, enterprising, and conventional. When a person's vocational interests match his or her work environment types, this is considered congruence. Congruence has been found to predict occupation and college major. The Theory of Work Adjustment (TWA), as developed by Dawis and Lofquist, hypothesizes that the correspondence between a worker's needs and the reinforcer systems predicts job satisfaction, and that the correspondence between a worker's skills and a job's skill requirements predicts job satisfactoriness. Job satisfaction and satisfactoriness together should determine how long one remains at a job. When there is a discrepancy between a worker's needs or skills and the job's needs or skills, then change needs to occur either in the worker or the job environment.

Social Cognitive Career Theory (SCCT) has been proposed by Lent, Brown and Hackett. The theory takes Albert Bandura's work on self-efficacy and expands it to interest development, choice making, and performance. Person variables in SCCT include self-efficacy beliefs, outcome expectations and personal goals. The model also includes demographics, ability, values, and environment. Efficacy and outcome expectations are theorized to interrelate and influence interest development, which in turn influences choice of goals, and then actions. Environmental supports and barriers also affect goals and actions. Actions lead to performance and choice stability over time.

Career development theories propose vocational models that include changes throughout the lifespan. Super's model proposes a lifelong five-stage career development process. The stages are growth, exploration, establishment, maintenance, and disengagement. Throughout life, people have many roles that may differ in terms of importance and meaning. Super also theorized that career development is an implementation of self-concept. Gottfredson also proposed a cognitive career decision-making process that develops through the lifespan. The initial stage of career development is hypothesized to be the development of self-image in childhood, as the range of possible roles narrows using criteria such as sex-type, social class, and prestige. During and after adolescence, people take abstract concepts into consideration, such as interests.

Career Counselling

Career counselling may include provision of occupational information, modelling skills, written exercises, and exploration of career goals and plans. Career counselling can also involve the use of personality or career interest assessments, such as the Myers-Briggs Type Indicator, which is based on Carl Jung's theory of psychological type, or the Strong Interest Inventory, which makes use of Holland's theory. Assessments of skills, abilities, and values are also commonly assessed in career counselling.

What Does a Guidance Counsellor do?

A guidance counsellor works in a school setting to help students better prepare for continuing education, or to help facilitate decisions made about future careers. The requirements for becoming a guidance counsellor varies among schools. Guidance counsellors tend to have at least a Bachelor of Arts (B.A.) in psychology, but may also have a B.A. in career counselling. Some places require high school counsellors to have a master's degree as well, and many schools require the counsellor to be licensed. In the college setting, counsellors may not have a B.A., but may be experts in their teaching area. Sometimes the guidance counsellor at the college level is called an academic advisor.

In the elementary setting, guidance counsellors are frequently catchall counsellors who help to facilitate testing for learning disabilities and may also manage Individualized Education Plans (IEPs) for students in need of them. They tend not to offer psychological assistance, but may participate in observation of students in classroom settings or in psychological or intelligence testing. Children in need of significant counselling for psychological issues usually meet with a school psychologist instead of a guidance counsellor, although in some schools, funding issues can mean that access to a psychologist may be significantly limited. Usually, a guidance counsellor in an elementary school is simply called a counsellor. Regardless of title, these employees can be an excellent resource for children and parents. If a parent is concerned about a child's learning abilities, contacting the elementary counsellor is a good first step. The counsellor may be particularly helpful if the administration of the school does not take the parent's concerns seriously.

In the middle school setting, the guidance counsellor may still participate in some educational testing for students deemed "at academic risk." The guidance counsellor usually also helps students make decisions regarding choices in electives and whether they are challenged enough or too much by their present classes. When courses are too hard or too easy, the guidance counsellor may be able to help the student change his or her schedule.

While the guidance counsellor at one time was an everyday presence on the junior high or middle school campus, funding cutbacks have forced many counsellors to work at more than one school on a part-time basis. The difficult years of beginning adolescence can be significantly aided by having a friendly guidance counsellor. Counsellors may meet with students with emotional problems regularly, simply to check in with them and see if assistance can be offered, although this role is often performed by a school psychologist, if one is available.

In high school, emphasis for the guidance counsellor is on helping students make decisions about their future careers or college plans. A guidance counsellor helps a student make out a plan of study that will best fit his or her plans after high school. For example, a student who wants to attend a university will likely be directed to take courses that will help achieve this end and make the student eligible for attendance. The high school guidance counsellor may give information about financial aid options for those who wish to attend trade schools or college after graduation. He or she can also help those students who are struggling and are at risk for failing to graduate.

While working with a guidance counsellor can be very helpful for many students, it can be important that the student not depend entirely on the counsellor's information. If a student is interested in applying to particular colleges or getting financial aid, for example, it is worthwhile for her to double-check information and ask for guidance from a perspective college. Sometimes information changes so quickly that the guidance counsellor simply cannot keep up. Usually guidance counsellors are best informed about local or regional schools, but may be less conversant with requirements necessary in other locations or in private colleges.

What Is Vocational Guidance?

A vocation is a career or calling and the word is derived from the Latin *vocare*, which means "to call." Vocational guidance means helping someone find his or her calling or at least a suitable career choice. Vocations or careers can be loosely categorized into areas such as service, technical, mechanical, creative, health and business.

Vocational training rather than vocational guidance is available at career colleges and this is usually for entry-level careers. For example, a career college with a health vocational curriculum may offer education and training programmes for nurse's aide and medical assistant careers, while business-oriented vocational schools may have marketing assistant and bookkeeping programme offerings. A career college or vocational school differs from regular colleges and universities as the focus isn't on academics, but rather on training students for a specific career. Vocational or career colleges are also sometimes referred to as community colleges or trade schools.

Vocational guidance is often started in high school although some high schools also have vocational training programmes. Vocational exploration courses offer students the opportunity to research different career possibilities as well as learn which vocational areas they have aptitude or talent in. For instance, many vocational guidance classes give tests to the students that test their ability with numbers, words, mechanical concepts and many more subjects.

Tests designed to measure an individual's personality traits, intelligence quotient (IQ) as well as his or her main values and interests are administered and analyzed by career counsellors.

Once career counsellors and the students have looked over the test results, career options can be chosen that fit best with each individual. Vocational guidance doesn't stop there as many other considerations must be made when deciding on a career direction. The type and number of years of education must be considered. Salary and working conditions are other important considerations in career selection. The likely demand for the occupation in the next decade or more is a crucial element when choosing a vocation since this affects the likelihood of finding jobs in a certain career field.

Vocational guidance isn't just for high school students. Rather it's for anyone either starting a career or changing careers. Some people may have several different careers in their life, while others may stay in the same field during all their working years.

What Does a School Guidance Counsellor Do?

A school guidance counsellor assists students in and out of school. Guidance counsellors work with students of all ages to help them succeed in school, make plans for the future, and address social and behavioural problems. Counsellors tend to focus on working with a specific age group, such as elementary age children, middle schoolers, or students in high school. This job requires a degree in counselling, as well as certification.

At the high school level, the school guidance counsellor meets with patients to discuss their strengths and weaknesses, as well as plans for the future. Guidance counsellors can talk with students about potential careers, assist students with college and job applications, and provide interventions for students who are struggling in school. This work can include observing students in class and meeting with faculty members to discuss students who may be having problems.

For students in middle school, the work of a school guidance counsellor is slightly different. Students at this age are often struggling with social problems. The counsellor's role may be as someone who provides advice and friendly assistance to students who have trouble making friends or navigating the middle school social environment. On the flip side, guidance counsellors can meet with bullies to stage interventions. Counsellors also work with faculty to identify students who need extra help with their schoolwork or who appear to be having problems at home.

Guidance counsellors who work with students in elementary and grammar school network with faculty and parents to keep an eye on students as they start their school careers. A school guidance counsellor is especially sensitive to students with learning disabilities and social problems who could benefit from early intervention. Identifying students with issues like auditory processing disorder, dyslexia, and other disabilities that can interfere with learning ensures that these students do not fall by the wayside and have a chance at getting treatment so that they can do well in school. Students of all ages can see a school guidance counsellor for help with social skills, test-taking skills, and study skills. Guidance counsellors are skilled at identifying potential areas of interest for students to get students active and involved, whether a student is a great fit for the theater department or a candidate for extra science classes. Counsellors think about how to work with students to help them succeed at life, not just in academic environments, and their work can be quite diverse on any given day.

Career Counselling

Career counselling, career guidance and career coaching are similar in nature to other types of counselling or coaching, e.g. marriage or psychological counselling. What unites all types of professional counselling is the role of practitioners, who combine giving advice on their topic of expertise with counselling techniques that support clients in making complex decisions and facing difficult situations. The focus of career counselling is generally on issues such as career exploration, career change, personal career development and other career related issues.

Around the globe, countless definitions, concepts and terminology exist for career counselling - particularly due to cultural and linguistic differences. This even affects the most central term *counselling* (or: *counselling* in British English) which is often substituted with the word *guidance* as in *career guidance.* For example, in the UK, *career counselling* would usually be referred to as *careers advice* or *guidance.* Due to the widespread reference to both *career guidance* and *career counselling* among policy-makers, academics and practitioners around the world, references to *career guidance and counselling* are becoming common. Accordingly, this article emphasizes a *broad understanding* of career counselling which involves a variety of professionals activities commonly associated with career counselling, guidance, coaching, and advise. More specific roles and activities associated with career counselling are explained below.

Related Professional Activities

Career counselling or career guidance includes a wide variety of professional activities which focus on supporting people in dealing with career-related challenges - both preventively and in difficult situations (such as unemployment). Career counsellors work with people from various walks of life, such as adolescents seeking to explore career options, experienced professionals contemplating a career change, parents who want to return to the world of work after taking time to raise their child, or people seeking employment. Career counselling is also offered in various settings, including in groups and individually, in person or by means of digital communication. Several approaches have been undertaken to systemize the variety of professional activities related to career guidance and counselling. In the most recent attempt, the Network for Innovation in Career Guidance and Counselling in Europe (NICE) - a consortium of 45 European institutions of higher education in the field of career counselling - has agreed on a system of professional roles for guidance counsellors. Each of these five roles is seen as an important facet of the *career guidance and counselling profession.* Career counsellors performing in any of these roles are expected to behave professionally, e.g. by following ethical standards in their practice. The NICE Professional Roles (NPR) are:

- The *Career Educator* "supports people in developing their own career management competences"
- The *Career Information & Assessment Expert* "supports people in assessing their personal characteristics and needs, then connecting them with the labour market and education systems"
- The *Career Counsellor* "supports individuals in understanding their situations, so as to work through issues towards solutions"
- The *Programme & Service Manager* "ensures the quality and delivery of career guidance and counselling organisations' services"
- The *Social Systems Intervener & Developer* "supports clients (even) in crisis and works to change systems for the better"

The description of the NICE Professional Roles (NPR) draws on a variety of prior models to define the central activities and competences of guidance counsellors. The NPR can, therefore, be understood as a state-of-the-art framework which includes all relevant aspects of career counselling. For this reason, other models haven't been included here so far. Models which are reflected in the NPR include:

- BEQU: "Kompetenzprofil für Beratende" (Germany, 2011)
- CEDEFOP "Practitioner Competences" (2009)
- ENTO: "National Occupational Standards for Advice and Guidance" (Great Britain, 2006)
- IAEVG: "International Competences for Educational and Vocational Guidance" (2003)
- Savickas, M.: "Career Counselling" (USA, 2011)

Benefits

Professional career counsellors can support people with career-related challenges in many ways. Through their expertise in career development and labour markets, they can put a person's qualification, experience, strengths and weakness in a broad perspective taking into consideration their desired salary, personal hobbies and interests, location, job market and educational possibilities. Through their counselling and teaching abilities, career counsellors can additionally support people in gaining a better understanding of what really matters for them personally, how they can plan their careers autonomously, or help them in making tough decisions and getting through times of crisis. Finally, career counsellors are often capable of supporting their clients in finding suitable placements/ jobs, in working out conflicts with their employers, or finding the support of other helpful services.

It is due to these various benefits of career counselling that policy-makers in many countries of the world publicly fund guidance services. For example, the European Union understands career guidance and counselling as an instrument to effectively combat social exclusion and increase citizens' employability.

History

Frank Parson's *Choosing a Vocation* (1909) was perhaps the first major work which is concerned with careers guidance. While until the 1970s a strongly normative approach was characteristic for theories (e.g. of Donald E. Super's *life-span approach*) and practice of career counselling (e.g. concept of *matching*), new models have their starting point in the individual needs and transferable skills of the clients while managing biographical breaks and discontinuities. Career development is no longer viewed as a linear process. More consideration is now placed on nonlinear, chance and unplanned influences.

Training

Up until now there is no standardized qualification path for professional career counsellors, although various certificates are offered nationally and internationally (e.g. by professional associations), and the number of academic degree programmes in career guidance and/ or career counselling is growing worldwide. Still, in most countries, basically anybody could call themselves a "career counsellor" (unlike engineers or psychologists whose professions are protected legally). At the same time, policy makers agree that the competence of career counsellors is one of the most important factors in ensuring that people receive high quality support in dealing with their career questions. Depending on the country of their education, career counsellors may have a variety of academic backgrounds: In Europe, for instance, degrees in (vocational/ industrial/ organization) psychology and educational sciences are among the most common, but backgrounds in sociology, public administration and other sciences are also frequent. At the same time, many training programmes for career counsellors are becoming increasingly multidisciplinary.

Professional Career Guidance Centres

There are many career guidance and counselling centres all over the world. They give services of guidance and counselling on higher studies, possibilities, chances and nature of courses and institutes. Also that these services are offered either fixing up a meeting with the Experts or having telephonic conversations with the guide or even the online guidance which is very common these days with the people getting services on click of their mouse. There are many such service providers all over the world providing online counselling to people about their career or conducting a psychometric test to know the persons aptitude as well as interests.

Career Testing

People who participate in career counselling can benefit from the use of aptitude tests, or career testing. Career testing is often done online and provides insightful and relatively objective information about which jobs may be suitable for the test taker based on combination of their interests, values and skills. Career tests usually provide a list of recommended jobs that match the test takers attributes with those of people with similar personalities who enjoy/are successful at their jobs. There are various ways to test an individual for which field he is suitable, psychometric testing being one among them.

Psychometric testing covers a wide range of skills, interests and values of people and can be of use in career counselling in different ways. For example, the information won from such tests can be of help for the professionals who mentor, coach or counsel individuals. With psychometric testing, there is no pass or fail, but the quality of the information won from the tests can vary. Psychometric testing uses in-depth psychological profiles to assess personality and intellectual levels. Different test companies use different theoretical approaches to testing, such as the psychometric approach, the psychodynamic approach, the social learning approach and the humanist approach. Different test companies have their own methods of testing, some of them being protected with copyrights. Two commonly used assessments are the Strong Interest Inventory and the MBTI, for example. Usually, psychometric testing uses multiple sets of questions relating to personality type, how the test taker would handle aspects of work and home life, what his or her goals are for the future and his or her strengths and weaknesses. If the test taker is honest and the employed tests follow scientific standards, the results should be fairly accurate and useful for career counselling activities.

Challenges

One of the major challenges associated with career counselling is encouraging participants to engage in the process. For example in the UK 70% of people under 14 say they have had no careers advice while 45% of people over 14 have had no or very poor/limited advice.

In a related issue some client groups tend to reject the interventions made by professional career counsellors preferring to rely on the advice of peers or superiors within their own profession. Jackson et al. found that 44% of doctors in training felt that senior members of their own profession were best placed to give careers advice. Furthermore it is recognised that the giving of career advice is something that is widely spread through a range of formal and informal roles. In addition to career counsellors it is also common for teachers, managers, trainers and Human Resources (HR) specialists to give formal support in career choices. Similarly it is also common for people to seek informal support from friends and family around their career choices and to bypass career professionals altogether. Today increasingly people rely on career web portals to seek advice on resume writing and handling interviews; as also to research on various professions and companies. It has even become possible to take vocational assessments online.

Career Guide

A career guide is an individual or publication that provides guidance to people facing a variety of career challenges. These challenges may include (but are not limited to) dealing with redundancy; seeking a new job; changing careers; returning to work after a career break; building new skills; personal and professional development; going for promotion; and setting up a business. The common aim of the career guide, whatever the particular situation of the individual being guided, is normally to help that individual gain control of their career and, to some extent, their life.

Career Guide Professionals

Individuals who work as career guides usually take the approach of combining coaching, mentoring, advising and consulting in their work, without being limited to any one of these disciplines. A typical career guide will have a mixture of professional qualifications and work experiences from which to draw when guiding clients. They may also have a large network of contacts and, when appropriate will put a particular client in touch with a contact relevant to their case. A career guide may work for themselves independently or for one or more private or public careers advisory services. The term 'Career Guide' has been first established and used by career consulting firm Position Ignition, which was created in 2009 and has been using the term for their career consultants and career advisors.

Career Guide Publications

Career guide publications may take a number of forms, including PDFs, booklets, journals or books. A career guide publication will typically be divided up into a number of chapters or segments, each one addressing a particular career issue. Career guides can also focus on a particular industry or profession. For instance, there is 'The fine artist's career guide: making money in the arts and beyond' and 'Professional Pilot's Career Guide'.

Career Guidance Standards

In Europe, career guidance as a public service is generally expected to meet a number of quality assurance standards. According to these standards, European career guidance should:

- Have regular review periods in which to assess guidance resources and processes
- Be transparent and open
- Create synergy and co-operation between education, training, employment and community sectors
- Ensure consistency between local and regional services so that all citizens are treated equally, regardless of geographical location.
- Strive for continuous improvement of tools, services and products.

2

The Principle of Guidance

Sequence

If I were asked which of all the spiritual principles I ranked first, I should feel inclined to say the Principle of Guidance, not in the sense of being more essential that the others — for every portion is equally essential to the completeness of a perfect whole — but in the sense of being first in order of sequence and giving value to all our other powers by placing them in their due relation to one another. "Giving value to our *other* powers", I say, because this also is one of our powers. It is that which, judged from the standpoint of personal self-consciousness, is above us; but which, realised from the point of view of the unity of all Spirit, is part and parcel of ourselves, because it is that Infinite Mind which is of necessity identified with all its manifestations.

Infinite Mind Is Internal

Looking to this Infinite Mind as a Superior Intelligence from which we may receive guidance does not therefore imply looking to an external source. On the contrary, it is looking to the innermost spring of our own being, with a confidence in its action which enables us to proceed to the execution of our plans with a firmness and assurance that are in themselves the very guarantee of our success.

Understanding

The action of the spiritual principles in us follows the order which we impose upon them by our thought; therefore the order of realisation will reproduce the order of desire; and if we neglect this first principle of right order and guidance, we shall find ourselves beginning to put forth other great powers, which are at present latent within us, without knowing how to find suitable employment for them. This would be a very perilous condition: for without having before us objects worthy of the powers to which we awaken, we should waste them on petty purposes dictated only by the narrow range of our unilluminated intellect. Therefore the ancient wisdom says, "With all thy getting, get understanding". The awakening to consciousness of our mysterious interior powers will sooner or later take place, and will result in our using them whether or not we understand the law of their development. The interior powers are natural powers as much as the exterior ones. We can direct their use by a knowledge of their laws; and it is therefore of the highest importance to have some sound principles of guidance in the use of these higher faculties as they begin to manifest themselves.

Will

If, therefore, we would safely and profitably enter upon the possession of the great inheritance of power that is opening out before us, we must before all things seek to realise in ourselves that Superior Intelligence which will become an unfailing principle of guidance if we will only recognise it as such. Everything depends on our recognition. Thoughts are things, and therefore as we *will* our thoughts to be, so we *will the thing* to be. If, then, we *will* to use the Infinite Spirit as a spirit of guidance, we shall find that the fact is as we have willed it, and in doing this we are still making use of our own supreme principle. And this is the true "understanding" which, by placing all the other powers in their correct order, creates one grand unity of power directed to clearly defined and worthy aims, in place of the dispersion of our powers, by which they only neutralise each other and effect nothing.

Truth

This is that Spirit of Truth which shall guide us into all Truth. It is the sincere Desire in us to reach out after Truth. Truth first and Power afterwards is the reasonable order, which we cannot invert without injury to ourselves and others; but if we follow this order we shall always find scope for our powers in developing into present realities the continually growing glory of our vision of the ideal.

From Ideal to Real

The ideal is the true real, but it must be brought into manifestation before it can be shown to be so, and it is in this that the *practical* nature of our mental studies consists. It is the *practical* mystic who is the man of power: the man who, realising the mystical powers within, fits his outward action to this knowledge, and so shows his faith by his works; and assuredly the first step is to make use of that power of infallible guidance which he can call to his aid simply by desiring to be led by it.

Career Guidance and Counselling: State of the Speciality

Štefan Vendel, Prešov University in Prešov

Mission: Vocational guidance and career counselling is a speciality within the profession of counselling, one that fosters career development and work adjustment of individuals at each life stage. They assist individuals to make suitable and viable choices.

Assistance with life-planning is a function that has come to professional counselling as heritage from its very beginnings. The progenitor of professional counselling, the Guidance Movement really began out of the conviction of many of the guidance pioneers that human beings, particularly young people, desperately needed help in planning for their entry into complicated, confusing world of work.

Thus vocational and educational planning activities are virtually at the core of professional counselling's legacy from the past. However, in recent years many counsellors strangely seem to have turned away from vocational/educational counselling and life planning as activities that are somehow unworthy of their time and attention. Nothing could be further of the truth. Vocational life is a wellspring of both some of the most pernicious problems and some of the most fulfilling satisfaction that contemporary life can afford.

When individual, who fail to cope adequately with the demands of vocational life, fail to achieve minimal success and satisfaction from work, it became almost impossible for them to achieve adequate levels of self/esteem, autonomy, or independence. A chronic failure to cope adequately with one's vocational life is almost certain to lead to punishing, criminality, and anxiety and depression are themselves both triggered and exacerbated by the experience of stress, anxiety, frustration, and failure in the work place. Many of the major developmental crises that people experience in the course of their lives are centred around challenges and discontinuities that affect their vocational role. Any attempt to provide professional help to an adolescent or adult human being that ignores his or her vocational life is almost bound to be partial and superficial.

The rapid changes that are now occurring in the organization of work and the arrangement of occupations, as well as the increasing globalization of the workforce foster career counselling's historic mission of helping individuals adapt to societal expectations and personal transitions in their work lives.

Career counsellors are employed in settings as varied as schools, universities, companies, advisories, community agencies, and government offices. They provide career services across the life cycle, including vocational guidance, work adjustment, career education, job placement, occupational information, academic advising, position coaching, employee assistance, retirement planning, vocational rehabilitation, and organizational consultation.

In one of writing devoted to career counselling, in the book *Applying Career development theory to Counselling*, emphasizes its author R. Sharf importance of career counselling by the apposite words: "*The knowledge that several hours spent in counselling can change the outcome of an individual`s life is an exciting challenge to the career counsellor. There are many types of counselling, such as personal and crisis, as well as psychotherapy, but few counselling situations are apt to have as potentially far-reaching effect as career counselling.*"

Training in Career Development and Career Counselling

Probably nothing is more important than providing adequate training to future career counsellors in order to meet the challenges.

The study Relation of Type and Amount of Training to Career Counselling Self-Efficacy conducted in 2004 in Italy examined the relation of self-efficacy to length and type of training in a sample of Italian career counsellors. Findings indicated that amount of career counselling training was positively related to counsellors' self-efficacy regarding their abilities to conceptualize vocational problems, deal with career indecision concerns, and provide educational counselling. In addition, counsellors who had participated in an in-service training course that focused on social cognitive/learning theories reported stronger self-efficacy regarding their skills at vocational problem conceptualization and at educational counselling than did those who received more eclectic training.

Some analytics regard the current state of training in career counselling that is provided by counsellor education departments as significant weakness. There is a widespread perception that career counselling has been marginalized because of disinterest among both faculty and students. Counsellor educators seem indifferent to career counselling. A startling example of this indifference occurs in what is called *The Handbook of Counselling* (Locke, Myers, & Herr, 2001), in which "career counselling" is absent from all 44 chapter titles and scarce in the index. The speciality that originated the modern field of counselling by differentiating itself from social work is now marginalized.

Of course, part of the indifference among counsellor educators may reflect the interests of their students who shun career counselling courses as they concentrate on family therapy, community counselling, mental health counselling, and substance abuse counselling. It is unfortunate, given the contemporary need for counsellors to help individuals adapt to dramatic changes in the economy and occupational structure.

Despite this societal need - and probably because of disinterested faculty and uninterested students - many counsellor education programmes offer only one course in career counselling, and often that course is taught by an adjunct instructor or new assistant professor. Only a small number of programmes offer a second course or an advanced practicum in career counselling. The programmes that do offer a second career course find it difficult to identify a suitable textbook. Thus, Euroguidance association should to develop training materials to improve courses and to publish more materials for advanced courses.

Emphasizing training standards and competencies is an important part of this work. Such action is particularly important in light of the emergence of "*substitute practitioners*." Given the societal need for career services, coupled with the disinterest of the counselling profession at large, career coaches are flourishing, and Internet sites offering career help are proliferating. Some analytics lament over the "deprofessionalization" that goes with the "anyone can do it" mentality of coaches and designers of Web sites. Partly in response to this situation some counsellors call for the profession to help the public differentiate between professional career counsellors, career development facilitators, and career coaches.

In summary counsellors respond to what is modelled for them in their training programmes, positively. Both faculty and training programmes that reflect excitement and support for vocational psychology appear to be most effective in engaging counsellors in career counselling activities. It is, therefore, not surprising that after participating in a counselling training programme; the counsellors report more positive feelings about career counselling and more positive comments about their self-efficacy as career counsellors.

Supervision

Together with the training there is the need for supervision over the counsellors working with clients. Everyone has its own individual flaws and blocks and career counsellors should receive appropriate supervision to ensure that these do not adversely affect their work. Together with continuing learning opportunities (perhaps through training and attending professional meetings), supervision is important for the career counsellor‘s development. Career counselling is a demanding occupation and counsellors need to look after themselves between, during and after sessions with clients. Good support is necessary from fellows, for improving methods, to share areas of common interests, to pool knowledge, and to reduce isolation. In addition, supervision plays a supportive role for the counsellor.

Constant self-monitoring and examination of the career counsellor's own work, which may usefully draw on feedback from clients is also important. Practicing counsellors can audio tape counselling sessions and receive supervision from more experienced fellows. The more experienced counsellors are able to role model for the less experienced ones. The practicing counsellors can also receive frequent feedback from their colleagues as they share case presentations in seminars whereby the practicing counsellors can profit from the cumulative expertise of all those involved in the praxis.

Competencies Needed by Counsellors

Primary areas (Competencies that guidance/career counsellors should possess in order to assist clients with their career development needs) covered in major texts for a beginning course in career counselling is:

- Career development theories
- Career assessment
- Career information resources
- Career development programming
- Field experiences
- Career interviewing-/Career counselling competencies

The discipline provides practitioners with a diverse group of clients. Together with the primarily undergraduate population seen in the educational counselling centres, most of the clients in the work offices are middle-aged. Because of this, client demographics cut across age, race, gender, and levels of socio-economic status. Since guidance counsellors will likely be working with diverse clients in the future, their experience with such clients can be critical for training goals. Let me to say some words concerning these and other points.

Theories: The Application of Career Development Theories to Practice

Many of the analytics who examined the current status and imminent future of the career counselling profession identified its foundational theories as a major strength.

Practitioners more readily accept some theories because they offer practical guidance. Osborn and Baggerly (J. of Career Development, 2004) looked at school counsellors to determine their preferred career counselling and testing activities. In their work, the school counsellors who were studied most preferred to use trait-factor theory, which in this study included Holland's theory. Person-environment correspondence theory and cognitive information processing theory were also preferences. However, it was found in this study that school counsellors spend limited time doing career development work.

In the study of Chris Brown from the 2002, participants – CC practitioners - responded on the question: "*What if any career counselling theory/theories do you use?*" 55% identified 2 to 3 theories that informed their work. Most noted were Holland, Super, Social Learning/Cognitive theories. Holland's RIASEC theory is the most popular, perhaps due to the number of applicable tools, such as the *Self-Directed Search.*

Ppractitioners indicated that they apply career theory to practice by (a) using assessment instruments, and (b) conceptualizing client issues from the basic theoretical tenets.

In addition, it has been suggested that practitioners likely apply career theory to practice by relating the theories to distinct career services (e.g., guidance, placement, education, counselling, etc.) In other words, career practitioners who provide vocational guidance use trait-and-factor theory to (a) interpret interest and ability assessments, (b) provide information regarding educational and vocational interests and (c) encourage career exploration, and suggest person/job fit options. For clients who are in need of career education services, developmental counselling models are used to orient the client to developmental tasks. Practitioners who provide placement services utilize Social Learning Theory to help clients secure employment in their chosen field by, for example, (a) reducing job search anxiety, (b) countering mistaken beliefs, and (c) increasing assertiveness.

The provision of career counselling from a theoretical framework is strongly recommended by the profession. Career development theories have definitely advanced and enriched the strategies and methods for helping people deal with career concerns. In addition, research on career counselling and career testing is essential to ensure effective implementation of a career development programme. Adherence to a counselling theory has been found to be a major characteristic associated with effective school counsellors. However, some practicing counsellors do not appear to value career theory or research, and regard heory as "not applicable".

Indeed, the analytics deplore the ineffective communication between practitioners and researchers. Extensive data pertaining to career development continue to accumulate yet not be used because career counsellors and vocational psychologists work in separate spheres. Career development researchers have already produced an impressive amount of content. Now may be the time to focus on helping career counsellors use that content in their practices.

The analytics recommended that in the next decade the career counselling profession should (a) expand the purview of its theories beyond the traditional focus on the vocational behaviour of white, middle-class men and should incorporate greater awareness of and sensitivity to race, sex, and culture; (b) concentrate more attention on adult transitions to supplement its emphasis on adolescent decision making; (c) promote a holistic view of life roles and emphasize "life structure counselling"; (d) integrate career development theories to make them more coherent and comprehensive; and (e) address the turbulence in the work world and soothe the anguish and ills experienced by workers.

Our experience suggest a strong need for training that provides counsellors with updates on career theories and current approaches that demonstrate practical applications of theories. *The Career Development Quarterly* has moved in this direction by asking the authors of the annual literature reviews to address one important question: How can the research published last year be useful to counsellors? Advances in this direction surely will be facilitated by *Career Convergence,* the exciting Web publication debuted by NCDA in February 2003. This electronic magazine provides a practical online resource for career counsellors in the form of "how to" and "best practices" articles, informational tips, and Web links. There is promis that this "practitioner-to-practitioner" forum will lead to collaborative reflection and research on the process of career counselling. This research on process would be best conducted by teams of practitioners and researchers working collaboratively.

Assessments

A common activity associated with career counselling is career testing. The Career Counselling practise tends to make far greater use of assessments than does the personal counselling. Assessments can enhance counsellors work; the use of assessments can often provide important insights into client concerns; and assessments can often play an important role in guiding and shaping counsellors work with their clients.

Practicing counsellors should learn to administer and interpret a wide range of assessment tools measuring: vocational interests, occupational values, career maturity, career identity, career decision making, and career self-efficacy. The most frequently used are the Strong Interest Inventory, the Self-Directed Search, the Career Transitions Inventory, My Vocational Situation, the Career Decision-Making Difficulties Questionnaire, the Myers-Briggs Type Indicator, Sigi-Plusand and so on. The counsellors also makes use of qualitative assessments such as the Career Genogram. Vocational assessment enables career counsellors to understand clients' vocational behaviour in a relatively objective way and improves the process of career intervention.

Regardless of level, most school counsellors report spending very little time on career testing. Approximately three-fourths of middle and high school counsellors participating in one published study reported spending very little time on career testing, an activity which is critical for accurate completion of students' educational and career plans, as well as for providing valuable information for both the college and non-college bound student.

School counsellors need to have opportunities and support to provide career counselling and testing. Career testing data guides middle and high school counsellors in programme development and evaluation. Therefore, it is crucial for school counsellors to gain support of administrators and policy makers in areas such as time for testing, specific training and clerical help to enable them to provide appropriate career tests. Additional training may enhance the perceptions of counsellors who prefer not to spend time devoted to career counselling to testing.

As to use diagnostic instruments beside school seting, as Frak Schmidt and John Hunter (1981) estimated, the use of cognitive ability tests for selection in hiring can produce large labour cost savings, ranging from $18 milion per year for small employers such as police department...to $16 bilion per year for large employers such as federal government.

Technology

Vocational assessment is enhanced by the use of technology. More specifically, the advancement in computer-assisted techniques greatly enriches career assessment and intervention. Counsellors are relieved from the tedious task of data entry and analysis, and, therefore, can focus more time on facilitating clients' awareness of themselves by explaining the assessment results. The wide use of the Internet makes it possible to share and distribute information in a much more efficient way.

Another achievement of technology is the development and improvement of computer-based career planning systems. They provide an important support tool for the career counsellors.

Today, systems of career assessment and career information are multiple and massive, and the Internet is the usual starting and end point for accessing them. In the business area, electronic résumés and electronic interviews have become common. Online counselling has found its niche, and its users are increasing in number. Testing on the Internet has been readily available and has increased in popularity since a greater variety of tests, translated into many languages, have been offered online.

The major threat from information technology and the wide use of the Internet is to the provision of career services and the training of career practitioners, but at the same time, information technology provides an exciting opportunity for a new application of career counselling and advances in the profession. Because of the information and communication technology, enormous amounts of information become available to the public. The occupational information that has traditionally been available in career centres is now accessible from home with a few keystrokes on the computer keyboard.

In a recent perusal of the Internet, I found interest inventories, assistance in developing a resume, occupational information, and sites that provide career counselling. I believe that the changes in technology offer many opportunities and possibilities for providing career counselling using new and nontraditional methods. The amount and characteristics of career-related resources available to individuals expand daily. As an example, the technology exists that allows clients to access over the Internet short and engaging videos depicting the typical work activities of individuals in various occupations. In my experience, many clients would find this type of occupational information more appealing than reading brief occupational descriptions. Similarly, online testing becomes much more appealing than boring pencil-and-paper testing.

Although technology may make career services more easily accessible for many people, it may also increase the possibility that individuals can be harmed. In the past, most career assessments were not readily available to individuals, and career counsellors had the responsibility for evaluating the psychometric characteristics of an instrument before giving it to a client. Now clients have access to many career assessments that may look legitimate but that, in actuality, have poor psychometric properties. Hence, individuals may be making career decisions that are based on invalid instruments. There can also be financial costs because some of these sites appear to charge hefty fees for what may be negligible services.

Career assessment provided over the Internet is just one example of interventions that can be problematic because they do exclude the help of a counsellor. In some high schools, career development activities consist solely of computer-assisted career guidance programmes. Whiston et al. (2003) found that counsellor-free interventions were not as effective as were other interventions that involved a counsellor (e.g., individual counselling, workshops, group counselling). They also found that individuals who used a career computer system supplemented by counselling had better outcomes than individuals who just used a computer system.

Some analytics regard the proliferation of counsellor-free interventions, both through the Internet and in other settings, as threat to the career counselling field and a disservice to clients.

Unless career counsellors are more active in informing others of the efficacy of career counselling, administrators and organizational decision makers may see counsellor-free services as a less expensive alternative to career counselling.

In essence, computer technologies significantly change the methods of delivering career services and provide an alternative avenue of offering career services. What is the role of counsellors then? Are they really obsolete? How can counsellors take advantage of advanced technologies to enhance career counselling services?

Technology should become career counsellors' best assistant, not their competitor. Computers will accomplish much of the tedious and labour-intensive work, such as record keeping, the management of assessment data, and searching for information. Discussion and consultation regarding cases can be done using multimedia technologies. I envision that technology will enhance career counsellors' performance by being an extension to what they are doing but not replacing their jobs. Computer technologies cannot substitute for the counsellor's role in facilitating self-awareness, self-exploration, and the construction of an individual's journey in a career path.

Career counsellors, being relieved from routine work by computers, can really use what they are trained for: helping people to make meaning of their life (with work as a part of life) and to develop coping skills to adjust well to their environment. Career counsellors do not just match people with work but also help people find their sense of self in relation to work and life.

Career Informations

Other services, in addition to assessmets, is producing and analyzing the Labour Marketing Information. Among the most inportant kinds of information pertain:

- Where informations about schools and vocations can be found.
- Description of work
- Work conditions
- Required education, knowledge, abilities and skills
- Entry and average incom in the occupation
- What is the future outlook of the occupation client are interested in
- Where the more information about a occupation can be obtained

- What are the possibilities of finding a job in region where a client lives

Demands for such information grow as the possibilities of education and work fulfilment get more diverse.

In conjunction with Information the counsellors need a psychologically based classification system of occupations. The change in occupational structure and labour demands makes it difficult for career counsellors to rely solely on the conventional classification system of job clusters. Many new occupations require that workers combine traits in a different way than has traditionally been done, possess more adaptive skills, and have the ability to learn quickly to adjust to new environments. The new occupational classification system that will replace the International Standard Classification of Occupations currently used in EU countries and incorporate the changes that are occurring in the world of work is yet to be developed and refined.

Holistic Model of Career Counselling

A wide range of presenting client problems should be encountered by career couselors. Career issues such as dealing with transitions, career indecision, underemployment, or unemployment are often compounded by other life circumstances. Clients who have career concerns are also frequently dealing with concurrent issues of poverty, abusive homesituations, depression, anxiety, ageism, and so on. Some clients are influenced by situational factors such as divorce, the global crisis, or the down sizing of companies. Career counselling clients are usually about 60 percent women. Many of these women are dealing with gender issues related to career choice and job satisfaction.

Recent discussions in the career literature have emphasized the importance of not separating career and personal counselling. Incorporating both career and personal issues is sometimes labelled as a *Holistic Model.*

An important aspect of the counselling work for many of counsellors, as they try to engage the holistic model, is to realize that there are often more psychologically related issues to attend to than they first realize. Under the guise of conventional career related concerns career clients often present more complex personal issues. A request for assistance with a resume or help with a job search may mask more profound developmental impasses, affective disorders, or other psychological concerns.

Dealing with the complexity of the holistic model, is often one of the biggest challenges for practicioners. For some it is a novel notion, one that runs contrary to their understanding of career counselling. Some career counselling practitioners may not be qualified to attend to the personal issues of their career clients due to the nature of their training.

Other counsellors appear to intellectually understand the holistic model; they find themselves, however, continuing to dichotomize career and personal issues in practice. This process often manifests in comments that suggest that they would feel reluctant to work with clients as "psychologically" in the career centre as they would in the counselling centre. At times the distinction is clinically appropriate, but more often, it appears to represent an internalized, false dichotomization of career and personal issues.

Furthermore, it is not unusual for practicing counsellors, particularly the more advanced counsellors, to initially experience the complexity of the career counselling as a threat to their sense of self-efficacy as counsellors. Often these advanced practicioners have developed solid therapeutic skills with the clients that they have seen in the counselling centres. Many of these practicioners then enter the praxis of vocational guidance and counselling thinking that it will be easier and less demanding than their work in the counselling centres. Counsellors often describe their experience here, initially, as "personal counselling plus all these 'add ons.' and are surprised to find it comparatively more difficult. Indeed, career counselling is often more complex and harder to do than personal counselling.

The philosophy of the Career Guidance and Counselling today should be a holistic one; particularly with regards to our approach to client concerns. That is, the training model of guidance counsellor should not compartmentalize clients concerns into dichotomized categories such as "career concerns" and "personal-social" concerns. I believe that career issues must be understood within overall personality context. As a result, the vocational guidance and career counselling should be comprehend as a part of counselling psychology.

More Unity and Collaboration

Career counsellors work in schools, vocational guidance institutions, centres of psychological services, employment offices, assessment centres, in private praxis and other institutions. This fragmentation of career services has isolated counsellors from each other. Career counsellors could begin to address this fragmentation by organizing a career summit meeting. In my vision for the future, not only would researchers and practitioners collaborate, but there would be more unity and alliance among professionals involved in career counselling. In my opinion, there is little contact among the vocational psychologists, career counsellors, and school counsellors whose responsibilities also include career development. In many instances, these groups are quite insular and tend to attend different conferences and draw from different professional publications. Thus, advancements in one area are not known in other areas, and individuals receive less than optimum career counselling and assistance. This fragmentation also hinders the advancements that could occur if there was more unity. For example, very few grant Euros have been directed toward providing career counselling to needy individuals.

I believe that further advancement could be made if there was more unity among the professionals interested in career counselling and if these professionals would exchange information and work together with the shared goal of advancing career counselling. In fact, maybe it is time to have more meetings like this one of the Euroguidance Association, the meetings where individuals from a variety of disciplines come together because of a shared belief that career counselling is not only a means for addressing individual quality of life issues but is, also, an avenue for addressing social issues and problems.

Weaknesses of Career Counselling

One overriding weakness that was identified by multiple analyses was the minimal training offered by counsellor education programmes for students who wish to specialize in career counselling. Many times the people who teach the career counselling courses do not have an appreciation and love and passion for career counselling. It is perceived as not as attractive as personal counselling.

Many of those who do have a passion for career counselling are unable to teach the course in an interesting, thought-provoking, and engaging way. Furthermore, counsellors-in-training have generally considered such courses as routine and boring. In a field in which there is such passion for career counselling by those who specialize in it, it is regrettable that some counsellor education programmes cannot have one faculty member who can teach a strong career counselling course. That‘s why Euroguidance should begin publish the books to support improvement in career counselling courses.

A somewhat related threat to career counselling concerns individuals who are ill prepared to provide career services. The popularity of job coaches who charge sizeable fees for finding individuals' dream jobs poses a direct threat to those who are well trained and knowledgeable about effective interventions. The popularity of job coaches, however, indicates that there are individuals who need career counselling; yet, career counselling professionals have failed to attract those individuals to career counselling venues. I believe that career counsellors have done an inadequate job of publicizing and informing the public about the benefits of career counselling.

Underutilization of Services and Inadequate Service

Whenever I have asked the students in my career counselling class how many of them had visited the guidance office in their high schools or the career development centre (or counselling centre) at the university for career counselling services, most of them have answered that they have never done so or sometimes have not even known where the career development centre was located. For those who have received service, all they remember is that they were given some types of assessment, and, most often, they do not remember the results or the meaning of them. Underutilization of services and inadequate service seem to be the other two issues that our profession needs to address.

Targeting Only College Students

Career counselling seems to overwhelmingly target college students and to lesser degree high school students. The centrality of career development across the entire life span is missing from the current research and practice in the field. The early and late portions of the life span in relation to career development have been poorly understood. Career education is integrated more often into the curriculum at the middle school and high school level but is very rarely included at the elementary school level. The needs of older individuals are neglected; information and resources for providing career counselling services to these populations are sparse at best.

Strengths of Career Counselling

A chief strength of career counselling as a profession is its relatively long history. The beginnings of the organized practice of vocational guidance in the United States date to the early 1900s. Because of this history, there is a large body of data, knowledge, theory, and skills, which provide the underpinnings for the effective practice of career counselling. This long history has also led to the availability of many career development theories. These theories and their derivatives inform the practice of career development.

A second strength of the career counselling profession is a very practical one - you can make money! People who specialize in career counselling can earn a lucrative salary. In fact, the independent practice of career counselling is one of the few applied psychology fields in which individuals can make substantial amounts of money. Yet because of that, the profession of career counselling can attract charlatans and foster greed in people. It is the bane of the career counselling profession, one founded in helping others solve their life problems, that it sometimes attracts this unsavory element. Not that there is anything wrong with making money working at something one loves, but where there is an opportunity for financial gain, a greedy, selfish group of people who put themselves before the good of their clients will also arise.

The third strength that analytics noted was that members of the counselling profession had produced excellent materials to use with clients in implementing career development models and counselling methods. There are many valid interest inventories, ability tests, value surveys, and developmental indices as well as some effective computer-system interventions. These tools have been so useful that, on the whole, the career counselling profession may have come to rely excessively on test interpretation as its central intervention.

Although test interpretation is a core activity, purchasing tests has become too expensive. A weakness that is particularly frustrating is that counsellors have insufficient funds to purchase these expensive tests and systems. Profit-seeking corporations now own and market the major career inventories and tests. Many counsellors would like to use these popular tools with their clients, but they cannot afford to purchase the "products" from commercial enterprises. Early in the last century, concerned psychologists, led by James McKeen Cattell, formed the Psychological Corporation to distribute tests because they feared the possibility of corporate entrepreneurs profiting excessively from the work of scholars and researchers. It would be a worthy project for Euroguidance to develop a set of psychometric tools for career interventions and distribute them free of charge over the Internet. The exciting possibility is that Euroguidance going even further to develop Web-based career centres, one for counsellors and one for clients. This type of decision-support system, delivered directly to counsellors in their offices by the Web, could allow counsellors to access tests, materials, evidence-based protocols, and other information quickly and conveniently. Perhaps counsellors could use such knowledge-delivery systems to use computer programmes to do the person-environment matching so fundamental to vocational guidance and to free career counsellors to do holistic life planning. This suggestion extends Holland's (1971) innovative idea of using a counsellor-free, self-directed search for educational and vocational guidance to relieve counsellors to do more complicated work with their clients.

Another strength of career counselling is that it is inherently positive. It focuses on a person's strengths and how to use those strengths appropriately. A "new" movement in psychology has named itself "positive psychology." It is no more than what career counsellors have been doing every day for more than 100 years.

Yet another strength is that individuals who are having career problems seek out career counsellors. Although there continue to be substantial shame and guilt attached to such mental health issues as depression or personality disorders, there is relatively little shame in not having all the skills to make an effective career decision. Career counselling has not been tainted with the mental illness, medical model approach to counselling.

Opportunities for Career Counselling

Because career counselling can touch every aspect of a person's life and because career counselling has not been tainted with the social stigma of mental illness, there is rarely a dearth of clients. Practitioners find that their client base is only constrained by their marketing skills, because the potential audience for such services is limitless. Furthermore, any time there is a social transition, there are even more clients. If helping people is what motivates a career counsellor, there is an important opportunity during social transitions to really help people who are suffering. Career counsellors can quite quickly make a very positive difference in people's lives.

Because career counsellors have generally focused their practice and research on the dominant culture in a country, there are important opportunities to significantly expand the base of career counselling by providing research on the career development of individuals who have not generally been offered career counselling services. These groups include members of nondominant domestic cultures in the EU, such as individuals in lower economic categories; gypsies, non-European racial and ethnic groups, individuals who are differently "able," and so on.

Implications for the Future: A Strategic Plan to Enhance Career Counselling

To continue its good work in the next decade, the career counselling profession must intensify efforts to serve the diverse clients in new settings, translate theory and research into knowledge about the career counselling process that can be used in practice, construct new tools that exploit the potential of informational technology, increase and improve the training offered by counsellor education programmes, infuse information and values into public policy debates, and assist counsellors worldwide who seek to internationalize the profession of career counselling. In this regard, I offer for consideration the following objectives and sample strategies.

To improve the training of career counsellors, Euroguidance should continue to publish materials itself and foster the development of materials to aid in teaching interesting and engaging career counselling classes. There are many ways to learn, and career counselling materials need to be presented in lively ways that engage the student in the learning process. Such materials might include experiential activities, cases, videos, lesson plans, and syllabi, all are important to provide opportunities for the active learning that is very important for adult learners, a group that includes many counsellors-in-training.

To broaden the focus beyond career decision making, Euroguidance should have a special invited conferences on the other aspects of career counselling (not career decision making), such as maintaining a job, different stages in the career development in a person's life, the latest ways of progressing in a career, and the career counsellor's actions and duties after clients have made their career decisions. Selected papers from such conferences should be published.

To improve the basic and advanced skills of career counsellor practitioners, Euroguidance should have at least one of its international conference themes focus on the "best practices" in career counselling and then turn the proceedings of that conference into a usable textbook on what works in career counselling and why it works. The Euroguidance conference should strive to have both beginning practice and advanced practice workshops, along with a strong multicultural emphasis infused into all presentations. Euroguidance should offer awards for best practices in career counselling and widely publicize that competition. Euroguidance should actively seek to market career development more effectively to external constituencies such as legislators, school counsellors, parents, and corporate, educational, governmental, and nongovernmental agencies. It should also actively work with counsellor educators who teach career counselling classes to infuse marketing skills into those courses.

These skills should not be simply private practice marketing skills, but they should also include how to market the idea of career development and planning into the societal institutions in which career counsellors have membership or that affect their lives. Euroguidance have to expand efforts to market the effectiveness of career counselling to the public - develop audio and video public service announcements that inform people about the good that career counselling can do in their lives. Individuals who know about career counselling want to avail themselves of the service. It carries no stigma in the public eye. The public may become even more interested in career services as increasingly employees are expected to manage their careers

To extend career counselling into underserved groups in the EU countries and other nations, Euroguidance must conducting a career development project for underserved groups (e.g., gypsy youth). It should also institute annual awards for "contributions to multicultural career counselling" and for "contributions to international development of career counselling."

Foster The International Growth of the Profession

One opportunity that is too important to miss is to make a significant contribution to the internationalization of the career counselling profession. In response to the globalization of the economy and the emergence of world workers, countries across the globe are instituting career services and university training programmes to prepare career counsellors to develop and deliver these services. No longer should the career counselling profession originated in USA "export" its models and methods to international colleagues who translate them for use in their own countries. Now, career counsellors in numerous countries should design and develop indigenous pôvodné models, methods, and materials that suit their culture and express their preferred ways of helping others. Euroguidance can do more to assist in the "globalocalization" of career counselling, which means adapting general knowledge about work, workers, and careers to the local language and caring practices of each country.

Scientist-practitioner Approach to the Field

It is also important for guidance counsellor to involved in career counselling research. The research have to investigate elements critical to the process and outcome of career counselling. By doing the research guidance counelors are able to contribute to the growing body of knowledge in our field. Possibility of doing research, particularly when counelors see the studies that they have helped collect data for, published in significant professional journals is exciting. Including research as part of the praxis is an important part, as the current trended model of guidance is the scientist-practitioner approach to the field.

Need to Show The Cost-benefits Of Career Counselling. Also, in my vision of the tasks to be accomplished is the collection of data that will allow career counsellors to show the cost-benefits of career counselling. In these days of increasing accountability and the movement toward empirically supported treatment or interventions, researchers must not only show that career counselling is effective, but also that it is cost effective. Although it is difficult to determine the economic benefits of career counselling, researchers need to investigate the cost of career counselling and compare it with variables such as welfare and unemployment costs, college student retention/ recruitment costs, and differential health care costs. The need for this type of research is critical and that more efforts should be invested in these types of studies.

If we look on the value of career counselling from this point of view, the price of work which at current average earnings levels a worker employed 40 years will produce, is in countries of The Visegrád Group – the Czech Republic, Hungary, Poland and Slovakia - more than 700000€ and in other EU countries even much more. About investing such a sum of money the board of expert consults a number of days. To students finishing his education devote attention in vast majority of cases only his/her parents. Career counsellors have therefore great deal of responsibility not only for the future of their clients but indirectly for effectiveness of economy, because resources of tomorrow are in today‘s schools. In the global community in which we now live, it seems essential that counsellors in the EU countries learn what is happening elsewhere. This kind of knowing will help us with our own multicultural and diversity issues and make us conversant with the growing world community of career counselling professionals.

Comprehensive School Counselling Programmes are Essential to Student Achievement and Successful Postsecondary Transition

Recent developments in technologies have driven worldwide economic changes that demand that all workers have 21st century knowledge and skills in order to be competitive and to manage inevitable life-career transitions. Data trends suggest that today's students and their parents understand that success in careers of all types now requires more training and education than was demanded of previous generations.

The number of students aspiring to postsecondary education has never been higher. Between 1980 and 2002, the percentage of national tenth-graders hoping to complete a bachelor's degree nearly doubled from 41 to 79 percent, across all ethnic groups. The numbers of students taking the SAT has risen from 8000 in 1926, the first year the SAT was administered, to 1,376,745 in 2006.

Unfortunately, an alarming gap exists between student's aspirations and their achievements. State and school data trends point out how many students are ill-prepared for post-secondary success. For example, for every 10 students entering 9th grade in the state of Florida, only six will complete high school. Of those six, only three will go onto college and only two will complete a baccalaureate degree programme within six years. For those students who do graduate from high school, a vast majority (61%) do not go on to earn a postsecondary certificate or degree within five years, if at all.

The Chicago Public Schools (CPS), the first major school system to track and publicly report the college enrollment patterns of its graduates, document similar outcomes. Mirroring the rising college aspiration rates noted above, nearly 92% of 1999 CPS graduating seniors said they planned to attain a postsecondary degree at a four- or two-year college or vocational/ technical school. However, almost half of the students who enter a CPS high school never make it to graduation. And only one-third of those who complete high school enroll in a four-year college; of the cohort that does enroll in college, just 35% graduate college within six years. Why?

Why did only six percent of the students who started in a CPS high school in the mid-1990s – in a situation that is not unique to Chicago – earn a four-year college degree by the time they were in their mid-twenties? What did or did not occur during students' high school years that contributed to such dismal postsecondary outcomes? Administrators and educators must work with partners in and outside the school to address this alarming gap between students' aspirations and their actual educational achievements. Emerging trends suggest that this is best accomplished through a comprehensive school counselling programme focused on career development.

The National Leadership Cadre (NLC) is an organization of nine states that supports school counselling reform with a focus on career development. The NLC maintains that graduation and postsecondary placement rates, in addition to other student achievement indicators such as Adequate Yearly Progress (AYP) reports and standardized test scores, improve when school administrators implement a comprehensive developmental guidance (CDG) programme that aligns with the American School Counselling Association's (ASCA) National Model and focuses on career development as its ultimate mission.

Implementation must begin at the state level, through leadership and coordination of partnerships comprised of government agencies, state school counselling associations, and institutions of higher education. With state policies, recommendations, and endorsements as necessary leverage, district and local administrators can call upon staffs for similar coordinated implementation of school counselling programmes that focus on students' life career development.

In this accountability-driven era, educational administrators at all levels want to support strategies that improve student outcomes and demonstrate results. Education focused on the life career development of students can be a means to those ends. For example Missouri, one of nine Cadre states, found that high schools implementing the ASCA Model and delivering educational and career planning documented higher gains in meeting AYP benchmarks than their counterparts who did not. In addition, the Missouri study documented better attendance rates, fewer discipline problems and higher math scores on the state assessment test among middle school students.

A Reform Primer for Administrators

School counselling is a profession in transition. Its vocational and career-focused heritage, dating back to the 1900's, was a response to the economic, educational, and social problems of the time. These same influences are placing enormous demands on schools once again and thus are reshaping the profession. Even service-based employers who need not fear outsourcing are demanding employees with the flexible higher-order thinking skills required to learn and adapt as technology-driven demands change their industries. Working against the demands for such a workforce are alarmingly high dropout and postsecondary remediation rates; deficient math, science and reading skills; and increases in youth risk behaviours and achievement gaps that separate students of colour and low-income students from white and more affluent students. In addition to efforts to revise curricula and instruction is a strategy too often overlooked: a well developed and implemented school counselling programme driven by needs assessment data and outcomes.

School counsellors' training and skills and their unique role in the school make them ideal coordinators and leaders in implementing a Comprehensive Developmental Guidance programme in which all staff play a role. In a comprehensive developmental guidance model, school counsellors develop and deliver curriculum and interventions that support life-career development. They collaborate with other educators and business/community partners to ensure that students transition to postsecondary education and the workplace with essential knowledge, attitudes and skills for success. Successful implementation of this model, however, requires that administrators understand the emerging role of school counsellors in the 21st century as outlined by ASCA as well as the basic tenets of a comprehensive developmental guidance programme.

Triangulated Leadership

Transforming the role of school counsellors within the school with a focus on career development requires buy-in and collaboration at all levels. To strengthen the pivotal role that school counsellors can play in promoting student achievement and future success, change must take place at the state, district, and school level. The National Leadership Cadre offers the following recommendations:

Leadership at the state level:

Department of Education offices:

- designate and publicize a leader or coordinator to support implementation of CDG programmes and work in partnership with state agencies, associations, and colleges, universities .

- point person to develop state school counselling programmes.
- mandate development of educational and career plans for all students, K-12.
- initiate and nurture partnerships with state school counselling associations and institutions of higher education to develop a state model that includes school counselling curriculum focused on promoting career development and academic achievement.
- support professional development of practicing school counsellors in order to actualize the Model.
- partner within the DOE as well as with other state agencies who are stakeholders in life career development (e.g. Special Education. Career and Technical education, State Departments of Labour, Economic and Workforce Development)
- align licensure requirements with state models.
- seek grant opportunities to fund state-wide school counselling initiatives that include implementation of new models, implementation of effective practices, and professional development needed for integration of career development and academic achievement.

State School Counselling Associations:

- work in partnership with to build good state policy to mobilize their members to fully participate in school counselling reform initiatives.
- lead statewide efforts to promote increased attention to career development by school counsellors.
- lead statewide efforts to promote the integration of school counselling programme with state educational reform initiatives.
- establish a task force to create a state model that aligns with the ASCA National Model.
- sponsor professional development opportunities at annual state conferences
- use a state association website to highlight and share best practices in life career development education.

Counsellor Education Training Programmes:

- encourage state school counselling training programmes to work with the Department of Education, the state school counselling association, and each other to build good state policy and to promote needed reforms in school counselling preparation.

- update the counsellor education curriculum to teach best practices in preventative interventions to increase academic achievement and enhance career development.
- update the counsellor education curriculum to teach best practices in organizing school counselling programmes to support student achievement and educational reform.
- partner with exemplary school districts to support school counselling innovation and reform.

Leadership at the school district level:

- adopt a comprehensive K-12 guidance model with an explicit focus on academic achievement and career development for all students.
- promote professional development that will enable school counsellors to fully implement this comprehensive guidance model.
- hold all schools accountable for creation of impactful educational and career plans for all students.
- establish a district wide policy for common planning time, if only during in-service, where counsellors can work with teachers and paraprofessionals to analyze needs, data etc.
- appoint or support existing district level guidance directors to coordinate linkages between community based organizations, businesses, postsecondary institutions, and regional employment boards

Leadership at the school building level:

- connect the school counselling programme to the school's goals in promoting academic achievement, career development, and successful transitions.
- restructure school counsellors' time to eliminate non-professional duties to promote the ability of the school counsellor to reach all students through classroom, large group, and small group interventions.
- provide common planning time on a regular basis.
- convey message that career curriculum is important and requires and integrated system-wide approach.

- establish and lead a team with representatives from the school counselling, special education, and technology departments to develop the most efficient method to create, store, and access career plans.
- work with school counsellors to identify times in the master schedule for delivering career guidance lessons at each grade level.
- work with school counsellors to develop opportunities for parents to give input to their child's educational/career plan.
- send a team of school counsellors to visit a school where a successful career planning process is already underway.
- allocate necessary funds for purchasing assessment tools and career software.

Co-counselling

Co-counselling (spelled co-counselling in American English) is a grassroots method of personal change based on reciprocal peer counselling. It uses simple methods. Time is shared equally and the essential requirement of the person taking their turn in the role of counsellor is to do their best to listen and give their full attention to the other person. It is not a discussion; the aim is to support the person in the client role to work through their own issues in a mainly self-directed way.

Co-counselling was originally formulated in the early 1950s by the American Harvey Jackins through a combination of his personal experiences gained through a wide range of counselling experience. Jackins founded the Re-evaluation Counselling (RC) Communities, with headquarters in Seattle, Washington, United States. His son, Tim Jackins, is currently the international leader of Re-evaluation Counselling and its main affiliates.

There are a number of smaller, separate, independent organizations that have resulted from breakaways from, or re-workings of, Re-evaluation Counselling. The principal one of these is Co-Counselling International (CCI).

General Description

The main activity in co-counselling involves participants arranging to meet regularly in pairs to give each other peer-to-peer counselling, in turn taking the role of counsellor and client, with equal amounts of time allocated to each. Co-counselling functions by giving people an opportunity to work on whatever issues they choose with the accepting support of another person, with whom they have no actual relationship. The person in the role of counsellor acts a facilitator to the client, sometimes as third-party observer and sometimes as second-party confidant. While co-counselling is sometimes practiced outside a formal organisation, formal co-counselling organisations have developed leadership and support structures, including trainings and retreats.

Safety (in the sense of being very low risk) and the sense that a co-counselling session is a safe space is important to the methods. There are strict rules of confidentiality. In most circumstances, the counsellor may not talk about a client's session without explicit and specific permission by the client. This is stricter than in other practices where practitioners discuss clients with supervisors, colleagues and sometimes with all sorts of other people. The peer relationship makes a considerable contribution to a sense of trust.

The nature of the co-counselling session opens up the possibility for people to get in touch with emotions that they would avoid in any other circumstance. A belief in the value of working with emotions has become a core focus of the approach. Co-counselling training emphasizes methods for accessing and working with emotions, and co-counsellors aim to develop and improve emotional competence through the practice. Evidence as to the actual effectiveness of this method is undemonstrated.

To get involved in co-counselling, it is usually first necessary to complete a course in The Fundamentals of Co-Counselling. The training involves learning how to carry out the roles of client and counsellor. Trainers may be counsellors or simply experienced members of the community. It also covers the guidelines or rules affecting co-counselling for the particular organization. Differences in approach mean that each organization normally requires completion of one of its own courses as a prerequisite for membership, even if someone has already completed a course with another organization.

Theoretical Framework and Assumptions

The original theory of co-counselling centres around the concept of distress patterns. These are patterns of behaviour, that is, behaviour that tends to be repeated in a particular type of circumstance, that are irrational, unhelpful or compulsive. The theory is that these patterns are driven by the accumulated consequences in the mind of (not currently) conscious memories of past events in which the person was unable to express or discharge the emotion appropriate to the event. Co-counselling enables release from the patterns by allowing "emotional discharge" of the past hurt experiences. Such cathartic discharge includes crying, warm perspiration, trembling, yawning, laughing and relaxed, non-repetitive talking. In day-to-day life, these "discharging" actions may be limited by social norms, such as, for example, taboos around crying, which are widespread in many cultures.

Having temporarily undivided supportive attention from another person often gives rise to strong feelings, apparently towards that person, typically of "falling in love" with them. This is similar to the phenomenon of transference, particularly when one of the partners is felt to have more authority because, for instance, they are more experienced, are teachers of co-counselling, or have authority roles within the organisation. The organisations differ in the ways that they handle this. The inability to trust and feel in real relationships is often exacerbated by the pseudo-intimacy of co-counselling, making transference more likely and more dangerous.

Therapeutic Context

Many co-counsellors take the view, often quite strongly, that co-counselling is not psychotherapy. In the beginning, this was because Re-evaluation Counselling decided not to draw on any discipline of psychotherapy for its theory and practice, although RC did incorporate some ideas from psycho-analysis such as "unconscious promptings" which Jackins adapted and relabelled "restimulation". A similar view is taken by some non-RC co-counsellors who regard psychotherapy as involving specialist techniques used by a therapist on a client and is therefore not peer and the client has little or no control over the process. Others consider that co-counselling is psychotherapeutic, in that it enables change or therapy to take place in the psyche, soul affect or being of an individual. Co-counselling takes a positive view of the person (i.e. we are all essentially good), considers the mind and body as an integrated whole and acknowledges the value of catharsis; it is regarded as an approach within humanistic psychology, a view that would be rejected by some within RC.

Re-evaluation Counselling

The core organization structure of RC consists of classes and local communities set up by experienced co-counsellors, which are in turn organized by regions and country. The term "re-evaluation" refers to the client's need to rethink their past distress experiences after the emotional hurt in those experiences have been discharged, and thereby regain ("re-emerge" with) their natural intellectual and emotional capacities. The RC organization and literature do not accept the description of its practice as psychotherapy, maintaining instead that the process of developing distress patterns that dissolve through emotional discharge in the context of appreciative attention is simply a natural process that does not imply either psychopathology on the part of the individual or the need for professional treatment. Re-evaluation Counselling regards other forms of "mainstream counselling" and psychotherapy in general as frequently inadequate attempts to bring about relief from distress using methods that do not focus on discharge and re-emergence.

In RC, the client and counsellor are expected to work co-operatively, participants are expected to provide non-judgemental active listening and to "contradict" the misinformation or other conditions thought to be associated with distress patterns. RC also engages techniques such as "non-permissive" counselling, in which the counsellor intervenes to "interrupt" client patterns without the consent of the client. The structure of RC is one of clearly defined leadership, to encourage clarity in the difficult struggles many people have to achieve breakthroughs against their distresses. RC encourages counsellors to think very hard about all possible ways to assist the client in discharging.

RC approaches the issue of feelings between co-counsellors by having a strict "no-socialising" rule. RC co-counsellors are expected not to socialise or have social or sexual relationships with other co-counsellors unless these relationships pre-dated their becoming co-counsellors. RC specifically rejects the label "transference" for this phenomenon, as this is seen as part of a "symptomatic" method typical in psychology; the original theory of co-counselling (from RC) teaches that the best thing to do in these circumstances is repeatedly counsel on, and "discharge" about, such feelings. In addition, methods of "getting attention out of distress" are available which help with the difficulty of "switching roles" between counsellor and client. When taught correctly, counsellors are soon able to grasp the difference between counselling relationships and those from outside life. However, sometimes there is a marked pull to "socialise" or confuse the boundaries of the co-counselling relationship with other types of relationships.

This is one reason why many consider a well-organised community of co-counsellors with clear rules to be essential in the successful practise of co-counselling.

Re-evaluation Counselling places a high importance on the need to understand and adhere to a comprehensive theory about the nature of the universe and of human beings (known in general as the "Benign Reality"), the best ways of assisting the discharge process and of pro-liberation attitudes in co-counselling. RCers believe that, when taken together, these enable the counsellor to keep a clear picture of the client's "re-emergence" and are therefore very effective. People disagreeing with the theoretical perspective are asked to think and discharge on the points at issue before actively challenging such perspectives. The main aim is to provide a safe, stable and supportive atmosphere within which people can client skillfully and also lead "re-emergent lives" where they are not dependent in a therapeutic sense, but instead become more energetic and effective (a state known as "zestfulness" in RC).

Co-Counselling International

Co-Counselling International (CCI) was started in 1974 as a breakaway from Re-evaluation Counselling by John Heron, who was at the time director of the Human Potential Research Project, University of Surrey UK, and a group of co-counsellors from Hartford, Connecticut, United States. Unlike other breakaways from RC, which involved changes of leadership but otherwise continued to practice in similar ways to RC, the CCI break was ideological, and CCI developed in significantly different ways. The differences are in practice, theory and organisation.

In practice, the client in CCI co-counselling is wholly in charge of the session. In other words, client and counsellor do not work co-operatively. The counsellor only intervenes in accordance with one of three levels of "contract"—free attention, normal and intensive—which are defined in CCI's principles. The only requirement of the counsellor is that they give "free attention" (that is, full supportive attention) to the client. The other two contracts constitute invitations to the counsellor to make interventions from within those permitted if they feel it is appropriate. The intensive contract can be similar to the RC way of working, although the counsellor is still not permitted to intervene as flexibly as in RC. The original theory of co-counselling is taught in the CCI fundamentals training courses, and participants learn techniques for releasing, or "discharging", emotions. However, the theory is not seen as a constraint within CCI, and co-counsellors draw on the whole range of psychotherapeutic theory and methods including analytical, cognitive-behavioural and transpersonal as well as humanistic approaches. The principal constraint is that the client must be able to work self-directedly.

Organisationally, CCI is a peer network with no core structure. Local and national networks have a variety of organisation. Classes and activities are organised by individuals or groups acting self-directedly. John Heron's status within the network has always been as an equal member, although inevitably as a founder member and activist for some 15 years and the person who developed much of the thinking behind CCI, there was a certain amount of transference on him. Heron now lives in New Zealand and is involved with the CCI network there.

CCI approaches the issue of personal relationships between co-counsellors as a matter for raising awareness. CCI co-counsellors may and do have the whole range of personal relationships with other co-counsellors. However, new co-counsellors are encouraged not to develop new non-co-counselling relationships with other co-counsellors until they have more experience and experienced co-counsellors will often have people with whom they only have a co-counselling relationship. Teachers of co-counselling are strongly discouraged from having sexual relationships with people they have taught.

Relations Between CCI and RC

The existence of other co-counselling organisations is generally not mentioned in RC, and RC co-counsellors are often not aware of their existence. Amongst those within RC who know about it, CCI is often seen as an "attack organisation" and was specifically condemned as such in many private and public conversations by Jackins, who claimed that Heron had started it against a specific agreement not to, and in breach of RC guidelines he had previously agreed to. In turn, Heron and many of his supporters claimed that RC was authoritarian and cult-like, and later, that Jackins engaged in sexual abuse of clients. RC supporters parried that CCI fostered a sexually-liberal atmosphere that blurred the boundaries of co-counselling and relationships. RC specifically bans membership to people who have participated in CCI groups actively. The history of co-counselling including its origins with RC is normally taught on CCI Fundamentals courses. CCI, by its nature, has no corporate opinion about RC, and individual CCI co-counsellors have their own views. Most CCI co-counsellors have a benevolent view toward RC, regarding it as a different, alternative approach to co-counselling. Membership of RC is not a bar to membership of CCI, and a few people manage to do both despite the RC ban.

Other Co-counselling Initiatives

- Focusing Partnerships. Co-counselling based on the focusing technique of Eugene Gendlin.
- The Association of Karen Horney Psychoanalytic Counsellors were the original publishers of *The Barefoot Psychoanalyst*, which allies the practice of co-counselling with the theories of Karen Horney. In 1987, the association became The Institute for Self-Analysis, a member of the International Karen Horney Society.
- Dror Co-Counselling was founded in Israel in 1998.
- Peer Listeners was an organisation set up following the resignation of Belgian Daniel Le Bon from RC in 1989.

Relationship Counselling

Relationship counselling is the process of counselling the parties of a relationship in an effort to recognize and to better manage or reconcile troublesome differences and repeating patterns of distress. The relationship involved may be between members of a family or a couple, employees or employers in a workplace, or between a professional and a client. Couple therapy (or relationship therapy) is a related and different process. It may differ from relationship counselling in duration. Short term counselling may be between 1 to 3 sessions whereas long term couples therapy may be between 12 and 24 sessions. An exception is brief or solution focused couples therapy. In addition, counselling tends to be more 'here and now' and new coping strategies the outcome. Couples therapy is more about seemingly intractable problems with a relationship history, where emotions are the target and the agent of change. Marriage counselling or marital therapy can refer to either or some combination of the above. The methods may differ in other ways as well, but the differences may indicate more about the counsellor/therapist's way of working than the title given to their process. Both methods also can be acquired for no charge, depending on your needs.

History

Marriage counselling originated in Germany in the 1920s as part of the eugenics movement. The first institutes for marriage counselling in the USA began in the 1930s, partly in response to Germany's medically directed, racial purification marriage counselling centres. It was promoted in the USA by both eugenicists such as Paul Popenoe and Robert Latou Dickinson and by birth control advocates such as Abraham and Hannah Stone who wrote 'A Marriage Manual' in 1935 and were involved with Planned Parenthood. Other founders in USA include Lena Levine and Margaret Sanger.

It wasn't until the 1950s that therapists began treating psychological problems in the context of the family. Relationship counselling as a discrete, professional service is thus a recent phenomenon. Until the late 20th century, the work of relationship counselling was informally fulfilled by close friends, family members, or local religious leaders. Psychiatrists, psychologists, counsellors and social workers have historically dealt primarily with individual psychological problems in a medical and psychoanalytic framework. In many less technologically advanced cultures around the world today, the institution of family, the village or group elders fulfil the work of relationship counselling. Today marriage mentoring mirrors those cultures.

With increasing modernization or westernization in many parts of the world and the continuous shift towards isolated nuclear families the trend is towards trained and accredited relationship counsellors or couple therapists. Sometimes volunteers are trained by either the Government or social service institutions to help those who are in need of family or marital counselling. Many communities and government departments have their own team of trained voluntary and professional relationship counsellors. Similar services are operated by many universities and colleges, sometimes staffed by volunteers from among the student peer group. Some large companies maintain a full-time professional counselling staff to facilitate smoother interactions between corporate employees, to minimize the negative effects that personal difficulties might have on work performance.

Increasingly there is a trend toward professional certification and government registration of these services. This is in part due to the presence of duty of care issues and the consequences of the counsellor or therapist's services being provided in a fiduciary relationship.

Basic Principles

Before a relationship between individuals can begin to be understood, it is important to recognize and acknowledge that each person, including the counsellor, has a unique personality, perception, set of values and history. Individuals in the relationship may adhere to different and unexamined value systems. Institutional and societal variables (like the social, religious, group and other collective factors) which shape a person's nature, and behaviour are considered in the process of counselling and therapy. A tenet of relationship counselling is that it is intrinsically beneficial for all the participants to interact with each other and with society at large with optimal amounts of conflict. A couple's conflict resolution skills seems to predict divorce rates. Most relationships will get strained at some time, resulting in their not functioning optimally and producing self-reinforcing, maladaptive patterns. These patterns may be called negative interaction cycles. There are many possible reasons for this, including insecure attachment, ego, arrogance, jealousy, anger, greed, poor communication/understanding or problem solving, ill health, third parties and so on.

Changes in situations like financial state, physical health, and the influence of other family members can have a profound influence on the conduct, responses and actions of the individuals in a relationship. Often it is an interaction between two or more factors, and frequently it is not just one of the people who are involved that exhibit such traits. Relationship influences are reciprocal - it takes each person involved to make and manage problems.

A viable solution to the problem and setting these relationships back on track may be to reorient the individuals' perceptions and emotions - how one looks at or responds to situations and feels about them. Perceptions of and emotional responses to a relationship are contained within an often unexamined mental map of the relationship, also called a love map by John Gottman. These can be explored collaboratively and discussed openly. The core values they comprise can then be understood and respected or changed when no longer appropriate. This implies that each person takes equal responsibility for awareness of the problem as it arises, awareness of their own contribution to the problem and making some fundamental changes in thought and feeling. The next step is to adopt conscious, structural changes to the inter-personal relationships and evaluate the effectiveness of those changes over time.

Indeed, "typically for those close personal relations there is a certain degree in 'interdependence' - which means that the partners are alternately mutually dependent on each other. As a special aspect of such relations something contradictory is put outside: the need for intimacy and for autonomy." "The common counterbalancing satisfaction these both needs, intimacy and autonomy, leads to alternately satisfaction in the relationship and stability. But it depends on the specific developing duties of each partner in every life phase and maturity".

Basic Practices

Two methods of couples therapy focus primarily on the process of communicating. The most commonly used method is active listening, used by the late Carl Rogers and Virginia Satir, and recommended by Harville Hendrix in *Getting the Love You Want*. More recently, a method called Cinematic Immersion has been developed by Warren Farrell in *Women Can't Hear What Men Don't Say*. Each helps couples learn a method of communicating designed to create a safe environment for each partner to express and hear feelings. When the Munich Marital Study discovered active listening to not be used in the long run, Warren Farrell observed that active listening did a better job creating a safe environment for the criticizer to criticize than for the listener to hear the criticism. The listener, often feeling overwhelmed by the criticism, tended to avoid future encounters. He hypothesized that we were biologically programmed to respond defensively to criticism, and therefore the listener needed to be trained in-depth with mental exercises and methods to interpret as love what might otherwise feel abusive. His method is Cinematic Immersion.

After 30 years of research into marriage John Gottman has found that healthy couples almost never listen and echo each other's feelings naturally. Whether miserable or radiantly happy, couples said what they thought about an issue, and "they got angry or sad, but their partner's response was never anything like what we were training people to do in the listener/speaker exercise, not even close."

Such exchanges occurred in less than 5 percent of marital interactions and they predicted nothing about whether the marriage would do well or badly. What's more, Gottman noted, data from a 1984 Munich study demonstrated that the (reflective listening) exercise itself didn't help couples to improve their marriages. To teach such interactions, whether as a daily tool for couples or as a therapeutic exercise in empathy, was a clinical dead end.

By contrast emotionally focused therapy for couples (EFT-C) is based on attachment theory and uses emotion as the target and agent of change. Emotions bring the past alive in rigid interaction patterns, which create and reflect absorbing emotional states. As one of its founders Sue Johnson says,

Forget about learning how to argue better, analysing your early childhood, making grand romantic gestures, or experimenting with new sexual positions. Instead, recognize and admit that you are emotionally attached to and dependent on your partner in much the same way that a child is on a parent for nurturing, soothing, and protection.

Research on Therapy

The most researched approach to couples therapy is behavioural couples therapy. It is a well established treatment for marital discord This form of therapy has evolved to what is now called integrative behavioural couples therapy. Integrative behavioural couples therapy appears to be effective for 69% of couples in treatment, while the traditional model was effective for 50-60% of couples .

Relationship Counsellor or Couple's Therapist

Licensed couple therapist may refer to a psychiatrist, clinical social workers, psychologists,pastoral counsellors, marriage and family therapists, and psychiatric nurses.

The duty and function of a relationship counsellor or couple's therapist is to listen, respect, understand and facilitate better functioning between those involved.

The basic principles for a counsellor include:

- Provide a confidential dialogue, which normalizes feelings
- To enable each person to be heard and to hear themselves
- Provide a mirror with expertise to reflect the relationship's difficulties and the potential and direction for change
- Empower the relationship to take control of its own destiny and make vital decisions
- Deliver relevant and appropriate information
- Changes the view of the relationship
- Improve communication

As well as the above, the basic principles for a couples therapist also include:

- To identify the repetitive, negative interaction cycle as a pattern.
- To understand the source of reactive emotions that drive the pattern.
- To expand and re-organize key emotional responses in the relationship.
- To facilitate a shift in partners' interaction to new patterns of interaction.
- To create new and positively bonding emotional events in the relationship
- To foster a secure attachment between partners.
- To help maintain a sense of intimacy.

Common core principles of relationship counselling and couple's therapy are:

- Respect
- Empathy
- Tact
- Consent
- Confidentiality
- Accountability
- Expertise
- Evidence based
- Certification, ongoing training and

In both methods, the practitioner evaluates the couple's personal and relationship story as it is narrated, interrupts wisely, facilitates both de-escalation of unhelpful conflict and the development of realistic, practical solutions.

The practitioner may meet each person individually at first but only if this is beneficial to both, is consensual and is unlikely to cause harm. Individualistic approaches to couple problems can cause harm. The counsellor or therapist encourages the participants to give their best efforts to reorienting their relationship with each other. One of the challenges here is for each person to change their own responses to their partner's behaviour. Other challenges to the process are disclosing controversial or shameful events and revealing closely guarded secrets. Not all couples put all of their cards on the table at first. This can take time.

Novel Practices

A novel development in the field of *couples therapy* has involved the introduction of insights gained from affective neuroscience and psychopharmacology into clinical practice. There has been interest in use of the so-called *love hormone* – oxytocin – during therapy sessions, although this is still largely experimental and somewhat controversial.

Popularized Methodologies

Although results are almost certainly significantly better when professional guidance is utilized, numerous attempts at making the methodologies available generally via self-help books and other media are available.

In the last few years it has become increasingly popular for these self-help books to become popularized and published as an e-book available on the web, or through content articles on blogs and websites. The challenges for individuals utilizing these methods are most commonly associated with that of other self-help therapies or self-diagnosis.

Using modern technologies such as Skype voip conferencing to interact with practitioners are also becoming increasingly popular for their added accessibility as well as discarding any existing geographic barriers. Entrusting in the performance and privacy of these technologies may pose concerns despite the convenient structure, especially compared to the comfort of in-person meetings.

Some resources include:

- Gottman's what makes marriage work
- The Five Love Languages - what spouses respond to.
- Please Understand Me - determining personal psychological makeup.
- Hold me Tight - 'Love demands the reassurance of touch. Most fights are really protests over emotional disconnection. Underneath the distress, partners are desperate to know: Are you there for me?
- Love & Respect - emotional needs of spouses.
- Divorce Busting - solutions for saving and restoring relationships.
- Men Are Like Waffles — Women Are Like Spaghetti
- Marriage Fitness

Relationship Counselling with Homosexual/bisexual Clients

"Marital Therapy" is now referred to as "Couples Therapy" in order to include individuals who are not married or those who are engaged in same sex relationships. Most relationship issues are shared equally among couples regardless of sexual orientation, but LGBT clients additionally have to deal with heteronormativity, homophobia and both socio-cultural and legal discrimination.

Individuals may experience relational ambiguity from being in different stages of the coming out process or having an HIV serodiscordant relationship. Often, same-sex couples do not have as many role models of successful relationships as opposite-sex couples. In many jurisdictions committed LGBT couples desiring a family are denied access to assisted reproduction, adoption and fostering, leaving them childless, feeling excluded, other and bereaved. There may be issues with gender-role socialization that do not affect opposite-sex couples.

A significant number of men and women experience conflict surrounding homosexual expression within a mixed-orientation marriage. Couple therapy may include helping the clients feel more comfortable and accepting of same-sex feelings and to explore ways of incorporating same-sex and opposite-sex feelings into life patterns. Although a strong homosexual identity was associated with difficulties in marital satisfaction, viewing the same-sex activities as compulsive facilitated commitment to the marriage and to monogamy.

Rehabilitation Counselling

Rehabilitation Counselling is focused on helping people who have disabilities achieve their personal, career, and independent living goals through a counselling process. Rehabilitation Counsellors can be found in private practice, in rehabilitation facilities, hospitals, universities, schools, government agencies, insurance companies and other organizations where people are being treated for congenital or acquired disabilities. While most rehabilitation counsellors focus on vocational services, in some states they qualify as both a Certified Rehabilitation Counsellor (CRC) and a Licensed Professional Counsellor (LPC), enabling them to focus on psychotherapy.

Over time, with the changes in social work being more psychotherapy-oriented, rehabilitation counsellors take on more and more community engagement work, especially as it relates to special populations.

History

United States: Historically, rehabilitation counsellors primarily served working-age adults with disabilities. Today, the need for rehabilitation counselling services extends to persons of all age groups who have disabilities. Rehabilitation counsellors also may provide general and specialized counselling to people with disabilities in public human service programmes and private practice settings. Initially, rehabilitation professionals were recruited from a variety of human service disciplines, including public health nursing, social work, and school counselling. Although educational programmes began to appear in the 1940s, it was not until the availability of federal funding for rehabilitation counselling programmes in 1954 that the profession began to grow and establish its own identity.

Education/Training

Though no specific undergraduate degree is required, the majority of rehabilitation counselling graduate students have undergraduate degrees in rehabilitation services, psychology, sociology, or other human services-related fields. As a Masters degree is required at a minimum, rehabilitation counsellors are trained at the graduate level, with most earning a Masters degree, and a few continuing on to the Doctoral level. The Council on Rehabilitation Education (CORE) accredits qualifying institutions, though not all programmes meet accreditation requirements, prohibiting some graduates from professional certification/licensure. Rehabilitation counsellors are trained in the following areas:

- Individual and group counselling
- Medical and psychosocial information
- Problems and community engagement of special populations
- Evaluation and assessment
- Research utilization
- Employment and occupational choice
- Case and caseload management
- Job development and placement

Accredited rehabilitation counsellor education programmes typically provide 60 credit hours of academic and field-based clinical training. Clinical training consists of at least a semester of practicum and a minimum of 600 hours of supervised internship experience. Clinical field experiences are available in a variety of community, state, federal, and private rehabilitation-related programmes.

Professional Certification/Licensure

The Commission on Rehabilitation Counsellor Certification (CRCC) grants certification to counsellors who meet educational requirements and have passed an examination indicating that they possess the competency and skill to become a Certified Rehabilitation Counsellor, (CRC in the United States; CCRC in Canada). A Masters degree is required to obtain certification. Certification as a rehabilitation counsellor is not mandated by any state or federal laws, however eligibility to sit for the certification exam is mandated by federal law for those wishing to work for state/federal vocational rehabilitation systems. Some states have Licensed Rehabilitation Counsellors (LRC), which places LRCs at the same level as other licensed social service professionals. In other states the CRC qualifies the rehabilitation counsellor to obtain the Licensure as a Professional Counsellor (LPC). Certification is highly desirable to many employers.

Social Relevancy

Community service to a culturally and ethnically diverse population, professional functions, critical thinking, advocacy, applied research activities, and ethical standards are integrated throughout rehabilitation counsellor preparation and development. Though rehabilitation counsellors are adept at understanding medical issues surrounding the disability (as proven by certification/licensure), they are trained in the social model of disability, which identifies systemic barriers, negative attitudes and exclusion by society (purposely or inadvertently) that mean society is the main contributory factor in disabling people.

Rehabilitation Counsellors are often advocates in the community for people with disabilities outside of the workplace, with most doing some form of community engagement. As a good portion of counsellors have disabilities themselves, the counselling process often emphasizes self-advocacy skills. Rehabilitation counsellors can be found in the leadership of many prominent organizations that support human rights and civil rights for people with disabilities such as American Coalition of Citizens with Disabilities, National Black Deaf Advocates, etc.

3

Rehabilitation Counselling Careers

Careers in the Profession

In the United States, many rehabilitation counsellors work in a variety of arenas. The predominant placement of rehabilitation counsellors are state rehabilitation programmes as Vocational Counsellors, social service agencies as Administrators, and at the collegiate level as Disability Counsellors/Specialists:

State Rehabilitation Programmes

The predominant need for rehabilitation counsellors is within federal/state funded vocational rehabilitation programmes. While the Veterans Benefits Administration has its own vocational rehabilitation programme, the rest of Federal/State Vocational Rehabilitation Programmes are funded and regulated by the Rehabilitation Services Administration (RSA), a division of the U.S Department of Education. Although policies vary from state to state, rehabilitation counsellors who work in the federal/state systems typically must hold a masters degree in rehabilitation counselling, special education or a related field, and are required to be certified or be eligible to sit for the certification examination. People accepting employment in the federal/state Vocational Rehabilitation programmes do so with the agreement they will meet these qualifications by a specified date to maintain employment.

Social Service Agencies/corporate Sector

Rehabilitation Counsellors can work in the non-profit/corporate sector in various ways. Though the majority start as counsellors, specializing in career counselling, most rehabilitation counsellors that work in the non-profit arena rise to the administration level, either in supervising staff or directing programmes for people with disabilities. Others supervise staff that work in case management programmes that serve people with disabilities. Some rehabilitation counsellors work with Independent Living Centres, doing community engagement, advocacy, outside referrals, and social service provision for people with disabilities. Entrepreneurial rehabilitation counsellors also work as consultants, establishing their own private service agencies. Counsellors in working with corporations focus on community relations or corporate service, serving as liaisons between companies and charities or service programmes.

College Disability Counsellors/specialists

By law all community colleges, colleges and universities are required to make reasonable accommodations for students with disabilities. To satisfy this requirement most collegial settings have a Disability Resources Centre, a Special Needs Coordinator or a similar office. Staff are responsible for coordinating services that *may* include but are not limited to: advocacy/liaison, computer access, counselling (academic, personal, vocational), equipment loan, information/referral services, in-service awareness programmes, notetakers, on campus orientation and mobility training for visually impaired students, priority registration assistance, readers, scribes, shuttle (on-campus), sign language interpreters, test proctoring/testing accommodations, and tutors. Some adaptive technological accommodations *may* include but are not limited to: Adaptive computer technology (including voice activated and speech output), Assistive listening devices, Films/videotapes about disabilities, Kurzweil personal reader, Large print software,Print enlargers (CCTV), Raised-line drawing kit, Tactile map of campus, Talking calculators, Tape recorders/ APH Talking Book Machine, TDD for hearing impaired, Wheelchair, Wheelchair access maps.

Students who have documentation proving their disability status and the staff are trained to access or have knowledge of the necessary services according the students' unique need. As the college level is different from the primary school system, the same services that a student may have received within a special education programme in high school may not be required at the collegiate level. A wide variety of students with disabilities can be served, some examples are individuals with: learning disabilities, sensorial disabilities (hearing loss, vision loss, etc.), physical disabilities (cerebral palsy, etc.) and psychological disabilities.

The Growth of the Field

Job outlook: As of 2010 there were 129,800 working in the field. Jobs for rehabilitation counsellors are expected to grow by 28 percent, which is much faster than the average for all occupations.

Professional Development

There are several professional organizations Rehabilitation Counsellors and other rehabilitation professionals belong to, including the American Rehabilitation Counselling Association, National Rehabilitation Counselling Association, and American Rehabilitation Action Network. Though there is no nationwide union or lobbying organization supporting rehabilitation counsellors (such as is the case with social workers, or psychologists), the Commission on Rehabilitation Counsellor Certification (CRCC) does a lot of work in organizing rehabilitation counsellors that pursue the professional advancement of the young field.

Re-evaluation Counselling

Re-evaluation Counselling or RC is an organization founded in the United States by Harvey Jackins in the 1950s and led by him and others until his death in 1999, though his activity decreased greatly before his death. It introduced a procedure called "co-counselling", which Jackins said was a new and effective method of helping people and bringing about social reform. RC teaches co-counselling and runs workshops throughout the world. It is owned by Re-evaluation Counselling Community Resources, Inc., a company based in Seattle, Washington, USA.

History

Jackins is said to have developed Re-evaluation Counselling after observing a troubled friend change through being patiently listened to while he cried. Curious about the effect of this crying, he worked with others to develop a method of peer counselling based on the recollection of psychological traumas (or "hurts") accompanied by various types of emotional catharsis (or "discharge"). He came to believe that discharge led to clear thinking (or "re-evaluation"). He held that repeated discharge through co-counselling, in which two people counsel one another in turn, could remove the accumulated effects of past hurts and bring about re-evaluation, a process called "re-emergence". The objective of RC became the dissemination of this method of creating rational thinking. Re-evaluation Counselling later put more emphasis on the removal of "oppression", which it considers to lie at the root of many of the world's problems. Jackins systematized re-evaluation counselling during the 1950s and 1960s. From the late 1960s, Jackins spread RC beyond Seattle by means of workshops, and in the mid-1970s travelled outside the US, teaching in the UK, Scandinavia and the rest of Europe. RC is now practiced in most countries.

After Jackins' death in 1999, the leadership passed to his son, Tim Jackins.

Ideas

Re-evaluation Counselling describes itself as "a process for freeing humans and society as a whole from distress patterns so that we may resume fully-intelligent functioning." Counselling is practiced in pairs ("co-counselling"), in which the participants listen to one another in turn and help one other to "discharge". No money is exchanged by the co-counsellors but they pay a fee to the Re-evaluation Counselling organization when attending classes or workshops.

RC believes that everyone is born completely good or innocent, and that all human hurts are acquired. Inappropriate or hurtful behaviour is caused by the unconscious "restimulation" of past hurts that have not been properly discharged. If discharge can be completed, the behaviour will not be repeated. RC believes that, as a result of these past hurts, the average person "is operating on about ten percent of his or her original resources of intelligence, ability to enjoy life and ability to enjoy other people."

The RC counsellor aims to remember the fundamental goodness of the client. Client and counsellor are expected to work co-operatively. The counsellor is expected to listen in a non-judgemental way but also to "contradict" errors and other conditions associated with distress so as to facilitate discharge. The counsellor also intervenes to "interrupt" the client's patterns. Each co-counsellor has to be emotionally healthy and well-versed in co-counselling in order to work effectively together.

RC has been criticized for encouraging emotional display and discouraging analysis of its ideas or research into its effectiveness. Although its advocates refer to the theory of Re-evaluation Counselling, it has been said that RC derives from Harvey Jackins' counselling experience and that "there has been no independent attempt to verify or otherwise the key constructs of RC theory." There have been occasional papers about RC in scholarly journals.

RC does not describe itself as psychotherapy and does not ally itself with any other self-help, counselling, or psychotherapy practice. RC opposes the use of psychiatric drugs and says that "mental illness does not exist." though it acknowledges that physical cerebral differences cause behaviours that are not the result of learned "hurts". John Heron compared RC with and distinguished it from primal therapy, Wilhelm Reich and Freud's early psychoanalysis when he made use of abreaction. The editor of the Brunner-Routledge series of books on "Advancing Theory in Therapy" says that while Re-evalulation Counselling is not generally regarded as a psychotherapy, "it has made and continues to make an important contribution to our understanding of human beings and human situations."

RC considers that co-counselling does not imply psychopathology on the part of co-counsellors or the need for professional treatment, and that there is a need for lay counsellors because of the shortage of professionals. RC says that, for the average person, co-counselling can heal emotional hurts, increase rational thought and increase one's capacity for a joyful and positive life. It has been said that, unlike professional organizations, RC lacks standards for assessing the competence of counsellors or any process for handling grievances. However, teachers must apply to the central organization in Seattle and be accepted as competent before they are allowed to lead groups.

RC's has ambitious social and environmental objectives, including, "The transformation of society to a rational, peaceful, non-exploitative, classless form world-wide. The preservation of all existing species of life and the re-creation of extinguished species. The preservation of wilderness areas and the creation of a completely benign environment over most of the earth, the oceans, and the atmosphere. The exploration of, and eventually becoming at home in, space."

Organization

The organization's official title is "The International Re-evaluation Counselling Communities". It is owned by Re-evaluation Counselling Community Resources, Inc., with headquarters in Seattle. Its President is Tim Jackins and its Vice President is Sarah Elizabeth Jackins. The corporation owns copyright in the terms "Re-evaluation Counselling", "RC" and "United to End Racism". It also controls the Re-evaluation Foundation, a non-profit 501(c) organization, and Rational Island Publishers. Within RC, Tim Jackins is called the "International Reference Person". He is a former mathematics teacher from Palo

Alto, California, and a graduate of Yale and Stanford. He has been a co-counsellor, leader and teacher of RC for most of his life. The International Reference Person appoints senior leaders, who appoint local leaders ("reference persons") in consultation with local groups. Reference persons decide who can attend events, teach RC, lead groups, and, to some extent, who may counsel together. They are not paid. RC considers that this form of centralized leadership is essential for uniformity of practice.

RC runs classes in co-counselling and local groups are set up by people experienced in the ideas and methods of RC who have been approved by the leaders. New members are invited to join "fundamentals" classes by existing members. They are expected to be well-functioning and emotionally healthy so that they can be effective counsellors as well as being able to benefit from counselling. Fees are fixed at a low hourly rate per person, and there are scholarships for people on low incomes. Twenty-five per cent of fees are sent to the central body in Seattle. Participants are asked not to use caffeine or alcohol and must abstain from mind-altering drugs so as to be attentive and to have access to their feelings. People who counsel together are prohibited from socializing with one another. It has been said that, in discussing clients' "distress patterns" in classes and workshops, RC violates the standard of confidentiality that is normally expected in counselling. Classes and local communities are organized into regions and loose, country-wide affiliations, although RC does not organize on national lines. RC is committed to spreading RC practices and insights "as widely as possible in the general population". RC does not seek publicity and states that it keeps a "low profile". Local publicity has to be approved by the regional leader and national and international publicity by the leader of RC. RC does not list local contact information on its website.

RC does not publish membership figures or comment on estimates. On one occasion, Jackins claimed that more than a million had attended RC "Fundamentals" classes. The April 2007 edition of the RC publication *Present Time* listed 243 RC groups (each with about 45 members) and 428 teachers in groups of about 10 people, making an active membership of about 15,000. RC tends not to co-operate with attempts at independent investigation and is sensitive to criticism, either external or internal, which it often regards as an attack on the organization. Jackins believed that much criticism was inspired by the US government, who feared RC's "profoundly progressive nature and its effectiveness". RC instructs members to "to quickly interrupt both attacks and gossip." It says that such attacks are "dramatizations of distress and are not acceptable behaviours within the RC Community. An attack is not an effective way to resolve disagreements or difficulties." "People who participate in an attack must first stop the attack and apologize for having participated in it. Only after they have done this should counselling resource be offered to them." Critics who persist "should be made to leave the group and their attacks ignored."

RC's system of unelected leadership and strict central control have been criticized by ex-members. John Heron, who was an RC leader and teacher, left the organization in 1974 to set up his own co-counselling organization, Co-Counselling International. He said he did so because he realized that RC "systematically conditioned its members to associate a certain kind of beneficial human development with centralized authoritarian control of theory and community policy. It was clear to me that this was pseudo-liberation." He considered that the authoritarianism of RC derived partly from the Leninist doctrines of central control that Jackins had learned in the Communist Party of America and partly from the autocratic example of his former associate L. Ron Hubbard. RC has also been criticized for suppression of internal debate. In an article analysing RC's "attack theory" Steve Carr says that "To counter attacks on RC and its leaders, RC members are instructed to interrupt the person, approach the accusation as the personal problem of the accuser, and vigorously come to the defence of the person or people being attacked." Richard Childs describes how he was treated in this way and expelled from RC when he tried to discuss allegations of sexual abuse within the organisation. However, other RC members have accused leaders or young leaders with sexually inappropriate comments, and there were no negative consequences, and any misunderstandings were resolved amicably.

Re-evaluation Counselling has been listed as a cult while some say that it is like a cult in some respects. The Study Group on Psychotherapy Cults, an organization of ex-members hostile to RC, described it as "cult-like". Denis Tourish and Pauline Irving in a 1994 article considered the characteristics that RC shared with psychotherapeutic cults, namely, a charismatic leader, idealization of the leader, followers regarding their belief system as superior to others, followers joining the group at times of stress, the therapist becoming central to the follower's life, the group absorbing increasing time, illusions of superiority to other groups and the group becoming suspicious of other groups. They concluded: "Given its hostility to such pluralistic notions of participation and democracy, RC has the potential to become a fully fledged and harmful cult, despite its original humanistic aims."

Re-evaluation counselling encourages its members to play an active role in public life and has set up groups to promote its ideas, which it calls "naturalized" groups. The main groups promoting RC methods are United to End Racism" (UER), formed in 2000, and the National Coalition Building Institute, formed in 1984. UER is part of RC and shares its HQ in Seattle. It participated in the 2001 Durban World Conference against Racism, the 2006 Caracas World Social Forum and the 2006 Vancouver World Peace Forum. The National Coalition Building Institute is formally independent of RC but is linked through its Founder-Executive Director, Cherie R. Brown, who is a member of RC and active in UER.

The Re-evaluation Foundation aims "To provide opportunities for people to participate in Re-evaluation counselling who otherwise could not afford to participate." Founded in 1972, it supports projects based on the theory and practice of Re-evaluation Counselling that apply "bold, thoughtful action to freeing human beings from the distresses associated with past hurtful, unjust experiences." Its president is Michael Markovits, a former vice-president of IBM. Its assets at the end of 2006 were $1,063,634. "The Foundation considers grant requests only from members of the Re-evaluation Counselling Communities who are seeking financial assistance that will further the dissemination of the theory and practice of RC." In 2007, the foundation made grants totaling about $240,000 to several organizations controlled by Re-evaluation Counselling, including "People-of-Colour Leadership Development, Global Initiatives, Young People Leadership Development/Family Counselling Work, Elimination of Racism, and Mental Health."

Relationship Counselling

Relationship counselling is the process of counselling the parties of a relationship in an effort to recognize and to better manage or reconcile troublesome differences and repeating patterns of distress. The relationship involved may be between members of a family or a couple, employees or employers in a workplace, or between a professional and a client. Couple therapy (or relationship therapy) is a related and different process. It may differ from relationship counselling in duration. Short term counselling may be between 1 to 3 sessions whereas long term couples therapy may be between 12 and 24 sessions. An exception is brief or solution focused couples therapy. In addition, counselling tends to be more 'here and now' and new coping strategies the outcome. Couples therapy is more about seemingly intractable problems with a relationship history, where emotions are the target and the agent of change.

Marriage counselling or marital therapy can refer to either or some combination of the above. The methods may differ in other ways as well, but the differences may indicate more about the counsellor/ therapist's way of working than the title given to their process. Both methods also can be acquired for no charge, depending on your needs.

History

Marriage counselling originated in Germany in the 1920s as part of the eugenics movement. The first institutes for marriage counselling in the USA began in the 1930s, partly in response to Germany's medically directed, racial purification marriage counselling centres. It was promoted in the USA by both eugenicists such as Paul Popenoe and Robert Latou Dickinson and by birth control advocates such as Abraham and Hannah Stone who wrote 'A Marriage Manual' in 1935 and were involved with Planned Parenthood. Other founders in USA include Lena Levine and Margaret Sanger.

It wasn't until the 1950s that therapists began treating psychological problems in the context of the family. Relationship counselling as a discrete, professional service is thus a recent phenomenon. Until the late 20th century, the work of relationship counselling was informally fulfilled by close friends, family members, or local religious leaders. Psychiatrists, psychologists, counsellors and social workers have historically dealt primarily with individual psychological problems in a medical and psychoanalytic framework. In many less technologically advanced cultures around the world today, the institution of family, the village or group elders fulfil the work of relationship counselling. Today marriage mentoring mirrors those cultures.

With increasing modernization or westernization in many parts of the world and the continuous shift towards isolated nuclear families the trend is towards trained and accredited relationship counsellors or couple therapists. Sometimes volunteers are trained by either the Government or social service institutions to help those who are in need of family or marital counselling. Many communities and government departments have their own team of trained voluntary and professional relationship counsellors. Similar services are operated by many universities and colleges, sometimes staffed by volunteers from among the student peer group. Some large companies maintain a full-time professional counselling staff to facilitate smoother interactions between corporate employees, to minimize the negative effects that personal difficulties might have on work performance.

Increasingly there is a trend toward professional certification and government registration of these services. This is in part due to the presence of duty of care issues and the consequences of the counsellor or therapist's services being provided in a fiduciary relationship.

Basic Principles

Before a relationship between individuals can begin to be understood, it is important to recognize and acknowledge that each person, including the counsellor, has a unique personality, perception, set of values and history. Individuals in the relationship may adhere to different and unexamined value systems. Institutional and societal variables (like the social, religious, group and other collective factors) which shape a person's nature, and behaviour are considered in the process of counselling and therapy. A tenet of relationship counselling is that it is intrinsically beneficial for all the participants to interact with each other and with society at large with optimal amounts of conflict. A couple's conflict resolution skills seems to predict divorce rates.

Most relationships will get strained at some time, resulting in their not functioning optimally and producing self-reinforcing, maladaptive patterns. These patterns may be called negative interaction cycles. There are many possible reasons for this, including insecure attachment, ego, arrogance, jealousy, anger, greed, poor communication/understanding or problem solving, ill health, third parties and so on.

Changes in situations like financial state, physical health, and the influence of other family members can have a profound influence on the conduct, responses and actions of the individuals in a relationship. Often it is an interaction between two or more factors, and frequently it is not just one of the people who are involved that exhibit such traits. Relationship influences are reciprocal - it takes each person involved to make and manage problems.

A viable solution to the problem and setting these relationships back on track may be to reorient the individuals' perceptions and emotions - how one looks at or responds to situations and feels about them. Perceptions of and emotional responses to a relationship are contained within an often unexamined mental map of the relationship, also called a love map by John Gottman. These can be explored collaboratively and discussed openly. The core values they comprise can then be understood and respected or changed when no longer appropriate. This implies that each person takes equal responsibility for awareness of the problem as it arises, awareness of their own contribution to the problem and making some fundamental changes in thought and feeling.

The next step is to adopt conscious, structural changes to the inter-personal relationships and evaluate the effectiveness of those changes over time. Indeed, "typically for those close personal relations there is a certain degree in 'interdependence' - which means that the partners are alternately mutually dependent on each other. As a special aspect of such relations something contradictory is put outside: the need for intimacy and for autonomy."

"The common counterbalancing satisfaction these both needs, intimacy and autonomy, leads to alternately satisfaction in the relationship and stability. But it depends on the specific developing duties of each partner in every life phase and maturity".

Basic Practices

Two methods of couples therapy focus primarily on the process of communicating. The most commonly used method is active listening, used by the late Carl Rogers and Virginia Satir, and recommended by Harville Hendrix in *Getting the Love You Want*. More recently, a method called Cinematic Immersion has been developed by Warren Farrell in *Women Can't Hear What Men Don't Say*. Each helps couples learn a method of communicating designed to create a safe environment for each partner to express and hear feelings.

When the Munich Marital Study discovered active listening to not be used in the long run, Warren Farrell observed that active listening did a better job creating a safe environment for the criticizer to criticize than for the listener to hear the criticism. The listener, often feeling overwhelmed by the criticism, tended to avoid future encounters. He hypothesized that we were biologically programmed to respond defensively to criticism, and therefore the listener needed to be trained in-depth with mental exercises and methods to interpret as love what might otherwise feel abusive. His method is Cinematic Immersion. After 30 years of research into marriage John Gottman has found that healthy couples almost never listen and echo each other's feelings naturally. Whether miserable or radiantly happy, couples said what they thought about an issue, and "they got angry or sad, but their partner's response was never anything like what we were training people to do in the listener/speaker exercise, not even close."

Such exchanges occurred in less than 5 percent of marital interactions and they predicted nothing about whether the marriage would do well or badly. What's more, Gottman noted, data from a 1984 Munich study demonstrated that the (reflective listening) exercise itself didn't help couples to improve their marriages. To teach such interactions, whether as a daily tool for couples or as a therapeutic exercise in empathy, was a clinical dead end.

By contrast emotionally focused therapy for couples (EFT-C) is based on attachment theory and uses emotion as the target and agent of change. Emotions bring the past alive in rigid interaction patterns, which create and reflect absorbing emotional states. As one of its founders Sue Johnson says, Forget about learning how to argue better, analysing your early childhood, making grand romantic gestures, or experimenting with new sexual positions. Instead, recognize and admit that you are emotionally attached to and dependent on your partner in much the same way that a child is on a parent for nurturing, soothing, and protection.

Research on Therapy

The most researched approach to couples therapy is behavioural couples therapy. It is a well established treatment for marital discord This form of therapy has evolved to what is now called integrative behavioural couples therapy. Integrative behavioural couples therapy appears to be effective for 69% of couples in treatment, while the traditional model was effective for 50-60% of couples .

Relationship Counsellor or Couple's Therapist

Licensed couple therapist may refer to a psychiatrist, clinical social workers, psychologists,pastoral counsellors, marriage and family therapists, and psychiatric nurses. The duty and function of a relationship counsellor or couple's therapist is to listen, respect, understand and facilitate better functioning between those involved.

The basic principles for a counsellor include:

- Provide a confidential dialogue, which normalizes feelings
- To enable each person to be heard and to hear themselves
- Provide a mirror with expertise to reflect the relationship's difficulties and the potential and direction for change
- Empower the relationship to take control of its own destiny and make vital decisions
- Deliver relevant and appropriate information
- Changes the view of the relationship
- Improve communication

As well as the above, the basic principles for a couples therapist also include:

- To identify the repetitive, negative interaction cycle as a pattern.
- To understand the source of reactive emotions that drive the pattern.
- To expand and re-organize key emotional responses in the relationship.
- To facilitate a shift in partners' interaction to new patterns of interaction.
- To create new and positively bonding emotional events in the relationship
- To foster a secure attachment between partners.
- To help maintain a sense of intimacy.

Common core principles of relationship counselling and couple's therapy are:

- Respect
- Empathy
- Tact
- Consent
- Confidentiality
- Accountability
- Expertise
- Evidence based
- Certification, ongoing training and

In both methods, the practitioner evaluates the couple's personal and relationship story as it is narrated, interrupts wisely, facilitates both de-escalation of unhelpful conflict and the development of realistic, practical solutions. The practitioner may meet each person individually at first but only if this is beneficial to both, is consensual and is unlikely to cause harm. Individualistic approaches to couple problems can cause harm. The counsellor or therapist encourages the participants to give their best efforts to reorienting their relationship with each other. One of the challenges here is for each person to change their own responses to their partner's behaviour. Other challenges to the process are disclosing controversial or shameful events and revealing closely guarded secrets. Not all couples put all of their cards on the table at first. This can take time.

Novel Practices

A novel development in the field of *couples therapy* has involved the introduction of insights gained from affective neuroscience and psychopharmacology into clinical practice. There has been interest in use of the so-called *love hormone* – oxytocin – during therapy sessions, although this is still largely experimental and somewhat controversial.

Popularized Methodologies

Although results are almost certainly significantly better when professional guidance is utilized, numerous attempts at making the methodologies available generally via self-help books and other media are available. In the last few years it has become increasingly popular for these self-help books to become popularized and published as an e-book available on the web, or through content articles on blogs and websites. The challenges for individuals utilizing these methods are most commonly associated with that of other self-help therapies or self-diagnosis.

Using modern technologies such as Skype voip conferencing to interact with practitioners are also becoming increasingly popular for their added accessibility as well as discarding any existing geographic barriers. Entrusting in the performance and privacy of these technologies may pose concerns despite the convenient structure, especially compared to the comfort of in-person meetings.

Some resources include:

- Gottman's what makes marriage work
- The Five Love Languages - what spouses respond to.

- Please Understand Me - determining personal psychological makeup.
- Hold me Tight - 'Love demands the reassurance of touch. Most fights are really protests over emotional disconnection. Underneath the distress, partners are desperate to know: Are you there for me?
- Love & Respect - emotional needs of spouses.
- Divorce Busting - solutions for saving and restoring relationships.
- Men Are Like Waffles — Women Are Like Spaghetti
- Marriage Fitness

Relationship Counselling with Homosexual/bisexual Clients

"Marital Therapy" is now referred to as "Couples Therapy" in order to include individuals who are not married or those who are engaged in same sex relationships. Most relationship issues are shared equally among couples regardless of sexual orientation, but LGBT clients additionally have to deal with heteronormativity, homophobia and both socio-cultural and legal discrimination. Individuals may experience relational ambiguity from being in different stages of the coming out process or having an HIV serodiscordant relationship. Often, same-sex couples do not have as many role models of successful relationships as opposite-sex couples. In many jurisdictions committed LGBT couples desiring a family are denied access to assisted reproduction, adoption and fostering, leaving them childless, feeling excluded, other and bereaved. There may be issues with gender-role socialization that do not affect opposite-sex couples.

A significant number of men and women experience conflict surrounding homosexual expression within a mixed-orientation marriage. Couple therapy may include helping the clients feel more comfortable and accepting of same-sex feelings and to explore ways of incorporating same-sex and opposite-sex feelings into life patterns. Although a strong homosexual identity was associated with difficulties in marital satisfaction, viewing the same-sex activities as compulsive facilitated commitment to the marriage and to monogamy.

Vocational Choice

If we are to help a person find work even though he is handicapped, how do we know what is best for him? How can we help them make decisions about work and education? What kind of problems will they have to overcome to get work? Early theories of occupational choice were based on an economic perspective and today that is also a large factor in determining the occupation a person chooses. However, there are psychological and sociological aspects of occupational choice.

Many times persons are offered advice that does not take into account religious views, history of one's mother country, and attitudes about work based in the literature of one's home country. There are several theories of occupational choice - that is what job is right for a person with certain characteristics? The theories are based on the view of a normal person who progresses through stages of human development. Each theory emphasizes certain factors:

- the person has to select his own occupation,
- there are certain factors that influence occupational choice,
- choosing an occupation is a very distinct event in one's life.

One of the most popular theories is trait-factor. This means that a person has certain distinct traits that are needed for success in a certain job. For example, a bookkeeper should be a person who likes accuracy, detail, mathematics, and quiet work area. If a person's traits can be measured, there is a direct way to predict success in certain job.

When this theory is applied to helping people find jobs, there are the following implications:

1. Each person has traits that are for one or a few correct occupations.
2. If left alone, a person should naturally make the correct occupational choice.
3. Without assistance though, a person might choose the wrong occupation and waste his time.
4. During the teen-age years, a person should learn what traits he has.
5. When the person knows his traits and the jobs that correlate with his traits, his educational choices should be based on those traits.
6. The choice of occupation and decisions that affect achieving that occupation should remain constant over a period of time. For example, if a young person decides to become a doctor, he will make decisions about his education (which medical institute

is best, what speciality interests him the most, and what is necessary for him to know to pass entry exams) so that he will eventually be the doctor he wants to be.

Another theory is that a person has certain needs that drive him toward a certain job. The motivation to satisfy these needs may be logical or emotional, conscious or unconscious, and directly or indirectly expressed in words. It is said that work is a way to satisfy one's needs. For example, a person may have a need for stability so that he finds a job that pays him well, and he stays in that job all of his life. He is content to be in one place and have reliable pay every month. Some vocational scientists have developed six basic interests or needs that can be measured. They are:

1. Theoretical - An overriding interest in the discovery of truth and an experimental, rational, and intellectual approach.
2. Economic - This is an emphasis on practical values and doing business activities.
3. Aesthetic - Placement of highest value on form and harmony; evaluating experience from its gracefulness, symmetry, or fitness.
4. Social - Emphasizing altruism and philanthropy
5. Political - An interest in personal power, influence, and renown.
6. Religious - Interest in unity of experience and in attempting to understand people and the universe in a whole system.

Theory of Early Parent-Child Relationships

Ann Roe developed three types of psychological climates that affect the work children eventually choose. If a parent is focuses on the emotional aspects of a child's growth, the result is an over-protecting or over-demanding atmosphere for the child. For example, the parent may be so concerned that the child has quiet, non-threatening life experiences as he grows, the child grows up in an over-protecting environment, not one that usually helps him adapt to different types of people and experiences. These children may choose occupations that have to do with emphasis on their own importance such as a political or governmental occupation.

The avoidance of a child results in his growing up in a neglectful or rejecting climate. Oftentimes these children have difficult behaviour as babies and their parents try everything to satisfy them without being very successful. These children tend to choose those jobs that involve objects (technology), animals (outdoor life occupations), or ideas (science). The parent who is relaxed and accepting of his child tries to provide a loving atmosphere for growth. These children tend to choose those professions that relate to people such a teachers, professors, doctors, social workers, and church workers.

Vocational Development

The main idea of all the theories of occupational choice is that one, several, or a group of factors influence the person and at some point in live each person chooses an occupation in association with these factors or as a reaction to them.

There is another group of theories that states that a person proceeds through various stages in life with vocation as only one part of his human development. For example, as people age and gain life experience, they may turn to another occupation. An engineer may become a teacher or pastor. A person does not choose an occupation for the whole of life, but chooses a series of occupations related to his life stage. People are not designated for a correct occupation - everyone can be satisfied with many jobs. These theories are known as theories of vocational development.

For example, each person goes through a course of development psychologically and socially. Through what he experiences, he grows in different ways. There are some basic assumptions about vocational development:

1. Individual development is continuous, and there are distinct life stages.
2. People in each stage of life have certain common traits.
3. Most people in a specific culture pass through similar developmental periods.
4. Society places certain demands on individuals and they are similar for all people in that society.
5. Developmental crises occur when people become aware of the need to change current behaviour and learn new coping skills.
6. As individuals learn new skills, they become more mature.
7. Preparations for overcoming a developmental crisis are made in the stage prior to next new crisis.
8. The crisis must be met successfully before the individual can pass to another developmental stage.

9. Learning required tasks gives the individual approval from society and helps a person pass through other crises successfully.

There may be a series of different tasks for a person to complete in society. An adolescent faces the task of choosing an occupation, but he must also master several other tasks concurrently:

- Accept his physical appearance,
- Accept the masculine or feminine role,
- Establish relationships with both sexes,
- Depend less on his parents for emotional support,
- Develop socially responsible behaviour,
- Prepare for marriage and family,
- Establish his own life values.

Another theory is that occupational choice is a long-term process that becomes progressively irreversible. A final choice in occupations is the compromise of an ideal and the available realistic alternatives. For example, a person may want to become a doctor after having an illness from which he recovered. However, his age may limit him since medical study requires long preparation. Instead, he may become a laboratory researcher or help with funding a research group that is trying to conquer a certain disease.

Also, when an occupational choice is made, other choices are eliminated. As time goes by, the ability to change professions is limited. The responsibilities of family, finances, and use of one's energies limits choices. Other factors that affect occupational choice are role models, coping with reality of certain occupational environments, and if a person thinks of work as enjoyment or a task.

Another theory is that a person develops an image of himself as he works. Through different work activities, people learn about their own unique style and similarity to others. Sensations, perceptions, and experiences all help a person to build an adult image of himself. People work to earn a living, to gain recognition as a person, to express themselves, and for satisfaction. So vocational development occurs in a social and economic sphere of work.

How Do These Theories Relate to Disabled Persons?

Disabilities affect a person's ability to do a certain type of work. Adjustment to disability affects how a person works. For example, a person who loses a leg may not have the ability to return to his former job assembling cars. He must find other work where he is not required to stand for long periods of time. Adjustment to a disability may be positive in that a person strives to work after the disability occurs. It may be negative because a person sees himself as unable to work and must sit at home for the rest of his life. The vocational development of the person before his disability has a direct effect on how he sees himself after the disability happens. The rehabilitation specialist needs to know what residual abilities the person has after an accident and identify the disabled persons needs (independence, adequate income, care for family, etc.). By knowing these abilities and needs, the specialist can help a person find work that fits abilities and needs.

How do we know if a person is successful in a new job or in training? In a new job, we see that he is using his abilities and gaining some new ones. His work pleases him and he is a stable worker. If he decides on training, we verify that he attends classes, he finishes his course of training, and finds a job that gives him stability.

There are four potential problem areas for the individual with a disability as he begins his search for work.

1. Most kinds of work are done away from home and require travel to the place of work
2. Work is done in a public place, so that privacy from others is limited.
3. The work situation is impersonal and work is done regardless of a person's personal characteristics.
4. Work is bound by time commitments, that is, a person has to be on a job for so many hours per day or complete so many tasks per day.

Each work situation is special in that there are certain customs, rules, and traditions that come from the culture a person lives in and from the specific work place's history and place in society. For example, a car repairman has certain procedures he follows in fixing a car and there are certain prices paid for his knowledge and expertise. The car repairman's work place may be his own yard by his own home, which is not a high level place in society, or it may be with a dealer repairing BMW cars which is more prestigious.

How Do We Help a Person Understand How to Look for Different Work?

As we get to know the person, we are able to collect data about his medical history, his level of education, interest inventories, behaviour descriptions of himself and what others think of him, his likes and dislikes, and his sense of values. From all this information, we have a picture of who the person is and help him understand himself.

The process of finding a good job or career is not exact, but then neither is the choice of a marriage partner. Both of these choices maybe emotionally influenced, based on inadequate sampling of what is available, and scientifically unsound, but they can produce happy outcomes.

In many developing countries in the world, types of work are constantly changing. Professions we never heard of 10 years ago are now established. Many older types of work are vanishing as machines now do them or there is not a need for this work anymore. People with or without disabilities need to think about the type of work they do because the world of work is always changing. It changes drastically after an accident. For example, a person who is injured as a builder may not be able to work at his former job anymore. Therefore, he needs to find a job that will use his skills from earlier jobs. He may become a building inspector or order supplies for a builder.

In the modern world, the idea of having a job for all of one's life is no longer an option. Persons may change jobs every few years since the needs of a country change. The types of jobs that may be practiced over a lifetime are those associated medicine and government. Most other jobs will change in form over the years. For example, many engineers and university researchers lost their jobs in Russia during the 1990's. Some of these people became drivers since they have a good work record and ability to learn new habits. Some of these people have gone on to other jobs, but others have remained in their work as drivers and make a good income.

How Do We Find Information About Jobs?

There are local information centres in each region that provide information about jobs available. The disadvantage about this system is that the information may be out of date and the bureaucracy is not willing to help you find the information you need. However, that may be the first place to begin looking for jobs for your client.

There is also local information in your towns. There maybe employers who list job needs in their offices of personnel. For example, Perekriostik, a grocery store chain in Moscow, lists needs for persons with disability near their manager's office. When looking at such a job, you must observe the workers in this job while they are at work, find out how much training is needed for the job, find out about the rate of pay, and hours of work. Sometimes people with disabilities are hired simply as a tax break for an employer. The disabled worker gets very little pay and very little time actually working.

Newspapers and television are also sources of information. For example, there are ads in newspapers for work and special newspapers about types of jobs that need workers. Sometimes special announcements are made on television or radio about new businesses or factories that are opening. If the business is legitimate, it is good to keep a file of each one, its location, and telephone number.

How can you help the client know about a specific job? Gathering information becomes specific when one needs to know about a specific job. There are:

- legal qualifications - is a license required to do this job, are there legal restrictions that prevent a disabled person from doing this job?
- medical qualifications - what are the specific physical demands for this job? For example, a watch repairman needs finger dexterity to do his job. By actually looking at a person doing the job, you can observe what physical demands are made on his body to do this job.
- social skill requirements - one must be able to get along with others in a job, especially, the boss, co-workers, and supervisors.
- education - usually the completion of high school is necessary to get any type of job, however, once a person is in a job, advancement depends on practical learning rather then educational credentials
- job duties - analyze what is each mini-task of a job is, for example, working on an assembly line is not merely one big job, but may involve putting a certain number of items in a box, closing a box, and putting it on a different conveyer.
- working conditions - this includes the amount of time spent on the job each day, special hazards of the job, the social climate of the job meaning that certain types of clothing may be necessary or certain relationships are important in doing one's job, and accessibility to transport to a job.
- payment for work

- availability of this job over a period of time - is it a short term job that will be finished in a period of months, does it depend on weather conditions (such as construction work), or would it be better for a person to have his own independent work?

How Does a Person Make a Choice of a Job or Occupation?

A person must be familiar with his own strengths and liabilities. He must know about the job he wants to do. His goals must fit with the job he wants to do.

If a person is over the age of 35 years and enjoyed his former work, he can use the skills he has now and apply them to another job. For example, if he worked on a construction site, he may be able to use the skills he learned there in a store or market helping people estimate the quantity of materials needed for a certain remodelling job or he may simply work in a place that sells building materials.

There are several types of decision-making processes that can be taught to help a person make a decision. Here is one of them:

1. The person must be willing to make a decision to solve a problem.
2. The problem must be defined and the goals identified - for example, a problem could be "finding a job that is suitable for me" and the goal would be to find the job in 2 months.
3. Alternatives to the decision are identified - for example, a person could say that actually working on a job is not his choice and he would rather take a government pension and play cards or watch television for the rest of his life.
4. Information is collected about the decision through interviews with prospective employers, other workers in the same jobs, or written materials.
5. The results of this data and the various possible choices are reviewed and compared.
6. There is a comparison of the person's values, family situation, and practicality of a job with the choices. For example, a man may want to drive a truck for a living, but if he has children, what kind of driving will he choose: does he want to be away from his family for weeks or does he want to drive locally and be at home every night?
7. The person makes a choice.

8. The chosen alternative is tried and the person evaluates whether or not he needs to change his situation or stay with the job he chose.

Career Development Theory

Think for a Minute: What is a Theory?

When the age-old question, "What am I going to be when I grow up?" is asked, how do we help our clients/students find the answer? What is the process that will help facilitate satisfying career decisions? What methods/activities are effective? How do we identify problem areas? What is career maturity? A theoretical perspective of career development provides the foundation, a starting point, to understanding the answers to these questions.

"A theory is a system of general concepts that provides a framework for organizing and interpreting observations. Theories help us to identify the orderly relationships that exist among many and diverse events" (Newman & Newman, 1984, p. 5). "

Counselling theories are conceptual frameworks for describing or understanding complex human developmental processes. Theories describe, explain, generalize, and summarize what we do in counselling to help clients make constructive changes that lead to success and satisfaction" (ICDM, 1991, p. 4-2). Theories give us a mental model from which to organize and interpret information to help determine what approach might be most appropriate.

This focuses on theories of career development. It will emphasize the role theory plays in designing career development programmes, creating assessment tools, and selecting methods to aid in the decision process. It will provide a knowledge base for the career development paraprofessional, and hopefully will stimulate a desire to go beyond, by reading and attending classes or workshops in order to build a greater understanding of the process and to expand helping skills.

Before we address future planning, we first need to identify the client's/student's current situation. That is, what is the starting point, what are his or her specific needs and what is the preferred way to approach the client/student? Demonstrating empathy helps build rapport and trust and provides a reference point with which to plan an individualized career planning strategy. The first two general theoretic concepts (discussed below) are meant to help clarify and provide insight into these issues.

Career Development Theory Overview

"We use theories to help us reduce or manage uncertainty and make more responsible decisions" (ICDM, 1991, p. 4-2). Career development theories provide a set of assumptions about vocational development. Theories provide models to sort out the various factors involved in career development. They help us understand the process and offer a framework in which to organize activities that will facilitate insight and growth within the client. These theories give us a foundation for organizing information about the client to use in formulating appropriate goals. In summary, career development theory helps to:

- make sense of what we experience and learn;
- bridge gaps between knowledge and the unknown;
- summarize information;
- explain information;
- make predictions;
- point out relations between means and ends;
- formulate goals; and,
- "stimulate research aimed at improving the knowledge and skill bases for career counselling" (Shertzer and Stone, as cited in ICDM, 1991, p. 4-3).

To best help the client/student, understanding his/her career maturity, that is, where the individual is in the process and how effective he/she has been in the past, is an important start. Career development theory acts as a reference point for the facilitator: "Theoretical perspectives on career development have contributed a great deal to career-guidance programmes by providing insights into developmental stages and tasks associated with transitions between stages, identification of personality types and corresponding work environments, and decision-making techniques.

In addition, these theories have delineated the effects of sex-role stereotyping, provided special insights into the career development of women, ethnic minorities, and other groups, and clarified aspects of social learning theory and its relationship to career development" (Zunker, 1994, p. 12). A number of theories have been developed to aid in our understanding of career development, that is, how we "become" whatever it is that we "become". Jepsen (1984) developed a classification system to provide an organizational basis for understanding career development theories. He divided the theories into "two broad groups: structural and developmental" (ICDM, 1991, p. 4-4).

- o Structural theories focus on individual characteristics and occupational tasks.
- o Developmental theories focus on human development across the life span.

One word of caution: As you read descriptions of these theories, keep in mind they have a limiting factor in that much of the research was based on white males. Issues facing specific populations, i.e., women, minorities, etc. may be different and require different approaches. The following overview describes theories typical of this classification system. The format used comes from the Improved Career Decision-Making in a Changing World. The following is just a brief overview. Read Your Zunker text, some of the related reference material cited in your bibliography, and Feller and Walz text to enhance your theoretical foundations.

Structural Theories

Trait and Factor: This theory began with Parsons, who proposed that choice of a vocation depended upon (1) an accurate knowledge of yourself, (2) thorough knowledge of job specifications, and (3) the ability to make a proper match between the two. He wrote: "In the wise choice of a vocation there are three broad factors: (1) a clear understanding of yourself, your aptitudes, abilities, interests, ambitions, resources, limitations; (2) a thorough knowledge of the requirements and conditions of success, advantages and disadvantages, compensation, opportunities, and prospects in different lines of work; (3) true reasoning on the relations of these two groups of facts" (Parsons, 1909/1989, p. 5). Williamson (1939) and others expanded this theory through the use of tests and other assessment tools to measure people's traits and the traits required in certain occupations.

Two major assumptions of trait and factor theory are: (1) individuals and job traits can be matched, and (2) close matches are positively correlated with job success and satisfaction. These ideas are still part of our career counselling approach today.

John Holland — Vocational Personalities and Environments: This typology theory was developed to organize the voluminous data about people in different jobs and the data about different work environments, to suggest how people make careers choices and to explain how job satisfaction and vocational achievement occur. Holland suggests that "people can function and develop best and find job satisfaction in work environments that are compatible with their personalities" (ICDM, 1991, p. 4-4). Holland based his theory of personality types on several assumptions. People tend to choose a career that is reflective of their personality. Because they tend to be attracted to certain jobs, the environment then reflects this personality. He classified these personality types and work environments into six types that he labelled realistic, investigative, artistic, social, enterprising, and conventional (often referred to by the acronym RIASEC). He suggests that the closer the match of personality to job, the greater the satisfaction.

All types are part of each of us. However, one type is usually evidenced most strongly. We may even resemble up to three of the types. Holland developed a hexagon model that illustrates some key concepts: consistency, differentiation, identity, and congruence. A very brief overview of the six personality types, six work-related activities, and sample occupations is presented below. For an in-depth description, refer to The Self-Directed Search Professional Manual listed.

"Holland's theory places emphasis on the accuracy of self-knowledge and career information necessary for career decision making" (Zunker, 1994, p. 49).

Although the theory appears to be applicable to both male and female workers, there is some question of gender bias in that most females frequently tend to score predominately in three personality types: artistic, social, and conventional. Holland suggests that in our sexist society, females will display a greater interest in female-dominated occupations:

Type	*Activities*	*Occupations*
Realistic	Working with things. i.e. tools and machines	Farmer Carpenter Mechanical Engineer
Investigative	Working with informationi.e. abstract ideas and theories	Chemist
Artistic	Creating things	Painter Writer
Social	Helping people	Social Worker Teacher's Aide
Enterprising	Leading others	Sales Representative Entrepreneur
Conventional	Organizing data	Night Auditor Secretary

Socioeconomic Theory

"Sociologists and economists provide detailed explanations and descriptions of how one's culture, family background, social and economic conditions and other factors outside an individual's control strongly influence one's identity, values, and overall human and career development. Socioeconomic theory is also known as the "chance" or "accident" theory. This approach to understanding career development suggests that many people follow the path of least resistance in their career development by simply falling into whatever work opportunities happen to come their way" (ICDM, 1991, p. 4-4, 4-5).

Developmental Theories

Super's Theory: "Donald Super (1957) and other theorists of career development recognize the changes that people go through as they mature. Socioeconomic factors, mental and physical abilities, personal characteristics and the opportunities to which persons are exposed determine career patterns. People seek career satisfaction through work roles in which they can express themselves and implement and develop their self-concepts. Career maturity, a main concept in Super's theory, is manifested in the successful accomplishment of age and stage developmental tasks across the life span" (ICDM, 1991, p. 4-5).

Krumboltz's Social Learning Theory

Much growth takes place as a result of learning and imitating the behaviour of others. Krumboltz:

"developed a theory of career decision making and development based on our social learning, or environmental conditions and events, genetic influences and learning experiences. People choose their careers on the basis of what they have learned. Certain behaviours are modelled, rewarded and reinforced" (ICDM, 1991, p. 4-5).

Decision-Making Theories

"Some decision-making theories hypothesize that there are critical points in our lives when choices are made that greatly influence our career development. These decision-making points are such events as educational choices, entry-level job positions, changing jobs, etc. Other decision-making theories are concerned with ongoing choices across the life span. The decisions that we make are influenced by our awareness of the choices that are available to us and our knowledge of how to evaluate them" (ICDM, 1991, p. 4-5).

Others address our complex environment. For example, H.B. Gelatt says, "We make our decisions based upon what is actual and what is actual is never static" (Gelatt, 1991, p. 1).

Cognitive Theories

Cognitive Theories of Career Development: "are built around how individuals process, integrate and react to information. The ways in which individuals process information are determined by their cognitive structures. These structures influence how individuals see themselves, others and the environment. Cognitive theories suggest ways to help clients build or refine a hierarchy of thinking skills and decision making skills that influence career development" (ICDM, 1991, p. 4-5).

Emerging Theories and Beyond Theories

Zunker's Theory: Zunker asserts that the recent trend in career counselling places greater emphasis on a humanistic approach designed to expand one's awareness of life, bringing greater meaning to all aspects of life-style. "In essence, the more an individual is aware of his or her potential and experience, the greater the likelihood of self-assertion and direction" (Zunker, 1994, p. 13). There is always the need for continued research. Current theories need refining and "new theories must be developed that address the needs of specific populations, such as females, the gifted and talented, people of colour, ethnic minorities, ex-offenders and persons with disabilities" (ICDM, 1991, p. 4-6).

Bolles' Paradigm: Career theories, by their very nature, explore in depth and tend to focus on narrow issues. They play an important role in understanding human nature however, it is equally important to view the whole picture as the sum of its parts. Aside from theory, some career programmes (systems) are based on philosophy. Richard Nelson Bolles' life/work planning is such a model.

His holistic process evolved over the last twenty-five years and is continuously expanding. It encompasses the "total person", taking into consideration physical, intellectual, mental, emotional, and spiritual needs. In What Colour Is Your Parachute?, Bolles writes about the importance of knowing your mission, that is, finding purpose in life. He addresses how various life roles fit into the bigger life/work picture. He says that we need to challenge all assumptions, paying careful attention on two levels: the human level and the spiritual level. He speaks to the fulfillment of our psychological needs as well as the importance of addressing spiritual issues. In essence, there is both the trait and factor approach and developmental schema in his process.

Maslow's Theory of Motivation and Personality

What motivates us? Maslow believed that we move in the direction of growth by seeking fulfillment of our needs. He identified a hierarchy of needs the individual strives to fulfill. (HT-1.26) These include: (1) physiological (2) safety (3) social (love and belonging) (4) ego (self-esteem) and (5) self-actualization. Maslow maintained that first we seek to satisfy the lower, primary needs (physiological and safety). As this occurs, we to move on to the higher needs (social and ego), and finally we strive toward the pinnacle, self-actualization. As our clients/students are influenced, so are we. It is important to identify our own current status on the hierarchy, as well as that of our clients/students, and to understand our motivating factors as well as the motivations of those we are helping.

Left/Right Brain: How People Approach Learning

We all learn from both sides of our brain. The difference is in the emphasis or area that we tend to concentrate on and use most. How do we take in information? How do we learn? The left side of the brain "sees" in linear form and concentrates on expressing ideas with words as symbols. The right side is our creative side and expresses ideas with pictures. The following chart (HT-1.27) delineates some of the differences between the functions of the two sides of the brain:

Left Side	***Right Side***
verbal expression	non-verbal expression
structure	spontaneity
logic	intuition
reason	emotion
words	pictures
linear	non-linear
sequential, one at a time	simultaneous, all at once
analytical	creative

This has implications in the entire communication process: for developing the helping relationship, for developing rapport and trust, and for assisting clients/students through the decision making process. There is also richness to this concept in exploring occupational areas during the career planning process (Bolles, 1981, pp. 94-97, 99-101,140-141).

Blooms Taxonomy

In 1956, Benjamin Bloom headed a group of educational psychologists who developed a classification of levels of intellectual behaviour important in learning. This became a taxonomy including three overlapping domains; the cognitive, psychomotor, and affective.

Cognitive learning is demonstrated by *knowledge recall* and the intellectual skills: comprehending information, organizing ideas, analyzing and synthesizing data, applying knowledge, choosing among alternatives in problem-solving, and evaluating ideas or actions. This domain on the acquisition and use of knowledge is predominant in the majority of courses. Bloom identified six levels within the cognitive domain, from the simple recall or recognition of facts, as the lowest level, through increasingly more complex and abstract mental levels, to the highest order which is classified as evaluation. Verb examples that represent intellectual activity on each level are listed here.

1. Knowledge: arrange, define, duplicate, label, list, memorize, name, order, recognize, relate, recall, repeat, reproduce state.
2. Comprehension: classify, describe, discuss, explain, express, identify, indicate, locate, recognize, report, restate, review, select, translate,
3. Application: apply, choose, demonstrate, dramatize, employ, illustrate, interpret, operate, practice, schedule, sketch, solve, use, write.
4. Analysis: analyze, appraise, calculate, categorize, compare, contrast, criticize, differentiate, discriminate, distinguish, examine, experiment, question, test.
5. Synthesis: arrange, assemble, collect, compose, construct, create, design, develop, formulate, manage, organize, plan, prepare, propose, set up, write.
6. Evaluation: appraise, argue, assess, attach, choose compare, defend estimate, judge, predict, rate, core, select, support, value, evaluate.

Affective learning is demonstrated by behaviours indicating attitudes of awareness, interest, attention, concern, and responsibility, ability to listen and respond in interactions with others, and ability to demonstrate those attitudinal characteristics or values which are appropriate to the test situation and the field of study. This domain relates to emotions, attitudes, appreciations, and values, such as enjoying, conserving, respecting, and supporting. Verbs applicable to the affective domain include accepts, attempts, challenges, defends, disputes, joins, judges, praises, questions, shares, supports, and volunteers.

Psychomotor learning is demonstrated by physical skills; coordination, dexterity, manipulation, grace, strength, speed; actions which demonstrate the fine motor skills such as use of precision instruments or tools, or actions which evidence gross motor skills such as the use of the body in dance or athletic performance. Verbs applicable to the psychomotor domain include bend, grasp, handle, operate, reach, relax, shorten, stretch, write, differentiate (by touch), express (facially), perform (skillfully).

Case Management Skills

Case Management Skills: In a time of national trauma and a shrinking economy we need to work together to be caring and cost-effective helpers. To be able to provide services that will lessen clients' stresses, we must work together to address the needs of the people we serve. To prepare well-qualified, productive workers, we must collaborate with all segments of our communities. In this way we become better able to help people obtain meaningful employment.

Case management is a holistic, comprehensive, client-centred model that tailors programmes to the clients' needs and includes assessment, goal setting, strategizing, referrals, and follow-up. It is an on-going process that involves coordinating services that are necessary and appropriate to meet the goals of the client. For example, in Workforce Initiative Act programmes, case management involves the processes of career counselling, basic skills, job training and job placement, as well as linkages to other agencies. Oversight and coordination of the participants' activities are mandated throughout programme participation.

Case management involves linking and accessing various programme services, i.e., assisting with child care arrangements while a client attends a training programme, or coordinating training dollars with another agency.

"Career development is an integral part of the case management process. In the assessment phase using tests, card sorts, activities, worksheets, helping sessions and facilitator observation, we assist clients/students in assessing their roles, interests, values, skills and aptitudes, and preferred work environments. Identifying the client's personal realities and developmental needs will help to develop strategies and support for overcoming significant barriers to employment. These barriers can be lack of basic skills, lack of reliable transportation, inadequate housing, no child care, difficulty managing time and finances, lack of prior employment, or no background in making decisions." (Workforce in Transition, p. A-19)

Tasks involved in career development that also apply to case management include:

- o assisting the client in moving toward self-sufficiency and away from dependency on human service programmes and personnel
- o providing short- or long-term support as the client develops needed
- o skills and occupational/job search readiness
- o providing ways in which the client can experience successes, however
- o small, that build self-esteem
- o assisting the client in accessing information about occupations and the labour market which will increase the client's effectiveness in making realistic career plans

Often, your agency/school may be the first place of contact for a client who is seeking career development services. If your initial assessment indicates that your client is appropriate for some aspect(s) of your agency/school's services, you may be designated as the case manager or CDF. In other parts of this training, more specific case management activities will be described. If your agency is not totally equipped to meet the needs of your particular client, you may need to refer the client to other agencies for specific services.

Also bear in mind that man y clients seeking personal counselling, mental health counselling, or drug and alcohol counselling may present or require assistance with career-related issues in association with other changes they are making.

Collaboration/Linkages/Referrals

Supervisory support is critical. At all times, these activities should be carried out under the guidance of a counsellor or other supervisor. Sometimes your supervisor will suggest that you consult with related outside agency staff. For example, when working with an individual with a disability, consult a counsellor with rehabilitation service expertise. Some of these agencies are discussed below.

In successful case management, the client must be seen as a "total person". Specific concerns may be handled by cooperation with, and appropriate referral to, outside agencies. Personal concerns could encompass areas such as: family problems, child care, substance abuse, interpersonal relationships, health, behavioural problems, transportation, housing, or legal problems. It is important to connect with agencies and to develop relationships with the staff members within each agency. Referral systems are then in place so that when an issue surfaces, linkages are available to those supportive services. These might include organizations such as:

- o Services to Children and Families
- o Catholic Social Services
- o Probation Departments
- o County Health Departments
- o Counselling or Mental Health Services
- o Vocational Rehabilitation Services
- o Educational Institutions
- o Chamber of Commerce
- o Private Sector Employers

It is not enough to refer a client to another person or agency without providing appropriate support and follow-up. Research on making effective referrals shows that most clients never make it to the referral site without adequate support and encouragement. The most effective referral is one where the person is personally escorted to the referral and follow-up associated with the referral is promised and transpires (Career Information System, 1980).

The Uses of Tests and Non-test Techniques in Counselling

Counsellors use tests generally for assessment, placements, and guidance and appraisals to as assist clients to increase their self-knowledge, practice decision making, and acquire new behaviours.

They may be used in a variety of therapies e.g. individual, marital, group, and family and for either gathering of data on clients, assessing the level of some traits, such as stress and anxiety, or measuring clients' personality types.

The purpose of non-informational tests is to stimulate further or more in-depth interaction with the client. Although the published literature on testing has increased, proper test utilization remains a problematic area. The issue is not whether a counsellor uses tests in counselling practices, but when and to what end tests will be used (Corey, Corey, & Callanan, 1984).

Testing Process

Steps involved in the process of using tests in counselling include the following: - selecting the test, administering test, scoring the test, interpreting results, communicating the results.

Selecting: Having defined the purpose for testing, the counsellor looks to a variety of sources for information on available tests. Resources include review books, journals, test manuals, and textbooks on testing and measurement (Anastasi, 1988; Cronbach, 1979). The most complete source of information on a particular test is usually the test manual.

Administering: Test administration is usually standardize by the developers of the test. Manual instructions need to be followed in order to make a valid comparison of an individual's score with the test's norm group. Non – Standardization tests used in counselling are best given under controlled circumstances. This allows the counsellor's experience with the test to become an internal norm. Issues of individual versus group administration need to be considered as well. The clients and the purpose for which they are being tested will contribute to decisions about group testing.

Scoring: Scoring of tests follows the instructions provided in the test manual, the Counsellor is sometimes given the option of having test machine scored rather than hand scored. Both the positive and negative aspects of this choice need to be considered. It is usually believed that test scoring is best handled by a machine because it is free from bias.

Interpreting: The interpretation of test results is usually the area which allows for the greatest flexibility within the testing process. Depending upon the Counsellor's theoretical point of view and the extent of the test manual guidelines, interpretation may be brief and superficial, or detailed and explicity theory based (Tinsley & Bradley, 1986). Because this area allows for the greatest flexibility, it is also the area with the greatest danger of misuse. Whereas scoring is best done by a bias-free machine, interpretation by machine is often too rigid. What is needed is the experience of a skilled test user to individualize the interpretation of results.

Communicating: Feedback of test results to the client completes the formal process of testing. Here, the therapeutic skills of Counsellors come fully into play (Phelps, 1974). The Counsellor uses verbal and non verbal interaction skills to convey messages to clients and to assess their understanding of it.

Issues in Testing

Confidentiality: The ethical and legal restrictions on what may be disclosed from counselling apply to the use of tests as much as to other private information shared between client and counsellor. The trust issue, which is inherent in confidentiality, is relevant to every aspect of testing. No information can be shared outside the relationship without the full consent of the client. Information is provided to someone outside the relationship only after the specifics to be used from the testing are fully disclosed to the client. These specifics include the when, what, and to whom of the disclosure. The purpose of disclosure is also shared with the client and what the information will be used for is clearly spelled out. Issues of confidentiality are best discussed with the client before conducting any test administration. There should be no surprise when the counsellor asks, at a later time, for permission to share results. Clients who are fully informed, before testing takes place, about the issue of confidentiality in relation to testing are more active participants in the counselling process.

Counsellor Preparation: Tests are only as good as their construction, proper usage and the preparation of the counsellor intending to use them. The skills and competencies counsellors need or using tests in practice are to:

- Understand clearly the intended purpose of a test.
- Beware of the client's needs regarding the test to be given.
- Having knowledge about the test, its validity, reliability and the norm group for which it was developed.
- Have personally taken the test before administering it.
- Have been supervised in administering, scoring, interpreting, and communicating results of the tests to be given.

Supervision in the practice of providing testing services ideally encompasses all of the above areas of concern. This supervision needs to be conducted by the knowledgeable practitioner with experience in using tests in clinical practice.

Non-test Counselling

While it is most often used by certified counsellors, psychologists and psychiatrists, non-directive counselling provides a number of techniques which can be used effectively by teachers and staff when talking with students about their undesirable behaviour. Attributed to Carl Rogers, this technique was designed to allow the individual in emotional turmoil to talk out problems and resolved difficulties with a minimum of direction being provided by the person serving as counsellor. Rogers believed that everyone has the motivation and ability to change in order to become a better, more "self-actualized" person. To help our students to achieve this state, we as teacher-counsellors, act as a sounding board; observing, listening, and deliberately responding according to certain guidelines while the student explores and analyses the problem and devises a personal solution. The teacher-counsellor's demeanor is ALWAYS accepting and non-punitive. This style encourages the student to feel comfortable in expression of feelings and thus facilitates positive change.

There are five basic responses to student commentary. The first, reflection, is the restating of the student's comment. This may be done in the exact same terminology used by the student, the repeating of part of the comment, or by rewording the student's statement. Reflection lets the students know that you are listening and promotes continued commentary. The second response, a leading statement or question, is designed to encourage the student to elaborate on a topic or devise a solution to a specific problem. Examples of a leading remark include: "I would like to hear your opinion", "Tell me more about yourself", and "What happened then"?

The third response, clarification, involves the stating of implied feelings behind a student's verbal communication. Examples of clarification include: "You sound sad". Moreover 'It appears as if you are very angry at James". Clarification helps the students to deal with the emotions which are present. The fourth, summarization, is a review of what has been discussed thus far in your counselling session. This summary allows both participants to briefly reflect on what has occurred, view it clearly, and use it as a new starting point from which to build. The fifth response, questioning, is a review of what has been discussed thus far in your counselling session. This summary allows both participants to briefly reflect on what has occurred, view it clearly, and use it as a new starting point from which to build.

The fifth response, questioning, is comprised of two main types: closed questions which are intended to yield brief, specific information; and open ended questions which are used to encourage the student to talk at greater length on a topic. Examples of closed questioning include: "How old is Mark?" and "Did you complete your homework?" Examples of open questioning include: "How is it going in mathematics class?" and how do you feel about losing recess?"

Rogers believed that this non-opinionated approach helps others to resolve inner conflicts and feelings which manifest themselves in undesirable behaviour. Therefore, the reduction of this inner turmoil can reduce inappropriate behaviour. This technique is useful with students who can be "reasoned with" and are seeking a solution to their problems (or just want to talk). Certainly, the student must be motivated to be involved in a therapeutic discussion. This is not a technique which can be imposed upon the student. Yet, because the student is involved in the programme and chooses the most appropriate solution, she is more likely to follow the proposed solution.

The non-test approach is also useful with students of lower intelligence levels who have accompanying speech and language problems which make their verbalizations difficult to understand. Reflection can be useful in these situations. Repeat the words that are comprehended, continuing the conversation and allowing the students to vent his or her emotions.

How to Use Non-Test Counselling

i) Arrange for a time and place which will provide privacy for your conference.

ii) If the student does not open session, use a leading statement or question to focus him/her on the topic of concern.

iii) Listen to the student in an interested, non-punitive, accepting manner. Make no judgement.

iv) Respond when appropriate, using one of the recommended techniques.

v) After the concerns have been thoroughly voiced by the student, focus him/her on finding solution for the difficulty. (e.g. 'How will you handle this in the future?", 'What do you do now?" and "Have you got any ideas about how you might deal with this issue?"). Allow the student to choose the solution that is best for him or her.

How A Logo and A Former President Increased Uptake.

In collaboration with the national government and other stakeholders, FHI/Nigeria developed the heart-to-heart logo that now marks each counselling and testing sites in the country with a "seal of approval". The logo also appears on national media messages that encourage people to go for counselling and testing. To foster ownership, coordination and standardization, FHI handed this logo over to the government, which encourages its use by all partners and organizations providing counselling and testing services. The distinctive and instantly recognizable logo not only signals the availability slogan, "we listen, we care," promises that clients will meet discreet, friendly providers in stigma free setting.

President Olusegun Obasanjo launched the logo at the 2005 World AIDS Day commemoration. The following year, he marked the day by being publicly tested for HIV. That the test was administered by FHI/Nigeria's Association Director of HIV Counselling and Testing Simon Cartier testifies to the programme's national contributions and technical excellence. Cartier attests that this singular act increase uptake of counselling and testing services. Policy makers and opinion leaders took note, and governors in different parts of the country took turns being publicly tested.

Working With the Government of Nigeria.

On a day-to-day basis, FHI/Nigeria's counselling and testing programme directly supports and works closely with two arms of the government that coordinate and implements HIV/AIDS related activities throughout the country: the National Agency for the Control of AIDS and the National AIDS/STI Control Programme.

Through its work with these bodies, FHI supported Nigeria's efforts to create national VCT guidelines and a training curriculum, as well as to establish four VCT training centres. FHI/Nigeria later helped the government formulate its scale-up plan, provided technical assistance to provide VCT services at primary health centres, and helped the government develop VCT monitoring and evaluation tools that are now used nationally.

Cartier says that the "good working environment and support from the government" should be credited for the dramatic increase in the number of VCT clients over the past three years. He added, "FHI/Nigeria has enjoyed an excellent relationship with Nigeria, thereby providing better opportunities for the programme to succeed". In turn, this relationship and the arrival of the million counselling and testing clients in Nigeria would not have occurred without the commitment, unstinting effort, teamwork, resilience and creativity of FHI/Nigerian's staff.

4

Guidance and Education

The Need to Understand that Guidance and Counselling is an Integral Part of Education What should be the place of guidance and counselling within education in the 21st Century? The position/services model of the past century often placed guidance and counselling in an ancillary position; not as an integral part of education. Concern about this was expressed as early as the 1920s by Myers (1923) when he stated:

The first development to which I wish to call attention is a growing recognition of vocational guidance as integral part of organized education, not as something different and apart from education that is being wished upon the schools by a group of enthusiasts because there is no other agency to handle it. (p. 139)

During the same year, Payne (1923) asked, "Is guidance an integral part of our educational system or is it something just tacked on? (p. 62). Yet, over the next decades, guidance and counselling continued to be organized and practiced as a position within a set of services, placing school counsellors in an ancillary position to the rest of education. If guidance and counselling is going to make the contributions it can and should make to assist all students to achieve success in school academically and reach their goals personally and occupationally, the programme of guidance and counselling and the work of school counsellors within it must be seen and practiced as an integral part of education. That was the point that Myers (1923) and Payne (1923) made many years ago. It is time to put into practice their words of wisdom. Even though the words organized and centralized programme were used many years ago, the organizational pattern of a position within a set of services prevailed. While good work was done by the practitioners involved, the organizational structure provided by the position/ services oriented led them in a direction that caused many of them to be more management/ administratively focused than student focused.

The work done in the 1970s and the 1980s toward the development and implementation of comprehensive guidance and counselling programmes that tied directly to the mission of education makes it imperative that school counsellors spend full time working with all students in close collaboration with parents, teachers, and administrators, and other stakeholders in the community.

I believe that this is the direction that the professional needs to follow, and, while full programme implementation in all schools across the country has not yet been reached, substantial progress is being made. This work must continue as the century unfolds.

Guidance and counselling in the schools at the turn of the past century was seen as one way to respond to conditions in society, work, and education. According to Stephens (1970), "guidance purposes were formulated initially as correctives to social ills, correctives that people were willing to pay for" (p.160).

But then for a number of reasons, as Stephens pointed out, that the zeal for reform diminished as the decades of the 1900s unfolded. He wondered if guidance had "become so concerned about becoming professionally acceptable and so involved in maintaining its own organization that the reform of industrial occupations and the support of human values have been lost as goals" (p. 161)

Stephens' (1970) statement about the profession turning inward was made in the 1970s. Today some may disagree and say that the school counselling profession has spoken out directly and strongly on societal work, and educational issues.

While that may be the case, I believed it is good to be reminded about the need for advocacy, about the need to be actively involved in social, work, and education reform, particularly because such reform efforts can benefit directly from the expertise of school counsellors. And, after all it is the heritage of the profession.

If the profession chooses an inactive stance, it could lead to what Haley (1969) many years ago called "the five Be's that will guarantee dynamic failure— be passive, be inactive, be reflective, be silent, beware" (p695).

Need for Guidance

Guidance is an indispensable part of the educational programme, not just added to the programme. School guidance services are essential for children, beginning in the kindergarten and continuing throughout their school experiences. A number of grounds have been given for the necessity of guidance in schools; some of these are as follows:

(1) Guidance in a Changing World – Our world grows increasingly complex to young people. Beginning about the turn of the century the age old process of firsthand learning and guidance become impossible. The modern boy has little or no chance to learn about an occupation.

(2) Modern Complexity – The world of young people is complex and growing increasingly so. This growing confusion in every phase of modern living requires that children and youth have more and more need of guidance at all levels of their schools experience. According to Arellano (1975), the individual today is living in a very complex society. The conditions of living have changed very much and many of these conditions are still changing very rapidly. All these changes and development in industrial, economic, social, educational, and other aspects of life have increased the dependence of the individual upon outside help which is the guidance worker.

(3) Need for Personal and Social Guidance – The necessity for vocational and educational, personal, and social guidance are very tangible and important. They are also real. There is the urgent need to help in directing valuable human potentials in many ways in pupils/students. This help is urgently needed because many social forces are impinging upon the life of each pupil. It is therefore necessary to help boys and girls attain good social and personal adjustments. Personal guidance is particularly needed because modern pupils are overwhelmed by the battling complexities which lead to feelings of insecurity, inferiority, lack of confidence, and frustration. Many children are literally starved for personal and social guidance.

(4) Guidance Helps National Security – Boys and girls should be placed in the social, educational, and occupational position where they can make the greatest contribution in line with his interests, aptitudes, and trainings to national security and development. If we train and place our young people well; our

country will be strong and will survive. According to Lupdag (1984), guidance is important in that it is crucial for individual and national development; human resources being the most important resource any nation can have. He further mentioned that guidance facilitates learning among the learners and also increases the holding power of schools and minimize dropouts.

Kelly (1965) stated that fundamentally the boys and girls in school, particularly the secondary level need guidance and counselling because of the following reasons/grounds:

(1) They are immature.

(2) They are faced with the task of making decisions concerning the future, some of which may well be irreversible.

(3) They are passing through the process of growth and development which involves the unfolding and expansion of powers and capacities, changes, both structural and functional, and adjustments of a mental, moral, social and emotional nature.

(4) Throughout the process of growth and development, the child needs guidance and direction in order that he may better understand himself and his problems, may learn problem-solving methods, and thus make progress toward the attainment of effective self-direction.

(5) Basically, children and youth need guidance and counsel in order that they may know the meaning and purpose of life, and the goals which must be sought to attain that purpose.

(6) Guidance is essential in order that the individual may profit from his educational experiences and may develop fully all his powers, capacities and capabilities.

(7) Guidance is necessary in aiding the individual to choose and prepare intelligently, either wholly or in part, for a work life in which he will find satisfaction the means of self support, a place in which to render service, and to achieve a reasonable recognition of his worth by his fellowmen.

(8) Guidance is necessary because the individual needs and wants help in choosing the right objectives to fulfill the purpose of life and to aid him in everyway as he strives to attain these objectives.

Need and Focus of Guidance and Counselling in Higher Education

1. To improve the internal efficiency of the school system

Focus: Academic guidance for;

- less able students thus reducing repetition, dropout and wastage
- average students to sustain stability, and improve;
- able students to enhance progress from one level (class) to the other.

2. To reduce/ eliminate anti-social activities on campus

Focus: - Advice on social and academic clubs to join

- counselling and dialogue on matters that can generate friction and students' unrest
- Counselling on emotional problems

3. To enhance career and job prospects of learners

Focus: - job and career advising

- Relationship between course of study and world of work.

It is clear form a review of the guidance and counselling literature of the past three decades of the past century that guidance and counselling programmes were being designed to serve all students. An often stated goal was that "although immediate and crisis needs of students are to be met, a major focus of a developmental programme is to provide all students with experiences to help them grow and develop" (Gysbers & Henderson, 2000, p.26) This goal was based on the assumption that all students can and should profit from the activities and services of comprehensive guidance and counselling programmes to facilitate their academic, personal/social, and career development. What does serving all students mean today? It means that comprehensive guidance programmes serve equally all students, parents, teachers, and other recipients regardless of gender, race, ethnicity, cultural background, sexual orientation, disability, family structure and functionality, socio-economic status, learning-ability level, language, level of school involvement, or other special characteristics. It means understanding students' cultural, sociological, psychological economic and family backgrounds. This is critical because as Martin and House (2001) stated:

School counsellors are ideally positioned in schools to serve as conductors and transmitters of information to promote school-wide success for all students. When school counsellors aggressively perform actions that support entitlement to quality education for all students, they create a school climate where access and support for rigorous preparation is expected (p.4).

Bases of Guidance Work (Psychological, Sociological, Moral and Spiritual Needs of College Students)

Humpreys et al. (1967) gave the following as psychological bases for the need of guidance work:

(1) Many of the principles and methods of guidance are rooted in psychology.

(2) Individuals differ widely in aptitudes, achievements, interests, personality characteristics, rates and patterns of growth. The latter being true in most areas of development, including physical, mental, emotional and social.

(3) Learning involves the active participation of the individual. The learning process depends upon a person's developed abilities, his physical and mental state, opportunities and stimulation provided, and motivational and incentive conditions.

(4) Psychology has contributed theories and experimental evidences that are helpful to guidance workers in understanding personality; psychological aspects of personality include the self-concept, unconscious motivation and defence mechanisms.

Organization and Structure of Guidance

You are now aware of the evolution of guidance and were familiarized with pertinent terms used in guidance, and come to know the importance of guidance in education and the need for guidance work. This time, I'm sure you are now ready to start with an appropriate organizational structure of school guidance. Before you embark on that task, you should arm yourself with the following ideas and concepts: basic principles of organizing a guidance programme, personnel or staffing and their roles, alternative models, and problems you encounter in the process of preparing and implementing the guidance programme.

Principles of Guidance and Basic Principles of Organizing a Guidance Programme

One should understand the basic concept of guidance before knowing its importance in education. The concept of guidance includes the need to exercise foresight in order to prevent, as far as possible, the occurrence of situations which make it necessary for an individual to seek help in order to adjust to the circumstances. When disturbing or unhealthful conditions interfere with satisfactory patterns of behaviour, it becomes the responsibility of teachers and members of the guidance personnel to supply whatever service is needed. Whatever the function of the guidance supplied- prevention, preservation, or attempted cure achievements. This is to say that guidance services, in order to be effective and play its importance in education, one should know certain basic, significant and sound principles, as follows:

(1) Guidance is holistic, meaning to say guidance is focused on the total person and is not compartmentalized. Although a particular guidance technique is focused on a specific area like choosing a career, or in the health of the pupil, this is seen in terms of the total person (Lupdag, 1984). The chief concern of guidance is the development of the whole individual (Arellano, 1975). According to Crow and Crow (1960), every aspects of a person's complex personality pattern constitutes a significant factor of his total displayed attitudes and forms of behaviour. Guidance services which are aimed at bringing about desirable adjustment in any particular area of experience must take into account the all-round development of the individual.

(2) All individuals are unique. Understanding of the uniqueness of individuals is fundamental. Any guidance work that does not recognize this is futile. Even in group guidance, individual differences are respected (Lupdag, 1984). Although all human beings are similar in many respects, individual differences must be recognized and considered in any efforts aimed at providing help or guidance to a particular child, adolescent, or adult (Crow and Crow, 1960)

(3) Guidance is for all students, not merely for the problem or "special" or maladjusted student. Guidance is for every one- the superior, the dull, the rich, the poor, the physically sick or handicapped, or the healthy (Arellano, 1975). According to Crow and Crow (1960), guidance services should not be limited to the few who give observable evidence of its need, but should be extended to all persons of all ages who can benefit there from, either directly or indirectly.

(4) Guidance should be regarded as a continuing process of service to an individual from young childhood through adulthood. Guidance is necessarily a continuous process extending throughout the school life of the student. Effective school guidance begins at the time the child enters his first school and continuous until the time he stops schooling and starts

his occupational life. In the very broad sense, guidance starts from in family till the last stage in man's life (Crow and crow, 1960; Arellano, 1975). According to Lupdag (1984), human development is a continuous process. It follows then that guidance also is continuous to assist the individual in coping with developmental demands. Across time, the individual changes due to factors internal and external to him. Hence, the need for continuous guidance.

(5) The function guidance is to help a person- (a) formulate and accept stimulating, worthwhile, and attainable goals of behaviour, and (b) apply these objectives in the conduct of his affairs.

(6) Existing social, economic, and political unrest is giving rise to many maladjustive factors that requires the cooperation of experienced and thoroughly trained guidance counsellors and the individual with a problem.

(7) Guidance seeks to help the student attain a clearer understanding and be used upon recognition of his dignity, worth, and individuality.

(8) Guidance is concerned with choices, decisions, and adjustment to be made by the student.

(9) Guidance is counsel, not compulsion. It is not prescriptive, but it is designed to make the individual increasingly self-directive.

(10) Guidance takes into account both the immediate and remote objectives of the student.

(11) Guidance is concerned with the student's efforts, attitudes, and will to succeed as well as the data derived from measurements.

(12) Guidance seeks to develop initiative, responsibility, self-understanding, and self-direction, for its purpose is to make individual develop his own insight. The counsellor should serve as a guide, a stimulating force and an interpreter of facts, ideas, and attitudes.

(13) Guidance is essentially an educational process and is inherent in all education.

(14) Guidance consists of a series of supplementary services based upon mutual confidence and understanding in order to meet the real needs of students. Guidance should be organized according to integrated efforts. Although each staff member

should contribute according to his abilities, all staff members should concentrate their efforts. There must be whole-hearted cooperation. According to Lupdag (1984), guidance is integrative. All aspects of life emotional, mental, social, economic, physical and religious are looked into for the development of an integrated personality. One cannot be divorce from the other.

(15) Curriculum materials and teaching procedures should be evidence a guidance point of view.

(16) An effective guidance programme needs to have personnel who have had special preparation and adequate training for the work. Guidance workers need to develop certain competencies if they are to perform their guidance activities successfully and effectively.

(17) Consider most individuals as average and normal persons; the counsellor is concerned mainly with the development of persons who are so-called "normal", that is, they are relatively normal in intelligence, normal in emotional ability, and normal in physical constitution and ability. As far as possible, the wise counsellor refers definitely abnormal persons to appropriate specialists. Before the counsellor designates a counselee as abnormal, he should have definite evidence bearing on the latter's deviation from normality.

(18) Parents and teachers have guidance-pointed responsibilities.

(19) An organized guidance programme should be flexible according to individual and community needs.

(20) To administer guidance intelligently and with as thorough knowledge of the individual as is possible, programmes of individual evaluation and research should be conducted, and accurate cumulative records of progress and achievement should be made accessible to guidance workers. Through the administration of well-selected standardized tests and other instruments of evaluation, specific data concerning degree of mental capacity, success of achievement, demonstrated interests, and other personality characteristics should be accumulated, recorded, and utilized for guidance purposes.

(21) Periodic appraisals should be made of the existing school guidance programme. The success of its functioning should rest on outcomes that are reflected in the attitudes towards

the programme of all who are associated with it - guiders and guides - and in the displayed behaviour of these who have been served through its functioning.

(22) Although guidance touches every phase of an individual's life pattern, the generally accepted areas of guidance include concern with the extent to which an individual's physical and mental health interfere with his adjustments to home, school, and vocational and social demands and relationships, or to the extent to which his physical and mental health are affected by the conditions to which he is subjected in these areas of experience.

Principles of Organizing a Guidance Programme

In the organization and administration of a functional guidance programme, a number of basic principles should be kept in mind. Among such principles are the following, as stated by Arellano (1975):

(1) The guidance service should arise out of the interests, needs, and purposes of the students in the school which it serves.

(2) The guidance service should be continuous and serve all youth, not merely the maladjusted ones.

(3) Guidance service should be concerned with the whole individual in his total environment and with specific needs and problems.

(4) Guidance service should be organized to deal not only with serious problems after they arise, but also with causes of such problems, in order to prevent them from arising or to prepare better for their solution.

(5) It should provide for all phases of student problems and student study.

(6) It should provide for specialists; and the service of these specialists should be so organized and administered that they not only contribute in these special fields directly to the guidance programme but also constantly strengthen all other members of the school personnel and help them in their problems.

(7) It should provide for securing and recording through tests and other device, adequate information regarding occupational and educational requirements and opportunities.

(8) All guidance activities should be directed toward improved individual self-knowledge and self-direction.

(9) A functional guidance programme should be an integral part of the total school programme and be vitally related to home, community, and other out-of-school experiences of students. It should permeate the entire school.

(10) It should be a cooperative undertaking of the entire school and should enlist the interest and effort of every member of the school staff.

(11) It should be as simple as possible and should be easy to organize and administer.

(12) It should provide for leadership and for coordination of all the agencies of school and community for long term guidance of youth.

Guidance Personnel / Staffing : Roles and Functions

Qualifications of Guidance Personnel/ School Administrator:

(a) The administrator must have a clear concept of the meaning, philosophy and significance of guidance.

(b) He must have knowledge of the goals and characteristics of a good guidance programme.

(c) He must know the basic assumptions of guidance and the methods of rendering and conducting guidance service.

(d) He must be guided by a definite, sound, workable educational philosophy.

(e) He must remember that guidance programme cannot be built up, put on paper, and then forgotten.

(f) He must be a good leader and understands as well as knows how to bring together the school and the community.

(g) The school administrator should be well trained in the field and with a minimum educational attainment of masteral degree in Guidance/ Counselling. It is preferable that he is a holder of doctoral degree and with some years of experience.

Other qualifications that he should possess are:

1. He should be cheerful, accommodating, enduring, and patient.
2. He should be friendly and sympathetic.
    1. He should have a good foresight and also with good sense of judgement and prediction.
    2. He should possess technical preparation.

3. He should have some knowledge of Sociology, Psychology, Philosophy, and other subjects that are related to the guidance programme.
4. He should possess competencies in the analysis of the individual.
5. He should be competent in the guiding procedure.
6. He should be competent in maintaining administrative relationship; especially as this will be indispensable in his coordinating with inside and outside agencies.

Roles of Guidance Personnel's

(a) They assist teacher – counsellors in meeting serious pupil problems.

(b) They conduct meetings of teacher and parent groups to improve their understanding of young people's adjustment problems and to encourage their practice of guidance principles.

(c) They serve in a general liaison capacity between a school's guidance staff and other groups, such as administrators, teachers, specialists, and community leaders.

(d) They help graduating pupils/ students make a choice of the right job by helping them secure authentic information about such jobs.

(e) They help their clientele students/ pupils prepare for interviews by giving them (clientele) the necessary guidance.

(f) They play a key role in the activities which are involved in preparing students for transfer from elementary to junior high school and from senior high school to college or other post-high school experience. This involves visiting the sending schools and developing orientation programmes for new students and their parents to make the transition as smooth as possible.

(g) They play an important role in curriculum planning since they are in position to know individual needs and special learning and instructional problems of students.

Functions of Guidance Personnel

(b) He serves as a consultant to principal, teachers, parents, and other members of the school staff;

(c) Acts a liaison person between the school and the resources of social and other community agencies;

(d) Provides effective counselling services to pupils, individually or in small group;

(e) Contributes to the development of an effective pupil study service through observing case studies and class studies and through a well-developed standardized testing programme;

(f) Contributes to the school's programme of research;

(g) Assists the school to understand and make best use of the school;

(h) Assists the child to understand and assume responsibilities for himself;

(i) Assists the parents to understand the child and facilitate his development;

(j) Assists the school to understand its total student body;

(k) Assists the school in making provisions for the needs of children;

(l) Develops a cumulative record for each pupil, containing basic information regarding home background, aptitudes, abilities, previous achievements, and other pertinent data for counsellor and staff use;

(m) Undertakes periodic follow-up studies of both drop-outs and graduates and assists other designated staff members in doing so. He also maintains some contact with graduates and assists drop-outs in making as satisfactory an out-of-school adjustment as possible;

(n) Undertakes many research and evaluation projects both formal and informal, to provide useful information to administration, teaching staff, students, parents, and the community.

The Role of the Guidance Counsellor

The school counsellor is a support person whose role is to provide services for the school. The programme design focus is on problem-solving, decision making and promoting a positive personal self-concept for the school environment. The school counsellor provides a comprehensive developmental counselling programme. These services are based upon the following interventions:

Individual Counselling: Individual counselling is a personal and private interaction between a counsellor and a student in which they work together on a problem. A one-to-one meeting with a counsellor provides a student an opportunity to explore ideas, feelings, and behaviours. However, counsellors are obligated under law and ethical standards to report and refer a case when a person's welfare is in jeopardy.

Small Group Counselling: Small group counselling involves a counsellor working with two or more students together. Group size generally ranges from five to eight members. Group discussions may be relatively unstructured or may be based on structured learning activities. All members have an opportunity to learn from each other in this encounter.

Classroom Guidance: Large group meetings offer the best opportunity to provide guidance to the largest number of students at Allatoona. Large group work involves cooperative learning, in which the large group is divided into smaller working groups under the supervision of a counsellor and teacher. Teacher and counsellors in classroom advisory groups deliver the guidance and counselling curriculum.

Consultations: The counsellor as a consultant helps people to be more effective in working with others. Consultation helps individuals think through problems and concerns. This process can take place during individual or group conferences.

Coordination: Coordination as a counsellor intervention is the process of managing various indirect services, which may include community agencies. There are many planned special events, which involve parents, community resources, and community guidance projects. Some of these include the Mentor Programme, Red Ribbon Week Activities, and Career Day.

Functions of Guidance and Counselling

Guidance and counselling programmes consist of four primary functions:

Programme Design and Planning/ Leadership

I. Establishes and promotes a school guidance and counselling programme.

   1.1. Develops a written school-based guidance plan based on learners needs.

   1.2. Implements an individual plan of action.

Counselling

I. Facilitates and implements delivery of counselling services in areas of self-known educational and occupational exploration, and career planning to facilitate academic achievement.

   1.1. Adheres to established system policies and procedures in scheduling appointments and obtaining parental permission.

1.2. Schedules time to provide opportunities for counselling.

1.3. Counsels learners individually by actively listening, identifying and defining issues, discussing alternative solutions, and formulating a plan of action.

1.4. Leads counselling or support groups for learners experiencing similar issues.

1.5. Evaluates effectiveness of group counselling and makes revisions as necessary.

Guidance/ Collaboration

1. Coordinates with school staff to provide supportive instructional guidance activities to students: self-knowledge, educational and occupational exploration, and care to facilitate academic achievement.

1.1. Collaborates with school staff in planning and scheduling guidance activities.

1.2. Conducts classroom guidance activities related to identified goals and objectives.

1.3. Gathers and evaluates data to determine effectiveness of classroom guidance and student comprehension, making revisions where necessary.

1.4. Provides direct/indirect assistance to learners preparing for test taking.

1.5. Provides information to students, parents, and teachers on student test scores.

1.6. Provides information to students and parents on career planning.

1.7. Assists students in their transitions to the next educational/ career level.

1.8. Leads skill-building groups in student self-knowledge.

Consultation/ Coordination

I. Consults, as needed or requested, with system/staff, parents, and community about and concerns.

1.1. Exchanges relevant information about situations with school/system staff and parents.

1.2. Collaborates with school staff in developing a strategy or plan for improving school climate.

1.3. Follows up on counselling and consultative referrals.

1.4. Consults with school system in making referral to community agencies.

The Classroom Teacher as a Guidance Worker

(a) He is the key person in the actual guidance activities in the classroom.

(b) He occupies the position of giving definite and appropriate guidance to the individual pupil or student.

He helps his pupils to:

(c) Develop a realistic self-concept.

(d) Recognize and deal with their strengths and weaknesses effectively and intelligently.

(e) Begin to recognize and understand emotional responses and to learn how to deal with them.

(f) Face some of the problems and processes of social development and learn how to get along better with peers, adults, and younger people.

(g) Learn good study habits and skills.

(h) Discover and gain some perspective of the educational opportunities open to them and some notion of various fields of knowledge.

(i) Discover and gain some perspective of occupational possibilities.

Organizational Structure of School Guidance

Basic Concepts: There are certain fundamental concepts concerning the organization of the programme that need to be considered carefully before the actual task begins. These have to do with:

(1) The purposes to be achieved;

(2) The functions to be served;

(3) The allocation of responsibilities and the delegation of authority; and

(4) The techniques to be utilized in evaluating the ultimate success of the programme.

It is important to note that there are also some factors that are basic to the ways in which the guidance services in any institution or school community are organized and implemented. These factors which are considered general considerations are as follows: school level, individual needs and community interests, size of school, faculty attitudes, and budgetary provisions. The guidance needs of elementary-school children differ in extent from those of the secondary-school or college students. Hence, the programmes aimed at meeting pupil needs at different school levels will be organized differently and will include services of fewer or more guidance personnel, as the case may require. A rural school, a district school, a small city school, and a large city school differ in the extent to which facilities and money are available for providing personnel and equipment. One important point is the fact that the organization of guidance services should always be flexible and adapted to existing school and community needs, interest and financial status.

Problems : The Organization of School Guidance

Guidance in schools is beset with many problems as shown in numerous researches. Some problems encountered in school which necessitated the importance of guidance are the following:

1. Misunderstanding of the guidance concept.
2. Lack if not absence of administrative support.
3. Lack if not absence of qualified guidance personnel.
4. Inadequacy, if not absence of guidance facilities.
5. Non-cooperation or lack of cooperation of school staff.
6. Community apathy to guidance.
7. Teacher's philosophy of education and life.
8. Non-cooperation or the lack of it from parents.
9. Teacher's lack of time for guidance work.
10. Lack if not absence of funds for guidance activities.
11. Inadequacy of guidance personnel's training.
12. Absence of organized guidance programmes.
13. Negative attitudes of teachers towards guidance.
14. Negative attitudes of learners towards guidance.
15. Negative or distorted attitudes of parents towards guidance.

Organization and Administration of Guidance Services

Before organizing guidance services for a particular school, it is necessary to understand exactly what is to be organized. This statement may sound trite, but many guidance programmes stumble aimlessly from year to year without any clear cut objectives. The purpose of this lecturrete has been to outline appropriate organizational patterns in guidance and a point of view regarding five basic guidance services: 1) the counselling service; 2) the individual inventory service; 3) the information service; 4) the placement service; and the follow-up service.

Types of Guidance Organizational Patterns

Some type of definite organizational pattern is the first step in planning for adequate guidance services. Two types of such patterns are readily perceived by an examination of current guidance practices: 1) the counsellor assumes a quasi-administrative staff position, initiating policies through the principal or through his own powers of persuasion; and 2) the counsellor is a staff member who serves as consultant to and executor for a guidance committee. Whatever the administrative pattern followed by a particular school, the following concepts are worthy of consideration:

1. School administrators provide leadership both through direct support, such as personnel, budget, and facilities, and also in terms of their attitudes toward guidance services as an indispensable part of the total educational programme.
2. If a Guidance Committee or Guidance Council is used, its major function is policy making. This can be defended on the basis that guidance services involve all staff members. The development of guidance services, as well as other services in the school programme, is of much concern to staff members as to administrative officers.
3. The counsellor plays a dual role. First, he serves as consultant in the formulation of guidance policies and then he aids in carrying out these policies. Second, the counsellor provides professional counselling services to all pupils who may benefit from them. This counselling function must be protected from dilution resulting from use of incompetent counsellors, or the assignment of an untenable position to the counsellor through improper organization of the guidance programme.
4. Teacher develops the psychological climate which nourishes the optimum development of each pupil. Such a planned environment guarantees that attitudes, understandings, and skills learned as a result of counselling can be practiced and applied by pupils. Teachers also contribute much to the study and understanding of pupils referring some pupils to the counsellor whenever symptomatic behaviour indicates need for pupil planning and adjustment.

Counsellor's Qualification

Because of the fact that the choice of a counsellor is so important to the guidance programme's ultimate success, the major portion of this lecturette emphasizes the counsellor's qualifications as: 1) personal, 2) experience, and 3) training. During the past ten years, general agreement as to these qualifications has been reached by most authorities and by national organizations. Counsellor certification plans have become increasingly popular not only in the Philippines but in other countries. Other members of the guidance team, administrators and teachers, also need some type of preparation for carrying out their guidance functions. Their readiness for in-service preparation is an important consideration. Teacher attitudes may be changed provided teachers are recognized as individuals with differences as great as those of pupils. A programme of in-service preparation may be organized around group activities for the teachers, but some teachers require individual assistance, both of the incidental and the planned varieties. The key concept to their in-service preparation is "learning through participation."

Individuals who are chosen to teach classes is personal adjustment, whether the class is an occupations course or psychology course, need qualifications beyond the ordinary teaching certificate. Until certification of such individuals becomes sufficiently crystallized, the teacher's preparation might well parallel that of the counsellor.

Three Types of Plans in Planning the Guidance Services

There are many procedures suitable to planning for guidance service. An examination of these methods indicates three plans which have been used frequently and with some success.

First, all members of the staff may participate in committees which study various aspects of guidance services. After deciding upon desirable changes in existing conditions, the study committees make recommendations to their administrative officers through a coordinating Guidance Committee. Second, a single, small committee of staff members under the leadership of the school principal studies existing conditions and needed changes. On the basis of its study, the committee makes recommendations to their administrative officers through a coordinating team for future organizational steps to the staff as a whole. This group in turn, relays its recommendations to the administrative officers. Third, in situations in which the counsellor has already been employed without any previous planning activities, a committee or the school principal decides upon the process whereby plans can be made for the guidance services, utilizing eventually one or the other, or both, of the plans above. Whatever plan is followed, lines of communication are necessary between any committee(s) and other staff members. It is crucial that differences of opinion be discussed and brought into the open. Staff members should not be allowed to develop attitude of suspicion because of ignorance of decisions, plans, or functions.

Basic Guidance Services

1. Counselling service is considered the core of the guidance programme. Through this service the student is assisted in understanding himself, gaining deeper awareness of one's problems, making intelligent decisions, and helping one grow to become a self-sufficient and mature person.

Counselling is a unique school and guidance service which depends upon several important factors. Its potential usefulness is a function of counsellor's competency, the likelihood or privacy for interviewing pupils, the attitude of pupils toward the counsellor and his methods, the interpretation given the counselling service by pupils, provisions for sufficient counselling time during school hours, and the observance of ethical practices. In addition, the growth of the counselling service depends upon the teachers' and the principal's attitudes toward the service. All members of the school guidance can contribute to the evolution of policies and practices which enhance the utilization of the counselling service by pupils.

2. Individual inventory service encompasses the collection, recording, and use of pupil data for the pupil's own planning and adjustment, as well as for the teacher who wants to provide the best possible classroom climate for pupils.

Student Inventory is a continuous and cooperative process of accumulating and recording of information on each student. It provides data on the following: home and family background, personal and social development, scholastic progress, mental ability, vocational interests, aptitude, and personality profile for guidance and counselling purposes.

The collection and recording of pupil data are most economical when the two processes dovetail, i.e., the collection of data provides information which does not have to be transposed but becomes a part of the record once it is filed in the pupil's individual inventory folder.

All procedures in organizing the individual inventory service must also consider provisions for: 1) facilities, equipment, and materials; 2) clerical personnel for handling data; and 3) a budget in line with goals for the service.

Pupil data which are not used weaken the individual inventory service. The counsellor uses such data in his counselling functions, but this alone is not sufficient. Ways should be devised whereby teachers come in contact with pupil and learn to use it for the best interests of pupils.

3. Information service utilizes all types of data needed by pupils in their planning or quest for optimum adjustment. Systematic provision for all types of information involves budget, personnel, and facilities.

The uses of information materials are many, varying from those with individual pupils in counselling situations to a wide variety of group procedures. The one caution in a series of individual and group procedures is lack of coordination. Pupils must perceive all such activities in their perspective as only means to an end. Counselling can enhance benefits from group procedures; while the latter can provide information and encourage pupils to seek counselling for individual planning activities, as well as increase the values derived from the counselling experiences.

4. Placement and follow-up services provide the follow-through and evaluation to all planning activities undertaken as the result of the other guidance services. They are also closely interwoven at time that it is difficult to classify some activities as belonging exclusively to the placement or to the follow-up service.
5. Research. The Guidance and Counselling Programme conducts studies along some areas such as student needs, student problems, academic delinquency, academic achievement, and student-teacher relations. Results of these studies serve as guideposts for educational planning and improvement of services.
6. Testing. It covers administering, scoring, interpreting, and evaluating results of mental ability, aptitude, interest, and personality tests.

The placement service encompasses every type or follow-through to pupils in school or after they leave school. The follow-up service includes not only an evaluation of all placements but also many other attributes of the total educational programme. In organizing and planning the coverage of either service, the Guidance Committee is limited only in its ability to see placement and follow-up needs, and the personnel necessary to carry out any plans.

Other School Guidance Services

1. Career and Life Planning. It is a package of activities designed to develop skills in self exploration, values clarification, career planning and decision making, and life goal setting.
2. Phone Counselling. It is offered even on the phone through "Tawag Na!" This is especially convenient for those who feel uneasy to meet their counsellors face to face.
3. Freshmen Enhancement Programme. It is package of activities for freshmen designed to facilitate adjustment into college life, enhance self-awareness and understanding, and develop the basic skills in coping effectively with rigors of academic life. The components of this programme include psychological testing and evaluation; study skills development; time management; stress management; and group growth sessions.
4. Orientation and Information. It consists of accumulation and dissemination of information about the different guidance activities, vocational opportunities, and educational information for better adjustment and personal growth.
5. Referral. Special cases, which require service beyond the scope of guidance and counselling programme, are referred to other agencies.
6. Linkages. The Guidance and Counselling programme also carry out collaborative activities with school and community-based organizations.
7. Training/ Workshops. Various groups of students (i.e. blocks, student organization, etc.) are brought together by counsellors to teach them skills in dealing with development and life issues. These include but are not limited to: stress management, study skills, training, leadership, training, self search, peer counselling, career and life planning, interpersonal relationships, self-confidence-building; team building; dealing with homesickness; and conflict management.

8. Extension Services. The guidance staff functions and responsibilities go beyond the students. They extend themselves by helping others trough training, seminar/workshops, or conduct research as they are often invited in occasions needing their skills and knowledge. In most instances, they render the services for free.

Problems in the Administration of Guidance Services

The administration of guidance services involves a number of problems which are directly related to organizational problem. For example, administrative relationships are important considerations in the organization and administration of guidance services regardless of the level of development.

In addition to administrative relationships, the counsellor must be concerned with plans for the year's activities, for reporting these activities to administrators and staff members; for continuing public-relations activities; for service-research activities which can aid in improving all educational services and the psychological climate for each pupil; for the maintenance and improvement of facilities and equipment; and for establishing normal budgetary and guidance personnel procedures. Unfortunately, counsellors have not always collected the kinds of data necessary for a business-like approach to the administration of guidance institutions, such record and data become more and more essential to the study of adequate guidance programmes –and also their evaluation. They also may aid in any justification of this pupil personnel service to administrators, school boards, teachers, and parents.

An examination of research studies shows a trend toward the use of multiple criteria as well as several sources of and techniques for gathering data.

Evaluative procedures are extremely important to any guidance worker. Any new educational service is expected to produce desirable effects upon pupil adjustments – and guidance services are no exception. Unless guidance workers can demonstrate their worth they may find themselves caught in a backwash of public opinion; and guidance workers cannot expect to find painless procedures for evaluation. They can choose from a wide range of criteria, methods, sources of data, and data-gathering techniques. The precise ingredients for any given evaluation should be determined on the basis of local needs by the Guidance Committee, school administrators, counsellor, and other staff members. The size of the project is of less importance than the quality of the research and the constant accumulation of pertinent evaluative studies, for evaluation are a process and not a terminal point in the development of guidance services.

Techniques Used in the Guidance Process

Systematic and careful analysis of the individual has always been of paramount importance in the guidance programmes for 2 fundamental reasons: it helps students to better understand themselves, a basic objective of guidance; and it is the systematic analysis of student characteristics which permits teachers, counsellors, and parents to help them. These two goals can only be realized through sound techniques of collecting, organizing, interpreting, and using relevant individual information.

A variety of testing instruments have made significant contributions by emphasizing the quantitative dimensions of studying individual behaviour. However, there are limitations and imperfections of tests that make it desirable to use non-test techniques to appraise the behaviour. These are: observations; anecdotal records; rating scales; cumulative records; data questionnaires; interview; autobiographies; sociometric techniques; and case study.

Observation: Purposes, Difficulties, and Ways of Improving it.

Observation – It is the base for most non-testing appraisal techniques, and it is intimately connected with the objective testing techniques.

Purposes of Observations

a. It may yield data that can challenge tentative hypotheses about the individual and confirm others.

b. It provides a practical way of testing the worth of ideas that have been formulated about the individual.

c. It can be used to evaluate the effectiveness of steps being taken to facilitate the individual's learning development, and adjustment.

Effective observations involve grasping clearly, concisely and as completely as possible the essential behaviour of the individual within given situations. Careful, trained observation can supply meaning to a particular sample of behaviour which can then be put into words for further clarification and study. What is important in observation is the ability to determine the factors that initiate behaviour and to describe accurately the way the person observes and reacts to a given situation.

Difficulties in Observing

a. Unconscious biases in observation sometimes occur because observers fail to admit their own feelings and limitations or because they are unaware of them. Accurate observations require an ability to evaluate objectively what is being perceived as well as an awareness of one's own feelings and beliefs.

b. Adequate sampling. To insure that the behaviour observed is representative of the individual, a number of observations should be made in a variety of situations and at different times.

Ways of Improving Observations

a. Before observation takes place, determine what is to be observed. What dimensions of behaviour are being watched for? What traits are being investigated?

b. Observe only one person at a time. If group behaviour is being studied, film and recording equipment should be used to obtain a record of the multitude of happenings taking place simultaneously.

c. Watch for significant behaviour.

d. Spread observations across a period of time.

e. Learn to observe without resorting to written notes during the observation period.

f. If possible, record and summarize the observations immediately after it is completed.

Anecdotal Records and Rating Scales: Uses, Values and Limitations

Anecdotal Records – It is a brief informal report by the teacher of an observation of a critical incident. It describes a sample behaviour in a given situational context.

The behaviour maybe positive or negative but it must be the learner's behaviour that is described and not the teacher's interpretation of the behaviour. The characteristics of this record are: objective, factual, recorded accounts of observed behaviour, concise, and describe only one incident at a time, and are continuous and cumulative, and are descriptive.

A good anecdote that has been recorded possesses the following features:

a. it records the date and the situation in which the behaviour occurred;
b. it describes the actions or behaviour of the subject, the reactions of others involved, and the subject's responses to these reactions;
c. it quotes what is said by and to the subject in the situation;
d. it notes body postures, gestures, qualities of voice, and facial expressions that gives cues to the motions of the subject; and
e. it describes the situation sufficiently to present a behavioural moment in the life of the subject.

Values of Anecdotal Records

a. They describe the behaviour of an individual, usually in diverse situations, and thus contribute to a fuller understanding of the individual's personality.
b. Accurately recorded descriptions of behaviour contribute more to understanding of an individual than vague, unsupported, or broad generalizations.
c. They encourage and stimulate teachers to become interested and informed about individuals.
d. They supplement quantitative data and enrich interpretations of behaviour.

Limitations of Anecdotal Records

a. It can be valuable only to the extent that the observational description is accurate and comprehensive.
b. Such records may create serious problems for school personnel in the light of recent legislation. The access to records granted to parents and students over 18 years old may make recording of anecdotes hazardous.
c. A typical incidents in the life of the subject are too likely to be observed and recorded. These incidents create impressions about the person out of proportion to their importance.
d. Recording and then preserving behavioural descriptions no longer representative may adversely influence others toward the individual.
e. It takes time to write and process. They inevitably add to counsellor, teacher, and clerical loads.

What Incidents Should be Recorded?

Any incident that seems important to the observer should be recorded. It should cover a wide sampling of pupil behaviour in different areas: class, playground, cafeteria, gym, free time, bus, picnic, field trip, or auditorium.

Rating Scales – It is used by personnel to implement observations. This was devised by the British navy to describe weather conditions. The rating scale form presents a list of descriptive words or phrases to be checked by the rater.

Use of rating scale

a. To obtain personality ratings on students.
b. To secure annual ratings of specific classes such as all students in grades nine to twelve.

Guiding principles in the construction of rating scales

a. Is each factor or characteristic clearly defined?

Example: One rater may think of "cooperativeness" as the ability to get along with others, whereas another rater might consider it faithful adherence to classroom or school regulations.

b. Is each factor or characteristic observable? Traits are not readily apparent to all observers should be avoided.
c. Are the degrees of the characteristic defined? The degrees or different levels for each factor to be rated should be established.

Types of Rating Scales

a. Numerical scales – It could be set as follows: 1– apathetic, 2 – rarely enthusiastic,

3–sometimes enthusiastic, 4– usually enthusiastic, and 5 – intensely enthusiastic.

b. Descriptive Scales – It is constructed to employ a series of phrases describing various degrees of the characteristic rated.

Example: How would you rate industriousness?

_________ indolent expends little effort.

_________ frequently does not complete work.

_________ gets required work done, but no more

_________ eager, usually does more than required

c. Paired comparisons. The rater compares each person rated with respect to the trait to every other individual rated in general terms of "equal", "better" or "worse".

d. Graphic rating scales. The units or degrees are indicated in a continuum. Example: Leadership

/	/	/	/
Actively avoids	Prefers not accepts to lead	Occasionally prefers	Actively seeks

Advantages of Rating Scale

a. They are a means of quantifying observations.

b. They are a means by which several observers rate the same individual thus increasing the reliability of the ratings.

Limitations of Rating Scale

a. It is subject to error. Flaws have been described as errors of personal bias, halo effect, central tendency and logical error.

Personal bias – it is introduced when observers make sweeping generalizations about certain groups.

Errors of Central Tendency – is committed when raters avoid the extremes of any rating scale.

Halo Effect – occurs when the rater permits the influence of one or two outstanding characteristics, whether good or bad, to colour all judgements about an individual.

Logical Error – occurs when the rater does not understand the trait to be rated.

Cumulative Records and Pupil-Data Questionnaires:

Uses, Advantages, and Limitations

Cumulative Records – It presents an organized, continuous record of information about individual students that distinguishes them from all other students. Usually, the cumulative folder includes the following:

a. identifying data and family background information

b. medical and health information

c. date of school entry

d. school grades

e. transcripts from previous schools attended

f. schoolwide test results
g. personality and behaviour traits
h. school activities
i. anecdotal records
j. autobiographies written in class settings

Use of Cumulative Records

a. The use of the records depends on the relevance of the data contained within them.
b. If properly constructed, the record will become the basis for most guidance services.

Data Questionnaires – Usually, this questionnaire consist of items regarding the student's home, family, health, educational and vocational plans, out-of-school and in-school activities, study habits and the like.

This questionnaire represents a cross-sectional approach while the cumulative record is basically a longitudinal record.

This form gives the school personnel information that enables them to see students as they are now and they provide extensive data dealing with the student's present life situation. Examples are:

My school work ________ My hobbies are ________________

A real friend____________ I enjoy reading about ____________

I am considered _________ The people I like best ____________

Advantages: It is a means of obtaining:

a. information dealing with students as they are now,
b. comprehensive information,
c. idiographic and normative data,
d. missing or incomplete information about students,
e. collection of data in an efficient manner.

Limitations:

a. Issues such as to whether the school has a right to obtain information (personal) about students or members of their families.
b. Data collected may also be difficult to organize and interpret since conflicting information is sometimes obtained.

The Interview: Uses, Advantages, and Limitations

The interview – It is a method of securing information about an individual. It is sometimes labelled as "fact-finding" which differs from counselling interview in the greater amount of control exercised by the interviewer.

Uses of Interview

The information-gathering interview often is used

a. to collect information not easily or economically secured by other means,
b. used to supplement information gathered in other ways,
c. to verify information collected through other means,
d. to observe mannerisms, physical appearance, and other non-verbal cues not obtained through other appraisal techniques.

Limitations:

a. It is time consuming
b. It may distort information about themselves, their reactions, and their experiences.
c. The interviewers may be the source of errors. They may record information because of "selective listening."

Advantages:

a. Useful in obtaining information not only about factual items such as those normally covered by pupil-data questionnaires, but also about attitudes, ambitions, and other affective matters that constitute the case study.
b. It can be employed to gather information needed because previous data are not clear cut or because underlying feelings need to be uncovered and understood.

Autobiographies and Sociometric Techniques:

Uses, Advantages, and Limitations

Autobiographies – It is a tool for understanding individuals which reveals not only behaviour but perhaps even more important personal attitudes and emotions behind the behaviour. It is person's own written report of his/her life that may provide insight into the inner person –individual's experiences and knowledge about themselves.

Two types of autobiographies

a. structured

b. unstructured

Structured Autobiography is written according to an outline or in response to specific questions or topics, while the *unstructured* one is basically an account of the individual's life without regard to specific questions.

Interpreting autobiographies

The following questions may help guide the interpretation.

a. What general impression does the paper convey?

b. From your knowledge of the individual's history, have significant experiences or persons been omitted?

c. What is the length of autobiography?

d. How is the paper organized?

e. What is the level of expression?

f. Are there inaccuracies in the paper?

Use of Autobiographies

a. It is useful in gaining an understanding of pupils/ students since most of the autobiographies appear to be honest and accurate.

b. It is ranked number 9 among all the techniques used in understanding a person.

Sociometric Techniques – It is concerned with the measurement of interpersonal preferences among members of a group in reference to a stated criterion.

Purposes of sociometric techniques

a. To assess interpersonal relationships which are believed to be a function of personality.

b. It is a method of discovering and analyzing patterns of friendship within a group setting.

c. It is a way of measuring the overt group adjustment or acceptability.

Kinds of sociometric measurements

There are two major categories:

a. the use of choices or specific criteria to serve a particular purpose at a particular time;

b. questionnaires or rating instruments that measure interpersonal attitudes and feelings, but not in respect to a specific, functional type of criterion.

Advantages and limitations:

a. It does not give a final or exact answer. It merely gives indications or direction in their study of the individual.
b. It gives an indication of the social structure at one point in time.
c. A great deal of research is needed in order to fulfill its potential, since there is no standardized method of administration or of formulation of the criteria of choice have yet been developed.
d. There are limitations in interpreting and applying the results of the tests.
e. The greatest advantage is that they provide objective information about the functioning of individuals within their groups that is available from no other source.

Case Study: Uses, Advantages, and Limitations

Case study – It is a comprehensive method of collecting and summarizing data about an individual. It seeks to present a cumulative picture of both development and the interrelations of the factors governing current status. In broader terms, it is the collection and report of all available evidence- social, psychological, environmental; vocational that explains the individual including the analysis of the interrelationships among the various data.

Advantages:

a. Isolates key factors in situations wherein conflicting accounts become confusing.
b. Identifies multiple causation and a constellation of contributing factors.
c. Yields systematic diagnosis and treatment plans.
d. Results in predictive outcomes.

Disadvantages:

a. Requires extensive time and effort.
b. May contain inadequate or questionable past data.
c. May delay treatment
d. May focus undue attention upon a single troubled individual to the detriment of others.

Issues Related to Appraisal (Non-test Techniques)

Issues related to appraisal (non-test techniques)

a. Non-test data (autobiographies, pupil data questionnaires, and so on) are less valuable than standardized test data.

Information derived from both standardized and non-standardized sources is subject to measurement error and interpretation error. Both types of data provide only estimates, however, and demand careful and systematic interpretation.

b. Parents should have access to all data about their children collected by school counsellors.

Forcing disclosure of some kinds of information revealed by the child to a professional in confidence may be damaging to the child when the recipient is the parent.

5

Identifying and Guiding the Exceptional Learners

As guidance counsellors we will be faced with learners who are exceptional. As such, we should be able to identify and guide each one of them. The lecturette in Chapter V will give you an idea on how the exceptional learners are identified. Exceptional are commonly referred to as special children since they deviate from the norm. It's either they are above or below the norm. Having knowledge of their learning activities, skills, attitudes, and capabilities, we, as guidance counsellors can assist them such that they will be able to maximize their learning potentials.

Slow Learners

Slow learners have below average ability but do not have mental retardation. In general, IQ's for slow learners range between 71 and 85. They make up approximately 14 percent of the school population. Because they have IQ scores between 71 and 85, they function on too high a level to be classified as retarded but are frequently excluded from learning-disabled and remedial reading programmes because their scores are too low.

Slow learners manifest some of the same characteristics that mentally retarded students display, but to a lesser degree. They tend to be concrete in their thinking, need help with strategies and organization, and are eager for success. Their executive functioning is on a higher level than that of children with mental retardation. They are better able to decide when and where to use strategies and are better able to classify and group information. They also are more aware of their mental processes and can take more responsibility for their learning. In terms of instruction, these are "more so" students; they need the same instruction that regular students need, but more so. They must be given more guidance, more practice, and more time to complete learning tasks.

Students with Physical Disabilities

The term *disability* refers to an objective, measurable organic dysfunction or impairment, such as the loss of a hand or paralysis of speech muscles or legs. The term *handicap* refers to a limitation arising from environmental or functional demands placed upon a person with a disability in a given situation (Cartwright, Cartwright, and Ward, 1989, p.67). A disability is always present, whereas handicap need not be. A child who is unable to walk because of a spinal injury is not handicapped when it comes to learning to read because the disability does not interfere with reading, but she or he would be handicapped in tasks that involve mobility. Insofar as possible, teachers must make adjustments so that disabilities do not become handicaps.

Reading and writing are essentially mental activities. Children who have impaired sight, profound hearing loss, or other physical disability can and do learn to read and write. Because of advances in technology and techniques for teaching the physically disabled, most of these children can be taught in regular classrooms.

B.1 Students with Hearing Loss

Hearing loss ranges from mild to profound. Children with a mild loss may be unable to hear distant sounds; those with moderate to severe losses need hearing aids and training; those with a severe or profound loss have virtually no hearing and may only feel vibrations.

As inclusion becomes more widespread, greater numbers of students with mild or moderate hearing loss will be taught in the regular classroom.

Hearing-impaired students need help in all language areas, but especially in vocabulary, figurative language, and syntax; they may also need additional help with conceptual development. Because their ability to learn through language is restricted, hearing-impaired children may lag behind in conceptual development (Hardman, Drew,Egan, & Wolf, 1993). Hearing-impaired children must be given directions very clear and explicitly. The teacher should use gestures, pantomime, pictures, and real objects to illustrate directions and explanations. She or he should also make generous use of the chalkboard. Hearing-impaired children should be seated in the front of the class with an unimpeded view of the board. The teacher must speak distinctly and face the students directly, especially if they can read lips. The teacher might use some sign language if students understand it.

B.2 Students with Language and Speech Disorders

A language disorder is "the impairment or deviant development of comprehension and/or use of a spoken, written, and/or other symbol system" (Rice, 1988, p. 238). Language disorders that involve deficiencies in comprehension of speech also have a direct impact on reading, since reading involves understanding language.

The most prevalent speech disorder is difficulty articulating particular sounds. Other disorders involve fluency, or flow of speech and include stuttering and cluttering, which is disorganized speech or slurring.

Speech impairments do not directly affect reading or writing. The teacher's role is primarily one of being sensitive to the difficulty and helping the child apply skills in the classroom that she or he learned while working with a speech therapist. The teacher should also be supportive and help the child build confidence, providing opportunities for the child to take part in discussions and purposeful oral reading. Consultation with the speech therapist and "promotion of a classroom atmosphere conducive to unpressured verbal interaction" (Cartwright, Cartwright, & Ward, 1989, p. 174) are also recommended.

B.3 Students with Visual Impairments

Visually impaired students include children who are blind and those who have low vision. Children with low vision can see print but, even when their vision is corrected with glasses, their ability to see is less than that of average children.

For the benefit of all children, but especially for the visually impaired, the teacher should ensure that the room has adequate lighting with no glare. Students who need to sit up close should do so. The teacher should also check to see that students who have glasses are wearing them and those who need magnifying glasses or other special equipment are using it. Avoid using materials that have small print or fuzzy dittos that are hard too see. Supplement visual presentations with oral explanations.

Students with Other Physical Impairments

A wide variety of physical and health conditions, such as spinal injuries and cystic fibrosis, place limits on children's ability to participate fully or without assistance in school activities.

The teacher's role is to become familiar with the physically impaired child's condition and make necessary adjustments in the classroom. Field trips, visits to the library, and even the physical setup of the classroom will have to be planned so as to accommodate the child's needs.

Promote understanding of disabilities. Be considerate but not overprotective. Because of their condition, some physically disabled students may miss school for extended periods of time. Encourage their classmates to send get-well cards or perhaps a newsletter informing them of classroom activities. When a child returns, plan a welcoming activity. Keep the child "involved in as many activities as her condition allows" (Kirk & Gallagher, 1986).

Working with Gifted Pupils

Giftedness is a term for persons who have mental or other talents that are well above the ordinary. Approximately the top two (2) percent of the population is classified as being gifted or talented.

Renzulli (1978) defined giftedness as the interaction of above-average ability, a high level task commitment, and a high level of creativity brought to bear on a particular problem area.

The gifted are defined as follows: Children who give evidence of higher performance capability in such areas as intellectual, creative, artistic, leadership capacity, or in specific academic fields; and who require services or activities not ordinarily provided by the school in order to fully develop such capabilities (Title V, Part 13, 1988).

Gifted children may also have problems. Their interests may be narrow, and they may be bored by having to work on skills that they have already mastered. They may also have problems accepting their ability because it sets them off from their peers. Not wishing to be perceived as different, many hide their talents, often quite successfully. They may also have learning disabilities and may experience serious difficulties reading and writing, despite their intellectual ability. They often fail to get help with their learning problems because their ability enables them to compensate for deficits (Wallace & McLoughlin, 1988).

Gifted children display many of the same developmental qualities as most children. The gifted child is much more likely to:

1. Tolerate ambiguity and complexity.
2. Have a longer attention span.
3. Be a highly curious and sharp-eyed observer.
4. Be a top-notch reader who retains what is read.
5. Have a well-developed speaking and listening vocabulary.
6. Have learned well the basic skills.
7. Understand complex directions the first time around.
8. Be imaginative and receptive to new ideas.
9. Be interested in broad concepts and issues.
10. Have one or more hobbies that require thinking.

A common problem with having gifted children in regular classrooms is that the curriculum is restrictive and unchallenging for them. *One way to "take the lid off," and yet have the gifted manageably working with other children, use many open-ended investigations and activities.*

- Help the mainstreamed gifted is to encourage them to build a large knowledge base.
- Help the gifted is to let them manage their own learning through individual and small group projects, including those done for school science fairs.
- Help gifted pupils is by exposing them to persons in science and other professions who can serve as information sources and future role models.
- Help the gifted by attending to their social skills as they interact with other children.

Inclusion or Mainstreaming

Inclusion is the practice of educating within the regular classroom all students, including those with special needs. In full inclusion, all support services are provided within the classroom setting. In partial inclusion, the student may be pulled out of the classroom for special instruction. Inclusion is more than just an organizational pattern. It is a philosophy that values diversity and the worth and potential of each individual (Hardman, 1994). Inclusion is also a collaborative, cooperative venture, with professionals working together and students helping each other. For inclusion to work, the competitive atmosphere of the traditional classroom must give way to the caring, collaborative spirit of the inclusive classroom where students and teachers learn from one another.

Career

Career describes an individuals' journey through learning, work and other aspects of life. There are a number of ways to define a career and the term is used in a variety of ways.

Definitions and Etymology

Career is defined by the Oxford English Dictionary as a person's "course or progress through life (or a distinct portion of life)". In this definition career is understood to relate to a range of aspects of an individual's life, learning and work. Career is also frequently understood to relate only to the working aspects of an individuals life e.g. as in career woman. A third way in which the term career is used to describe an occupation or a profession that usually involves special training or formal education, and is considered to be a person's lifework. In this case "a career" is seen as a sequence of related jobs usually pursued within a single industry or sector e.g. "a career in law" or "a career in the building trade". The etymology of the term comes from the m. French word carriere (16 c.) ("road, racecourse") which, in turn, comes from the Latin word "(via) cararia" (track for wheeled vehicles) which originated from the Latin word *carrus" which means "wagon".*

Historic Changes in Careers

For a pre-modernist notion of "career", compare cursus honorum. By the late 20th century, a wide range of choices (especially in the range of potential professions) and more widespread education had allowed it to become possible to plan (or design) a career: in this respect the careers of the career counsellor and of the career advisor have grown up. It is also not uncommon for adults in the late 20th/ early 21st centuries to have dual or multiple careers, either sequentially or concurrently. Thus, professional identities have become hyphenated or hybridized to reflect this shift in work ethic. Economist Richard Florida notes this trend generally and more specifically among the "creative class".

Career Management

Career management describes the active and purposeful management of a career by an individual. Ideas of what comprise "career management skills" are describe by the Blueprint model (in the United States, Canada, Australia, Scotland, and England) and the Seven C's of Digital Career Literacy (specifically relating to the Internet skills). Key skills include the ability to reflect on one's current career, research the labour market, determine whether education is necessary, find openings, and make career changes.

Career Choice

According to Behling and others, an individual's decision to join a firm may depend on any of the three factors viz. objective factor, subjective factor and critical contact.

- Objective factor theory assumes that the applicants are rational. The choice, therefore, is exercised after an objective assessment of the tangible benefits of the job. Factors may include the salary, other benefits, location, opportunities for career advancement, etc.
- Subjective factor theory suggests that decision making is dominated by social and psychological factors. The status of the job, reputation of the organization and other similar factors plays an important role.
- Critical contact theory advances the idea that a candidate's observations while interacting with the organization plays a vital role in decision making. For example, how the recruiter keeps in touch with the candidate, the promptness of response and similar factors are important. This theory is more valid with experienced professionals.

These theories assume that candidates have a free choice of employers and careers. In reality the scarcity of jobs and strong competition for desirable jobs severely skews the decision making process. In many markets employees work particular careers simply because they were forced to accept whatever work was available to them.

Career (Occupation) Changing

Changing occupation is an important aspect of career and career management. Over a lifetime, both the individual and the labour market will change; it is to be expected that many people will change occupations during their lives. Data collected by the U.S. Bureau of Labour Statistics through the National Longitudinal Survey of Youth in 1979 showed that individuals between the ages of 18 and 38 will hold more than 10 jobs.

A survey conducted by Right Management suggests the following reasons for career changing.

- The downsizing or the restructuring of an organization (54%).
- New challenges or opportunities that arise (30%).
- Poor or ineffective leadership (25%).
- Having a poor relationship with a manager(s) (22%).
- For the improvement of work/life balance (21%).
- Contributions are not being recognized (21%).
- For better compensation and benefits (18%),
- For better alignment with personal and organizational values (17%).
- Personal strengths and capabilities are not a good fit with an organization (16%).
- The financial instability of an organization (13%).
- An organization relocated (12%).

According to an article on Time.com, one out of three people currently employed (as of 2008) spends about an hour per day searching for another position.

Career Support

There are a range of different educational, counselling and human resource management interventions that can support individuals to develop and manage their careers. Career support is commonly offered while people are in education, when they are transitioning to the labour market, when they are changing career, during periods of unemployment, and during transition to retirement. Support may be offered by career professionals, other professionals or by non-professionals such as family and friends. Professional career support is sometimes known as "career guidance" as in the OECD definition of career guidance:

The activities may take place on an individual or group basis, and may be face-to-face or at a distance (including helplines and web-based services). They include career information provision (in print, ICT-based and other forms), assessment and self-assessment tools, counselling interviews, career education programmes (to help individuals develop their self-awareness, opportunity awareness, and career management skills), taster programmes (to sample options before choosing them), work search programmes, and transition services."

However this use of the term "career guidance" can be confusing as the term is also commonly used to describe the activities of career counsellors.

Provision of Career Support

Career support is offered by a range of different mechanisms. Much career support is informal and provided through personal networks or existing relationships such as management. There is a market for private career support however the bulk of career support that exists as a professionalised activity is provided by the public sector.

Types of Career Support

Key types of career support include:

- Career information describes information that supports career and learning choices. An important sub-set of career information is labour market information (LMI), such as salaries of various professions, employment rate in various professions, available training programmes, and current job openings and .
- Career assessments are tests that come in a variety of forms and rely on both quantitative and qualitative methodologies. Career assessments can help individuals identify and better articulate their unique interests, personality, values, and skills to determine how well they may match with a certain career. Some skills that career assessments could help determine are job-specific skills, transferable skills, and self-management skills. Career assessments can also provide a window of potential opportunities by helping individuals discover the tasks, experience, education and training that is needed for a career they would want to pursue. Career counsellors, executive coaches, educational institutions, career development centres, and outplacement companies often administer career assessments to help individuals focus their search on careers that closely match their unique personal profile.
- Career counselling assesses people's interests, personality, values and skills, and helps them to explore career options and research graduate and professional schools. Career counselling provides one-on-one or group professional assistance in exploration and decision making tasks related to choosing a major/occupation, transitioning into the world of work or further professional training.

- Career education describes a process by which individuals come to learn about themselves, their careers and the world of work. There is a strong tradition of career education in schools, however career education can also occur in a wider range of other contexts including further and higher education and the workplace. A commonly used framework for careers education is DOTS which stands for decision learning (D), opportunity awareness (O), transition learning (T), and self-awareness (S). Oftentimes, higher education is thought of as being too narrow or too researched based and lacking of a deeper understanding of the material to develop the skills necessary for a certain career.

Some research shows adding one year of schooling beyond high school creates an increase of wages 17.8 percent per worker. However, additional years of schooling, beyond 9 or 10 years, have little effect on worker's wages. In summary, better educated, bigger benefits. In 2010, 90% of the U.S. Workforce had a high school diploma, 64% had some college, and 34% had at least a bachelor's degree.

The common problem that people may encounter when trying to achieve an education for a career is the cost. The career that comes with the education must pay well enough to be able to pay off the schooling. The benefits of schooling can differ greatly depending on the degree (or certification) obtained, the programmes the school may offer, and the ranking of the school. Sometimes, colleges provide students more with just education to prepare for careers. It is not uncommon for colleges to provide pathways and support straight into the workforce the students may desire. Much career support is delivered face-to-face, but an increasing amount of career support is delivered online.

Career Assessment

Career assessments are tools that are designed to help individuals understand how a variety of personal attributes (i.e., interests, values, preferences, motivations, aptitudes and skills), impact their potential success and satisfaction with different career options and work environments. Career assessments have played a critical role in career development and the economy in the last century (Whiston and Rahardja, 2005). Assessments of some or all of these attributes are often used by individuals or organizations, such as university career service centres, career counsellors, outplacement companies, corporate human resources staff, executive coaches, vocational rehabilitation counsellors, and guidance counsellors to help individuals make more informed career decisions. In part, the popularity for this tool is due to the National Defence Education Act of 1958, which funded career guidance in schools. Focus was put onto tools that would help high school students determine which subjects they may want to focus on to reach a chosen career path. Since 1958, career assessment tool options have exploded.

Types of Career Assessments

Career assessments come in many forms and vary along several dimensions. The assessments selected by individuals or administrators vary depending on their personal beliefs regarding the most important criteria when considering career choices, as well as the unique needs of the individual considering a career decision. Some common points of variance are:

- Methodology - Some assessments are quantitative in nature and precisely measure key attributes believed to influence an individuals potential success and satisfaction with a career. Others are qualitative exercises designed to help individuals clarify their goals and preferences, which can then be used to make more informed career decisions.
- Measured attributes - Assessments vary with regard to the specific personality attributes measured. Some assessments focus on an individual's interests, and perhaps aptitude, while others focus on skills or values.
- Validity - Many assessments, particularly those offered on the internet, lack evidence for "validity," which is the degree to which interpretation of the results of the assessment or decisions made from the results are useful. Typical evidence of validity is verified empirically. Users should evaluate any tests psychometric properties when assessing whether to use it for a particular purpose, and how much weight to give to the results. When the validity of the assessment for its intended purpose cannot be evaluated, results should be interpreted with appropriate caution.
- Target customer profile - Some assessments, such as the Strong Interest Inventory, the Myers Briggs Type Indicator, and Careerscope are designed to serve broad markets (i.e., virtually any individual choosing a vocational programme or Career Clusters, starting their career or considering a career change.

Benefits

Career assessments are designed to discover the skills, aptitude and talents of candidates. A self-assessment can be helpful in assessing the areas in which a candidate has strengths and where they are weak. The results can be useful in helping candidates to choose a career that is in tune with their goals and talents. While the validation of each instrument may vary from test to test, overall these types of assessments have been proven to introduce more career options, increase satisfaction in one's career plan and increase the understanding of oneself (Prince et al., 2003).

Data as to how often people change careers are unavailable while there's a considerable mythology about it, though no systematic studies have been undertaken. However, many people change careers more than once. Some make changes because the career path they chose is no longer viable (to wit, buggy whip makers are no longer in high demand). Or because as they mature throughout the lifespan their interests evolve. The biggest benefit of career assessment, therefore, is that it enables candidates to make the best career decision to grow both personally and professionally.

To make an assessment of their skills, candidates can pursue many avenues, the can take career interest tests such as the Strong Vocational Aptitude test, they can conduct a self-assessment, they can use the plethora of career books designed to help with this task. In fact, there are a myriad of helpful books, the most famous of which is, Richard Bolles, What Colour is Your Parachute. In addition, they can seek expert help from career counsellors, or when warranted, psychologists or other mental health professionals. These professionals use a variety of techniques to determine the talents of candidates. Also, career counsellors can guide candidates on how to go about planning their career to achieve professional success.

Many people who are unhappy in their work find themselves uncertain as to where to turn for help. They may have seen career counsellors or career coaches or read self-help books or even obtained psychotherapy to address their career concerns—and, still found that their difficulties did not yield to these interventions. In response to this uncertainty in 2000, Dr. Lynn Friedman, a clinical psychologist, psychoanalyst who has devoted her career to work-life concerns pioneered an exciting new approach to career assessment; psychoanalytically-informed, career assessment. As a clinical psychologist, psychoanalyst working with people around work-life concerns, Friedman, a Washington DC Psychologist found that many people devoted considerable time, energy and money to unhelpful services because their difficulties were not properly assessed at the outset. Friedman found that a careful psychological assessment aimed at asking the question, "what prompts these career difficulties" allowed the underlying nature of the difficulties to be clarified and understood. With this understanding a helpful intervention could be planned. For example, Friedman found that many people who sought psychotherapy when career coaching might have been the optimal intervention and conversely, many sought career coaching or career counselling when psychotherapy or even psychoanalysis would be more effective at resolving their difficulties. Unfortunately, most career coaches and counsellors are not trained to assess whether psychotherapy or psychoanalysis would be the appropriate intervention.

Drawbacks

Career assessment, in the form of tests and other structured and unstructured tools, can be very useful for those who are uncertain about the array of career possibilities. However, there are some drawbacks to each. At best, the results of individual career assessments provide targeted information that may not address a particular individual's needs. In addition, some of the best individual assessment tools require the help of a qualified professional to ensure the results are interpreted correctly and usefully.

Also, many of the tests are based on the person's view of himself or herself. If someone is not self-aware, the results may not be accurate. Many times they do not take into account that people have natural blind spots. The test is only as good as its user and individuals are often not clearly aware of their own strengths and weaknesses.

Job Description

A job description is a list that a person might use for general tasks, or functions, and responsibilities of a position. It may often include to whom the position reports, specifications such as the qualifications or skills needed by the person in the job, or a salary range. Job descriptions are usually narrative, but some may instead comprise a simple list of competencies; for instance, strategic human resource planning methodologies may be used to develop a competency architecture for an organization, from which job descriptions are built as a shortlist of competencies.

Creating a job Description

A job description is usually developed by conducting a job analysis, which includes examining the tasks and sequences of tasks necessary to perform the job. The analysis considers the areas of knowledge and skills needed for the job. A job usually includes several roles. The job description might be broadened to form a person specification or may be known as Terms Of Reference.

Roles and Responsibilities

A job description may include relationships with other people in the organization: Supervisory level, managerial requirements, and relationships with other colleagues.

Goals

A job description need not be limited to explaining the current situation, or work that is currently expected; it may also set out goals for what might be achieved in future....

Limitations

Prescriptive job descriptions may be seen as a hindrance in certain circumstances:

- Job descriptions may not be suitable for some senior managers as they should have the freedom to take the initiative and find fruitful new directions;
- Job descriptions may be too inflexible in a rapidly-changing organization, for instance in an area subject to rapid technological change;
- Other changes in job content may lead to the job description being out of date;
- The process that an organization uses to create job descriptions may not be optimal.

Career Guide

A career guide is an individual or publication that provides guidance to people facing a variety of career challenges. These challenges may include (but are not limited to) dealing with redundancy; seeking a new job; changing careers; returning to work after a career break; building new skills; personal and professional development; going for promotion; and setting up a business. The common aim of the career guide, whatever the particular situation of the individual being guided, is normally to help that individual gain control of their career and, to some extent, their life.

Career Guide Professionals

Individuals who work as career guides usually take the approach of combining coaching, mentoring, advising and consulting in their work, without being limited to any one of these disciplines. A typical career guide will have a mixture of professional qualifications and work experiences from which to draw when guiding clients. They may also have a large network of contacts and, when appropriate will put a particular client in touch with a contact relevant to their case. A career guide may work for themselves independently or for one or more private or public careers advisory services. The term 'Career Guide' has been first established and used by career consulting firm Position Ignition, which was created in 2009 and has been using the term for their career consultants and career advisors.

Career Guide Publications

Career guide publications may take a number of forms, including PDFs, booklets, journals or books. A career guide publication will typically be divided up into a number of chapters or segments, each one addressing a particular career issue. Career guides can also focus on a particular industry or profession. For instance, there is 'The fine artist's career guide: making money in the arts and beyond' and 'Professional Pilot's Career Guide'.

Career Guidance Standards

In Europe, career guidance as a public service is generally expected to meet a number of quality assurance standards. According to these standards, European career guidance should:

- Have regular review periods in which to assess guidance resources and processes
- Be transparent and open
- Create synergy and co-operation between education, training, employment and community sectors
- Ensure consistency between local and regional services so that all citizens are treated equally, regardless of geographical location.
- Strive for continuous improvement of tools, services and products.

What are Career Goals?

Career goals are important objectives or milestones people set to evaluate their progress along their career paths. They can be made both by employed people and those searching for jobs, and include things like acquiring training in specialized fields, or determining to reach a certain level of promotion in a set number of years. Though goals can be very useful, they do need to be periodically assessed to ensure that they don't become counterproductive.

Common Types

People set career goals both before and after they start working. Before a person starts working, he may try to get a certain level of education to become eligible for certain jobs. Someone in a job that he doesn't like may try to get certification in a different area so that he can eventually change jobs. Those in careers that they do like often set time or money-related targets, like working a certain amount of time for a company, or making a specific amount of money. Many people also set goals related to advancement in their company, or for flexibility in their work schedule.

It's usually best to have a mix of ambitions, both short-term and long-term as well as specific and general. Long-term goals tend to be more general, since circumstances may change over time, while short-term ones are more specific, since they can be planned for more easily. General career goals are those related to an end, like "become a doctor" or "work from home", while specific ones are related to the steps needed to reach the desired end. If a person wanted to become a doctor, then his first specific goal would be getting good enough grades to get into medical school.

Goal-Setting Process

When setting targets, it's important to consider the basic motivation and then think about what concrete things need to happen to achieve it. Once a person has a basic list of steps, he should set a time frame for meeting the objective that includes regular milestones and check-ups. Career planners and HR staff can often help make sure that plans are realistic.

For instance, if a person wanted to make $75,000 US Dollars (USD) a year, he would first need to think about whether his company can afford to pay him that much, and if so, what level of promotion he would need to get before that salary would be offered. He would also need to think about what kind of skills he would need to work in that position, and if there are any other things he could do to make himself stand out from others up for promotion. If he saw that all of the people earning that much in his company had worked in the company for five years and all made a particular quota, then his time frame would probably be around five years.

His steps might include taking courses to learn how to improve his quotas and participating in special projects to make himself stand out. He could then determine a timeframe for meeting specific milestones: for instance, increasing his quota by 20% in one year. He could also schedule six-month check-ins to see whether he is making progress and to determine if the goal is still important to him.

Assessment

It's important to regularly assess career goals to make sure that they're still relevant and useful. As people's priorities change over time, goals need to be updated too. For instance, if a person wanted to be transferred to an office in Madrid, he might make learning Spanish a target. If later on, he decides that he can advance further in his career by not transferring, then learning Spanish might not be as important.

Sometimes running into roadblocks can be a sign that an ambition is unrealistic or needs to be re-assessed. Though some obstacles are to be expected, repeatedly failing to meet a goal or feeling as though it is more trouble than its worth may be a sign that it needs to be revised. It's important to be somewhat flexible with career goals and willing to revise when they're not working out. Being too rigid can limit options and actually be counterproductive, as it can cause people to spend a lot of energy on something that's not really important to them.

What is Career Development?

Career development is an organized planning method used to match the needs of a business with the career goals of employees. Formulating a career development plan can help employees to do their jobs more efficiently. Additionally, these plans can be beneficial for employees who might want to move up in a company or look for other jobs in the future. In the business world, there are generally two groups that direct the career development process: upper management and human resource personnel. Managers, for example, might have the responsibility of making sure the needs of a business coincide with the employee's career goals to achieve an overall balanced work atmosphere. They will often identify the skills, experience, and knowledge employees need in order to provide their best possible work. Human resource (HR) personnel are often responsible for providing career development information programmes for employees. Professional networking is usually important, and as a result, employees might get tools to start networking from the HR department. HR managers also usually provide a compensation structure that compliments business needs but also allows individual career growth. For example, employees who have exhibited a certain improvement or growth in needed skills might be promoted and given a raise.

Regardless of company leadership, employees have the primary responsibility to make sure their career development goals proceed how they want them to. Typically, employees assess what they want from their job currently, as well as in the future. Employees often work with their supervisors to figure out what training, professional development, or continued education options are available to them.

Sometimes, career development is explored by people who are not employees of a business. Instead, these people might be interested in creating a set of guidelines to help them to choose a career and get hired by a desired company. This typically involves a self-assessment in which a person usually considers things that he or she is naturally good at or has experience in. Additional things to consider include interests and learning styles. The self-assessment generally helps an individual to select careers they are the most interested in pursuing.

Individuals often continue their career development plan by preparing strategies for job interviews. Candidates who are not naturally good speakers, for example, might choose to enroll in an interview preparation programme. In this kind of programme, a mock interview is often conducted to see how well individuals respond to questions. The results are typically analyzed to determine things that can be adjusted in preparation for real interviews.

6

Psychological Testing

Psychological testing is a field characterized by the use of samples of behaviour in order to assess psychological construct(s), such as cognitive and emotional functioning, about a given individual. The technical term for the science behind psychological testing is psychometrics. By *samples of behaviour*, one means observations of an individual performing tasks that have usually been prescribed beforehand, which often means scores on a test. These responses are often compiled into statistical tables that allow the evaluator to compare the behaviour of the individual being tested to the responses of a norm group.

Psychological Tests

A psychological test is an objective and standardized measure of an individual's mental and/or behavioural characteristics. A psychological test is an instrument designed to measure unobserved constructs, also known as latent variables. Psychological tests are typically, but not necessarily, a series of tasks or problems that the respondent has to solve. Psychological tests can strongly resemble questionnaires, which are also designed to measure unobserved constructs, but differ in that psychological tests ask for a respondent's maximum performance whereas a questionnaire asks for the respondent's typical performance. A useful psychological test must be both valid (i.e., there is evidence to support the specified interpretation of the test results) and reliable (i.e., internally consistent or give consistent results over time, across raters, etc.). It is important that people who are equal on the measured construct also have an equal probability of answering the test items correctly. For example, an item on a mathematics test could be "In a soccer match two players get a red card; how many players are left in the end?"; however, this item also requires knowledge of soccer to be answered correctly, not just mathematical ability. Group membership can also influence the chance of correctly answering items (differential item functioning). Often tests are constructed for a specific population, and this should be taken into account when administering tests. If a test is invariant to some group difference (e.g. gender) in one population (e.g. England) it does not automatically mean that it is also invariant in another population (e.g. Japan).

Psychological assessment is similar to psychological testing but usually involves a more comprehensive assessment of the individual. Psychological assessment is a process that involves checking the integration of information from multiple sources, such as tests of normal and abnormal personality, tests of ability or intelligence, tests of interests or attitudes, as well as information from personal interviews. Collateral information is also collected about personal, occupational, or medical history, such as from records or from interviews with parents, spouses, teachers, or previous therapists or physicians. A *psychological test* is one of the sources of data used within the process of assessment; usually more than one test is used. Many psychologists do some level of assessment when providing services to clients or patients, and may use for example, simple checklists to osis for treatment settings; to assess a particular area of functioning or disability often for school settings; to help select type of treatment or to assess treatment outcomes; to help courts decide issues such as child custody or competency to stand trial; or to help assess job applicants or employees and provide career development counselling or training.

History

The first large-scale mental test may have been the imperial examination system in China. The test, an early form of psychological testing, assessed candidates based on their proficiency in topics such as civil law and fiscal policies. Other early tests of intelligence were made for entertainment rather than analysis. Modern mental testing began in France in the 19th century. It contributed to separating mental retardation from mental illness and reducing the neglect, torture, and ridicule heaped on both groups. Englishman Francis Galton coined the terms psychometrics and eugenics, and developed a method for measuring intelligence based on nonverbal sensory-motor tests. It was initially popular, but was abandoned after the discovery that it had no relationship to outcomes such as college grades. French psychologist Alfred Binet, together with psychologists Victor Henri and Théodore Simon, after about 15 years of development, published the Binet-Simon test in 1905, which focused on verbal abilities. It was intended to identify mental retardation in school children.

The origins of personality testing date back to the 18th and 19th centuries, when personality was assessed through phrenology, the measurement of the human skull, and physiognomy, which assessed personality based on a person's outer appearances. These early pseudoscientific techniques were eventually replaced with more empirical methods in the 20th century. One of the earliest modern personality tests was the Woolworth Personality Data Sheet, a self-report inventory developed for World War I and used for the psychiatric screening of new draftees.

Principles of Psychological Testing

Proper psychological testing is conducted after vigorous research and development in contrast to quick web-based or magazine questionnaires that say "Find out your Personality Colour," or "What's your Inner Age?" Proper psychological testing consists of the following:

- *Standardization* - All procedures and steps must be conducted with consistency and under the same environment to achieve the same testing performance from those being tested.
- *Objectivity* - Scoring is free of subjective judgements or biases based on the fact that the same results are obtained on test from everyone.
- *Test Norms* - The average test score within a large group of people where the performance of one individual can be compared to the results of others by establishing a point of comparison or frame of reference.
- *Reliability* - Obtaining the same result after multiple testing.
- *Validity* - The type of test being administered must measure what it is intended to measure.

Interpreting Scores

Psychological tests, like many measurements of human characteristics, can be interpreted in a *norm-referenced* or *criterion-referenced* manner. Norms are statistical representations of a population. A norm-referenced score interpretation compares an individual's results on the test with the statistical representation of the population. In practice, rather than testing a population, a representative sample or group is tested. This provides a group norm or set of norms. One representation of norms is the Bell curve (also called "normal curve"). Norms are available for standardized psychological tests, allowing for an understanding of how an individual's scores compare with the group norms. Norm referenced scores are typically reported on the standard score (z) scale or a rescaling of it.

A criterion-referenced interpretation of a test score compares an individual's performance to some criterion other than performance of other individuals. For example, the generic school test typically provides a score in reference to a subject domain; a student might score 80% on a geography test. Criterion-referenced score interpretations are generally more applicable to achievement tests rather than psychological tests.

Often, test scores can be interpreted in both ways; a score of 80% on a geography test could place a student at the 84th percentile, or a standard score of 1.0 or even 2.0.

Types of Psychological Tests

There are several broad categories of psychological tests:

IQ/achievement Tests

IQ tests purport to be measures of intelligence, while achievement tests are measures of the use and level of development of use of the ability. IQ (or cognitive) tests and achievement tests are common norm-referenced tests.

In these types of tests, a series of tasks is presented to the person being evaluated, and the person's responses are graded according to carefully prescribed guidelines. After the test is completed, the results can be compiled and compared to the responses of a norm group, usually composed of people at the same age or grade level as the person being evaluated. IQ tests which contain a series of tasks typically divide the tasks into verbal (relying on the use of language) and performance, or non-verbal (relying on eye–hand types of tasks, or use of symbols or objects). Examples of verbal IQ test tasks are vocabulary and information (answering general knowledge questions). Non-verbal examples are timed completion of puzzles (object assembly) and identifying images which fit a pattern (matrix reasoning).

IQ tests (e.g., WAIS-IV, WISC-IV, Cattell Culture Fair III, Woodcock-Johnson Tests of Cognitive Abilities-III, Stanford-Binet Intelligence Scales V) and academic achievement tests (e.g. WIAT, WRAT, Woodcock-Johnson Tests of Achievement-III) are designed to be administered to either an individual (by a trained evaluator) or to a group of people (paper and pencil tests). The individually administered tests tend to be more comprehensive, more reliable, more valid and generally to have better psychometric characteristics than group-administered tests. However, individually administered tests are more expensive to administer because of the need for a trained administrator (psychologist, school psychologist, or psychometrician).

Public Safety Employment Tests

Vocations within the public safety field (i.e., fire service, law enforcement, corrections, emergency medical services) often require Industrial and Organizational Psychology tests for initial employment and advancement throughout the ranks. The National Firefighter Selection Inventory - NFSI, the National Criminal Justice Officer Selection Inventory - NCJOSI, and the Integrity Inventory are prominent examples of these tests.

Attitude Tests

Attitude test assess an individual's feelings about an event, person, or object. Attitude scales are used in marketing to determine individual (and group) preferences for brands, or items. Typically attitude tests use either a Thurstone scale, or Likert Scale to measure specific items.

Neuropsychological Tests

These tests consist of specifically designed tasks used to measure a psychological function known to be linked to a particular brain structure or pathway. Neuropsychological tests can be used in a clinical context to assess impairment after an injury or illness known to affect neurocognitive functioning. When used in research, these tests can be used to contrast neuropsychological abilities across experimental groups.

Infant and Preschool Assessment

Due to the fact that infants and preschool aged children have limited capacities of communication, psychologists are unable to use traditional tests to assess them. Therefore, many tests have been designed just for children ages birth to around six years of age. These tests usually vary with age respectively from assessments of reflexes and developmental milestones, to sensory and motor skills, language skills, and simple cognitive skills. Common tests for this age group are split into categories: Infant Ability, Preschool Intelligence, and School Readiness. Common infant ability tests include: Gesell Developmental Schedules (GDS) which measures the developmental progress of infants, Neonatal Behavioural Assessment Scale (NBAS) which tests newborn behaviour, reflexes, and responses, Ordinal Scales of Psychological Development (OSPD) which assesses infant intellectual abilities, and Bayley-III which tests mental ability and motor skills.

Common preschool intelligence tests include: McCarthy Scales of Children's Abilities (MSCA) which is similar to an infant IQ test, Differential Ability Scales (DAS) which can be used to test for learning disability, Wechsler Preschool and Primary Scale of Intelligence-III (WPPSI-III) and Stanford-Binet Intelligence Scales for Early Childhood which could be seen as infant versions of IQ tests, and Fagan Test of Infant Intelligence (FTII) which tests recognition memory. Finally, some common school readiness tests are: Developmental Indicators for the Assessment of Learning-III (DIAL-III) which assesses motor, cognitive, and language skills, Denver II which tests motor, social, and language skills, and Home Observation for Measurement of Environment (HOME) which is a measure of the extent to which a child's home environment facilitates school readiness.

Infant and preschool assessments, since they do not predict later childhood nor adult abilities, are mainly useful for testing if a child is experiencing developmental delay or disabilities. They are also useful for testing individual intelligence and ability, and, as aforementioned, there are some specifically designed to test school readiness and determine which children may struggle more in school.

Personality Tests

Psychological measures of personality are often described as either objective tests or projective tests. The terms "objective test" and "projective test" have recently come under criticism in the Journal of Personality Assessment. The more descriptive "rating scale or self-report measures" and "free response measures" are suggested, rather than the terms "objective tests" and "projective tests," respectively.

Objective Tests (Rating Scale or self-report Measure)

Objective tests have a restricted response format, such as allowing for true or false answers or rating using an ordinal scale. Prominent examples of objective personality tests include the Minnesota Multiphasic Personality Inventory, Millon Clinical Multiaxial Inventory-III, Child Behaviour Checklist, Symptom Checklist 90 and the Beck Depression Inventory. Objective personality tests can be designed for use in business for potential employees, such as the NEO-PI, the 16PF, and the OPQ (Occupational Personality Questionnaire), all of which are based on the Big Five taxonomy. The Big Five, or Five Factor Model of normal personality, has gained acceptance since the early 1990s when some influential meta-analyses (e.g., Barrick & Mount 1991) found consistent relationships between the Big Five personality factors and important criterion variables.

Another personality test based upon the Five Factor Model is the Five Factor Personality Inventory – Children (FFPI-C.). aa

Projective Tests (Free Response Measures)

Projective tests allow for a freer type of response. An example of this would be the Rorschach test, in which a person states what each of ten ink blots might be. Projective testing became a growth industry in the first half of the 1900s, with doubts about the theoretical assumptions behind projective testing arising in the second half of the 1900s. Some projective tests are used less often today because they are more time consuming to administer and because the reliability and validity are controversial.

As improved sampling and statistical methods developed, much controversy regarding the utility and validity of projective testing has occurred. The use of clinical judgement rather than norms and statistics to evaluate people's characteristics has convinced many that projectives are deficient and unreliable (results are too dissimilar each time a test is given to the same person).

However, many practitioners continue to rely on projective testing, and some testing experts (e.g., Cohen, Anastasi) suggest that these measures can be useful in developing t herapeutic rapport. They may also be useful in creating inferences to follow-up with other methods. The most widely used scoring system for the Rorschach is the Exner system of scoring. Another common projective test is the Thematic Apperception Test (TAT), which is often scored with Westen's Social Cognition and Object Relations Scales and Phebe Cramer's Defence Mechanisms Manual. Both "rating scale" and "free response" measures are used in contemporary clinical practice, with a trend toward the former.

Other projective tests include the House-Tree-Person test, the Animal Metaphor Test, the Roberts Apperception Test, and the Attachment Projective.

Sexological Tests

The number of tests specifically meant for the field of sexology is quite limited. The field of sexology provides different psychological evaluation devices in order to examine the various aspects of the discomfort, problem or dysfunction, regardless of whether they are individual or relational ones.

Direct Observation Tests

Although most psychological tests are "rating scale" or "free response" measures, psychological assessment may also involve the observation of people as they complete activities. This type of assessment is usually conducted with families in a labouratory, home or with children in a classroom.

The purpose may be clinical, such as to establish a pre-intervention baseline of a child's hyperactive or aggressive classroom behaviours or to observe the nature of a parent-child interaction in order to understand a relational disorder. Direct observation procedures are also used in research, for example to study the relationship between intrapsychic variables and specific target behaviours, or to explore sequences of behavioural interaction.

The Parent-Child Interaction Assessment-II (PCIA) is an example of a direct observation procedure that is used with school-age children and parents. The parents and children are video recorded playing at a make-believe zoo. The Parent-Child Early Relational Assessment (Clark, 1999) is used to study parents and young children and involves a feeding and a puzzle task. The MacArthur Story Stem Battery (MSSB) is used to elicit narratives from children. The Dyadic Parent-Child Interaction Coding System-II (Eyberg, 1981) tracks the extent to which children follow the commands of parents and *vice versa* and is well suited to the study of children with Oppositional Defiant Disorders and their parents.

Interest Tests

Psychological tests to assess a person's interests and preferences. These tests are used primarily for career counselling. Interest tests include items about daily activities from among which applicants select their preferences. The rationale is that if a person exhibits the same pattern of interests and preferences as people who are successful in a given occupation, then the chances are high that the person taking the test will find satisfaction in that occupation.

Aptitude Tests

Psychological tests to measure specific abilities, such as mechanical or clerical skills. Sometimes these tests must be specially designed for a particular job, but there are also tests available that measure general clerical and mechanical aptitudes. An example of Aptitude test is the Minnesota Clerical Test; it is a 15-minutes individual or group test in two parts: number comparison (matching 200 pairs of numbers) and name comparison. Applicants are instructed to works as fast as possible without making errors. The test measures the perceptual speed and accuracy required to perform various clerical duties. It is useful for any job that requires attention to detail in industries such as utility companies, financial institutions, and manufacturing.

Test Security

Many psychological tests are generally not available to the public, but rather, have restrictions both from publishers of the tests and from psychology licensing boards that prevent the disclosure of the tests themselves and information about the interpretation of the results. Test publishers consider both copyright and matters of professional ethics to be involved in protecting the secrecy of their tests, and they sell tests only to people who have proved their educational and professional qualifications to the test maker's satisfaction. Purchasers are legally bound from giving test answers or the tests themselves out to the public unless permitted under the test maker's standard conditions for administration of the tests.

The International Test Commission (ITC), an international association of national psychological societies and test publishers, publishes the *International Guidelines for Test Use*, which prescribes to "protect the integrity" of the tests by not publicly describing test techniques and by not "coaching individuals" so that they "might unfairly influence their test performance."

What is Vocational Education?

In today's economy vocational jobs are becoming more and more important. This is why vocational education programmes are popular. Vocational education training provides career and technical education to interested students. These students are prepared as trainees for jobs that are based upon manual or practical fields. Jobs are related to specific trades, occupations, and vocations.

Instructors teach students procedural knowledge requires for their field. Community colleges have long been instrumental offerings for vocational education. These colleges around the country provide certificates in various vocational fields. They also offer certain degree programmes that focus on some popular occupations. The vocational field expands each year to include fields that were at one time non-traditional to this area.

The training for vocational jobs requires less education than four year degree programmes. They are also significantly less expensive. Instructors at this level of education use traditional methods of teaching. They incorporate the use of lesson plans, teacher resources, worksheets, and other tools in this process. One difference to other education programmes is the on-the-job training component. Many students will have the opportunity to work in their field while being educated. Some will be accepted into valuable apprenticeship programmes.

Some of the jobs in vocational fields include construction workers, blacksmiths, and steel workers. Today, there are other great choices of vocational jobs. This umbrella has broadened and diversified to include retail, tourism, and cosmetology. Some portions of the information technology field are taught in vocational education programmes as well. This allows students to decide from a vast array of career choices.

- Home >
- Teacher Resource >
- Vocational Education

Share on favourites Bookmark It! Share on email Email It!

- Teacher Helpers
- Best Teacher Web Sites
- Teacher Articles
- Teacher Catalogue
- Teacher Dictionary
- Teacher Forum
- Teacher Newsletter

- Teacher Timesavers
- Teacher Web Sites
- Teaching Tips
- Weekly Teacher Poll

Email Newsletter

Receive free lesson plans, printables, and worksheets by email:

What is Vocational Education?

In today's economy vocational jobs are becoming more and more important. This is why vocational education programmes are popular. Vocational education training provides career and technical education to interested students. These students are prepared as trainees for jobs that are based upon manual or practical fields. Jobs are related to specific trades, occupations, and vocations.

Instructors teach students procedural knowledge requires for their field. Community colleges have long been instrumental offerings for vocational education. These colleges around the country provide certificates in various vocational fields. They also offer certain degree programmes that focus on some popular occupations. The vocational field expands each year to include fields that were at one time non-traditional to this area.

The training for vocational jobs requires less education than four year degree programmes. They are also significantly less expensive. Instructors at this level of education use traditional methods of teaching. They incorporate the use of lesson plans, teacher resources, worksheets, and other tools in this process. One difference to other education programmes is the on-the-job training component. Many students will have the opportunity to work in their field while being educated. Some will be accepted into valuable apprenticeship programmes.

Some of the jobs in vocational fields include construction workers, blacksmiths, and steel workers. Today, there are other great choices of vocational jobs. This umbrella has broadened and diversified to include retail, tourism, and cosmetology. Some portions of the information technology field are taught in vocational education programmes as well. This allows students to decide from a vast array of career choices. The retail field is one of those career opportunities that allow for growth. Workers can start off in training positions and work their way up to management. Most retail companies have their own training programmes for specific jobs. These possibilities make retail even more welcoming to new employees. Tourism is also a great field to consider in the vocational realm. This area includes planning trips to being a tour guide. Cruise lines are popular parts of this field and their employment opportunities are immense.

The Vocational Education Act of 1963 played a role in what this field has grown into. At that time, the government authorized an expansion and redirection of vocational education. The baby boomer generation was targeted to be supplied with multiple arenas for advancement. It was also the country's goal to retrain displaced workers, who had lost jobs because of technology advancements. Today vocational education programmes are rivaling those of four year universities. Students are enrolling at unheard of rates than in times past.

Parents find the offerings of these programmes and community colleges exactly what they were looking for. There are terrific fields to consider with these avenues. Many of these jobs will provide children with a great living. There are also possibilities to move into other specialized career opportunities. The overall expense of this sort of education will depend on the part of the country that you reside in. In most cases, the benefit well outweighs the expense.

Trait Theory

In psychology, trait theory is an approach to the study of human personality. Trait theorists are primarily interested in the measurement of *traits*, which can be defined as habitual patterns of behaviour, thought, and emotion. According to this perspective, traits are relatively stable over time, differ across individuals (e.g. some people are outgoing whereas others are shy), and influence behaviour.

Gordon Allport was an early pioneer in the study of traits, which he sometimes referred to as dispositions. In his approach, *central traits* are basic to an individual's personality, whereas *secondary traits* are more peripheral. *Common traits* are those recognized within a culture and may vary between cultures. *Cardinal traits* are those by which an individual may be strongly recognized. Since Allport's time, trait theorists have focused more on group statistics than on single individuals. Allport called these two emphases "nomothetic" and "idiographic," respectively. There is a nearly unlimited number of potential traits that could be used to describe personality. The statistical technique of factor analysis, however, has demonstrated that particular clusters of traits reliably correlate together. Hans Eysenck has suggested that personality is reducible to three major traits. Other researchers argue that more factors are needed to adequately describe human personality including humor, wealth and beauty. Many psychologists currently believe that five factors are sufficient.

Virtually all trait models, and even ancient Greek philosophy, include extraversion vs. introversion as a central dimension of human personality. Another prominent trait that is found in nearly all models is Neuroticism, or emotional instability.

The Two Taxonomies

Both approaches extensively use self-report questionnaires. The factors are intended to be orthogonal (uncorrelated), though there are often small positive correlations between factors. The five factor model in particular has been criticized for losing the orthogonal structure between factors. Hans Eysenck has argued that fewer factors are superior to a larger number of partly related ones. Although these two approaches are comparable because of the use of factor analysis to construct hierarchical taxonomies, they differ in the organization and number of factors.

Whatever the causes, however, psychoticism marks the two approaches apart, as the five factor model contains no such trait. Moreover, psychoticism, unlike any of the other factors in either approach, does not fit a normal distribution curve. Indeed, scores are rarely high, thus skewing a normal distribution. However, when they are high, there is considerable overlap with psychiatric conditions such as antisocial and schizoid personality disorders. Similarly, high scorers on neuroticism are more susceptible to sleep and psychosomatic disorders. Five factor approaches can also predict future mental disorders.

Lower-order Factors

Similarities between lower-order factors for psychoticism and the facets of openness, agreeableness, and conscientiousness (from Matthews, Deary & Whiteman, 2003)

There are two higher-order factors that both taxonomies clearly share: extraversion and neuroticism. Both approaches broadly accept that extraversion is associated with sociability and positive affect, whereas neuroticism is associated with emotional instability and negative affect.

Many lower-order factors, or facets, are similar between the two taxonomies. For instance, both approaches contain factors for sociability/gregariousness, for activity levels, and for assertiveness within the higher order factor extraversion. However, there are differences too. First, the three-factor approach contains nine lower-order factors and the five-factor approach has six. Eysenck's psychoticism factor incorporates some of the polar opposites of the lower order factors of openness, agreeableness and conscientiousness. A high scorer on tough-mindedness in psychoticism would score low on tender-mindedness in agreeableness. Most of the differences between the taxonomies stem from the three factor model's emphasis on fewer high-order factors.

Causality

Although both major trait models are descriptive, only the three-factor model offers a detailed causal explanation. Eysenck suggests that different personality traits are caused by the properties of the brain, which themselves are the result of genetic factors. In particular, the three-factor model identifies the reticular system and the limbic system in the brain as key components that mediate cortical arousal and emotional responses respectively. Eysenck advocates that extraverts have low levels of cortical arousal and introverts have high levels, leading extraverts to seek out more stimulation from socializing and being venturesome. Moreover, Eysenck surmised that there would be an optimal level of arousal, after which inhibition would occur and that this would be different for each person.

In a similar vein, the three-factor approach theorizes that neuroticism is mediated by levels of arousal in the limbic system and that individual differences arise because of variable activation thresholds between people. Therefore, highly neurotic people when presented with minor stressors, will exceed this threshold, whereas people low in neuroticism will not exceed normal activation levels, even when presented with large stressors. By contrast, proponents of the five-factor approach assume a role of genetics and environment but offer no explicit causal explanation. Given this emphasis on biology in the three-factor approach, it would be expected that the third trait, psychoticism, would have a similar explanation. However, the causal properties of this state are not well defined. Eysenck has suggested that psychoticism is related to testosterone levels and is an inverse function of the serotonergic system, but he later revised this, linking it instead to the dopaminergic system.

List of Personality Traits

Personality	*Traits*
Openness to experience	Composed of two related but separable traits, Openness to Experience and Intellect. Behavioural aspects include having wide interests, and being imaginative and insightful, correlated with activity in the dorsolateral prefrontal cortex. Considered primarily a cognitive trait.
Conscientiousness	Scrupulous, meticulous, principled behaviour guided or conforming to one's own conscience. Associated with the dorsolateral prefrontal cortex. Anorexics are noted to have higher levels of conscientiousness.
Extraversion	Gregarious, outgoing, sociable, projecting one's personality outward. The opposite of extraversion is introversion. Extraversion has shown to share certain genetic markers with substance abuse. Extraversion is associated with various regions of the prefrontal cortex and the amygdala.
Agreeableness	Refers to a compliant, trusting, empathic, sympathetic, friendly and cooperative nature.
Neuroticism	"Refers to an individual's tendency to become upset or emotional" (Hans Eysenck) "Neuroticism is the major factor of personality pathology" (Eysenck & Eysenck, 1969). Neuroticism has been linked to serotonin transporter (5-HTT) binding sites in the thalamus: as well as activity in the insular cortex.
Self-esteem (low)	A "favourable or unfavourable attitude toward the self" (Rosenberg, 1965). An individual's sense of his or her value or worth, or the extent to which a person values, approves of, appreciates, prizes, or likes him or herself" (Blascovich & Tomaka, 1991).
Harm avoidance	A tendency towards shyness, being fearful and uncertain, tendency to worry. Neonatal complications such as preterm birth have been shown to affect harm avoidance. People affected by eating disorders exhibit high levels of harm avoidance. The volume of the left amygdala in girls was correlated to levels of HA, in separate studies HA was correlated with reduced grey matter volume in the orbito-frontal, occipital and parietal regions.

Contd...

Personality	***Traits***
Novelty seeking	Impulsive, exploratory, fickle, excitable, quick-tempered, and extravagant. Associated with addictive behaviour.
Perfectionism	"I don't think needing to be perfect is in any way adaptive" (Paul Hewitt, PhD) Socially prescribed perfectionism – "believing that others will value you only if you are perfect."Self-oriented perfectionism – "an internally motivated desire to be perfect. Perfectionism is one of the traits associated with obsessional behaviour and like obsessionality is also believed to be regulated by the basal ganglia.
Alexithymia	The inability to express emotions. "To have no words for one's inner experience" (Renÿ J. Muller PhD).In studies done with stroke patients, alexithymia was found to be more prevalent in those who developed lesions in the right hemisphere following a cerebral infarction. There is a positive association with post-traumatic stress disorder (PTSD), childhood abuse and neglect and alexithymia. Utilizing psychometric testing and fMRI, studies showed positive response in the insula, posterior cingulate cortex (PCC), and thalamus.
Rigidity	Inflexibility, difficulty making transitions, adherence to set patterns. Mental rigidity arises out of a deficit of the executive functions. Originally termed frontal lobe syndrome it is also referred to as dysexecutive syndrome and usually occurs as a result of damage to the frontal lobe. This may be due to physical damage, disease (such as Huntington's disease) or a hypoxic or anoxic insult.
Impulsivity	Risk taking, lack of planning, and making up one's mind quickly (Eysenck and Eysenck). A component of disinhibition. Abnormal patterns of impulsivity have been linked to lesions in the right inferior frontal gyrus and in studies done by Antonio Damasio author of Descartes Error, damage to the ventromedial prefrontal cortex has been shown to cause a defect in real-life decision making in individuals with otherwise normal intellect. Those

Contd...

Personality	***Traits***
	who sustain this type of damage are oblivious to the future consequences of their actions and live in the here and now.
Disinhibition	Behavioural dis-inhibition is an inability or unwillingness to constrain impulses, it is a key component of executive functioning. Researchers have emphasized poor behavioural inhibition as the central impairment of ADHD. It may be symptomatic of orbitofrontal lobe syndrome, a subtype of frontal lobe syndrome which may be an acquired disorder as a result of traumatic brain injury, hypoxic ischemic encephalopathy (HIE), anoxic encephalopathy, degenerative diseases such as Parkinson's, bacterial or viral infections such as Lyme disease and neurosyphilis. Disinhibition has been consistently associated with substance abuse disorders, obesity, higher BMI, excessive eating, an increased rate of eating, and perceived hunger.
Psychoticism	Psychoticism is a personality pattern typified by aggressiveness and interpersonal hostility, one of four traits in Hans Eysenck's model of personality. High levels of this trait were believed by Eysenck to be linked to increased vulnerability to psychosis such as schizophrenia. He also believed that blood relatives of psychotics would show high levels of this trait, suggesting a genetic basis to the trait.
Obsessionality	Persistent, often unwelcome, and frequently disturbing ideas, thoughts, images or emotions, rumination, often inducing an anxious state. Obsessionality may result as a dysfunction of the basal ganglia.

Two-factor Theory

The two-factor theory (also known as Herzberg's motivation-hygiene theory and dual-factor theory) states that there are certain factors in the workplace that cause job satisfaction, while a separate set of factors cause dissatisfaction. It was developed by Frederick Herzberg, a psychologist, who theorized that job satisfaction and job dissatisfaction act independently of each other. Two-factor theory fundamentals: Attitudes and their connection with industrial mental health are related to Maslow's theory of motivation. His findings have had a considerable theoretical, as well as a practical, influence on attitudes toward administration. According to Herzberg, individuals are not content with the satisfaction of lower-order needs at work, for example, those associated with minimum salary levels or safe and pleasant working conditions. Rather, individuals look for the gratification of higher-level psychological needs having to do with achievement, recognition, responsibility, advancement, and the nature of the work itself. So far, this appears to parallel Maslow's theory of a need hierarchy. However, Herzberg added a new dimension to this theory by proposing a two-factor model of motivation, based on the notion that the presence of one set of job characteristics or incentives leads to worker *satisfaction* at work, while another and separate set of job characteristics leads to *dissatisfaction* at work. Thus, satisfaction and dissatisfaction are not on a continuum with one increasing as the other diminishes, but are independent phenomena. This theory suggests that to improve job attitudes and productivity, administrators must recognize and attend to both sets of characteristics and not assume that an increase in satisfaction leads to decrease in unpleasurable dissatisfaction.

The two-factor, or *motivation-hygiene theory*, developed from data collected by Herzberg from interviews with a large number of engineers and accountants in the Pittsburgh area. From analyzing these interviews, he found that job characteristics related to what an individual *does* — that is, to the nature of the work he performs — apparently have the capacity to gratify such needs as achievement, competency, status, personal worth, and self-realization, thus making him happy and satisfied. However, the *absence* of such gratifying job characteristics does not appear to lead to unhappiness and dissatisfaction. Instead, dissatisfaction results from unfavourable assessments of such job-related factors as company policies, supervision, technical problems, salary, interpersonal relations on the job, and working conditions. Thus, if management wishes to increase satisfaction on the job, it should be concerned with the nature of the work itself — the opportunities it presents for gaining status, assuming responsibility, and for achieving self-realization. If, on the other hand, management wishes to reduce dissatisfaction, then it must focus on the job environment — policies, procedures, supervision, and working conditions. If management is equally concerned with both, (as is usually the case), then managers must give attention to both sets of job factors.

The theory was based around interviews with 203 American accountants and engineers in Pittsburgh, chosen because of their professions' growing importance in the business world. The subjects were asked to relate times when they felt exceptionally good or bad about their present job or any previous job, and to provide reasons, and a description of the sequence of events giving rise to that positive or negative feeling.

Here is the Description of this Interview Analysis: Briefly, we asked our respondents to describe periods in their lives when they were exceedingly happy and unhappy with their jobs. Each respondent gave as many "sequences of events" as he could that met certain criteria—including a marked change in feeling, a beginning and an end, and contained some substantive description other than feelings and interpretations...

The proposed hypothesis appears verified. The factors on the right that led to satisfaction (achievement, intrinsic interest in the work, responsibility, and advancement) are mostly unipolar; that is, they contribute very little to job dissatisfaction. Conversely, the dis-satisfiers (company policy and administrative practices, supervision, interpersonal relationships, working conditions, and salary) contribute very little to job satisfaction.

Two-factor theory distinguishes between:

- Motivators (e.g. challenging work, recognition, responsibility) that give positive satisfaction, arising from intrinsic conditions of the job itself, such as recognition, achievement, or personal growth, *and*
- Hygiene factors (e.g. status, job security, salary, fringe benefits, work conditions) that do not give positive satisfaction, though dissatisfaction results from their absence. These are extrinsic to the work itself, and include aspects such as company policies, supervisory practices, or wages/salary.

Essentially, hygiene factors are needed to ensure an employee is not dissatisfied. Motivation factors are needed to motivate an employee to higher performance. Herzberg also further classified our actions and how and why we do them, for example, if you perform a work related action because you *have* to then that is classed as "movement", but if you perform a work related action because you *want* to then that is classed as "motivation". Unlike Maslow, who offered little data to support his ideas, Herzberg and others have presented considerable empirical evidence to confirm the motivation-hygiene theory, although their work has been criticized on methodological grounds.

Workarounds

Herzberg's theory concentrates on the importance of internal job factors as motivating forces for employees. He designed it to increase job enrichment for employees. Herzberg wanted to create the opportunity for employees to take part in planning, performing, and evaluating their work. He suggested to do this by:

- Removing some of the control management has over employees and increasing the accountability and responsibility they have over their work. Which would in return increase employee autonomy, authority and freedom.
- Creating complete and natural work units where is it possible. An example would be allowing employees to create a whole unit or section instead of only allowing them to create part of it.
- Providing regular and continuous feedback on productivity and job performance directly to employees instead of through supervisors
- Encouraging employees to take on new and challenging tasks and becoming experts at a task.

Validity and Criticisms

In 1968 Herzberg stated that his two-factor theory study had already been replicated 16 times in a wide variety of populations including some in Communist countries, and corroborated with studies using different procedures that agreed with his original findings regarding intrinsic employee motivation making it one of the most widely replicated studies on job attitudes.

While the Motivator-Hygiene concept is still well regarded, satisfaction and dissatisfaction are generally no longer considered to exist on separate scales. The separation of satisfaction and dissatisfaction has been shown to be an artifact of the Critical Incident Technique (CIT) used by Herzberg to record events. Furthermore, it has been noted the theory does not allow for individual differences, such as particular personality traits, which would affect individuals' unique responses to motivating or hygiene factors. A number of behavioural scientists have pointed to inadequacies in the need hierarchy and motivation-hygiene theories. The most basic is the criticism that both of these theories contain the relatively explicit assumption that happy and satisfied workers produce more, even though this might not be the case. For example, if playing a better game of golf is the means chosen to satisfy one's need for recognition, then one will find ways to play and think about golf more often, perhaps resulting in an accompanying lower output on the job. Another problem is that these and other statistical theories are concerned with explaining "average" behaviour, despite considerable differences between individuals that may impact one's motivational factors. For instance, in their pursuit of status a person might take a balanced view and strive to pursue several behavioural paths in an effort to achieve a combination of personal status objectives.

In other words, an individual's expectation or estimated probability that a given behaviour will bring a valued outcome determines their choice of means and the effort they will devote to these means. In effect, this diagram of expectancy depicts an employee asking themselves the question posed by one investigator, "*How much payoff is there for me toward attaining a personal goal while expending so much effort toward the achievement of an assigned organizational objective?*" The expectancy theory by Victor Vroom also provides a framework for motivation based on expectations.

This approach to the study and understanding of motivation would appear to have certain conceptual advantages over other theories: First, unlike Maslow's and Herzberg's theories, it is capable of handling individual differences. Second, its focus is toward the present and the future, in contrast to drive theory, which emphasizes past learning. Third, it specifically correlates behaviour to a goal and thus eliminates the problem of assumed relationships, such as between motivation and performance. Fourth, it relates motivation to ability: Performance = Motivation*Ability.

That said, a study by the Gallup Organization, as detailed in the book *First, Break All the Rules: What the World's Greatest Managers Do* by Marcus Buckingham and Curt Coffman, appears to provide strong support for Herzberg's division of satisfaction and dissatisfaction onto two separate scales. In this book, the authors discuss how the study identified twelve questions that provide a framework for determining high-performing individuals and organizations. These twelve questions align squarely with Herzberg's motivation factors, while hygiene factors were determined to have little effect on motivating high performance.

Developmental Stage Theories

Developmental stage theories are theories that divide child development into distinct stages which are characterized by qualitative differences in behaviour.

There are a number of different views about the way in which psychological and physical development proceed throughout the life span. In addition to individual differences in development, developmental psychologists generally agree that development occurs in an orderly way and in different areas simultaneously.

Continuous Versus Discontinuous Development

One of the major controversies in developmental psychology centres whether development is continuous or discontinuous. Those psychologists who support the continuous view of development suggest that development involves gradual and ongoing changes throughout the life span, with behaviour in the earlier stages of development providing the basis of skills and abilities required for the next stages.

Not all psychologists, however, agree that development is a continuous process. Some view development as a discontinuous process. They believe development involves distinct and separate stages with different kinds of behaviour occurring in each stage. This suggests that the development of certain abilities in each stage, such as specific emotions or ways of thinking, have a definite starting and ending point. However, there is no exact time at which an ability suddenly appears or disappears. Although some types of thinking, feeling or behaving may seem to appear suddenly, it is more than likely that this has been developing gradually for some time.

Stage theories of development rest on the assumption that development is a discontinuous process involving distinct *stages* which are characterized by qualitative differences in behaviour. They also assume that the structure of the stages is not variable according to each individual, however the time of each stage may vary individually. Stage theories can be contrasted with continuous theories, which posit that development is an incremental process.

Importance of Choosing a Career for Early Focus

How many times have we heard a graduating senior state he/she has no idea what the future holds for a career. Kids often go to college for the basic foundational classes in hopes of discovering their niche somewhere along the way. In the process, a lot of unnecessary electives are chosen, majors are changed, and it generally leads to a few years of uncertainty and tension. Instead, students need to learn early on the importance of choosing a career for early focus.

Planning

A child who has no vision for the future usually has difficulty in high school. While everyone has to take the same core classes, how does one decide what electives to take? It definitely helps to know where one hopes to be after college. It can never be too early to choose a particular area of interest and forge a path to a promising future. For example, a girl discovers at a young age an overwhelming love for music. From that day forward, all her electives centre around the classes best suited to help her reach the goal of becoming a professional musician, or work in some position related to music. She definitely has the focus to make the necessary strides toward achieving her desire to play instruments for a living.

Time

For the people who cannot decide what to be when they grow up, much of the educational experience can be a waste of time. For instance, a young man chooses a major course of study in college. Half way through the programme, he decides his vision of the future has changed. But, along with a change in the career course also comes additional classes required to gain a degree in the new area of interest. Sometimes, people actually graduate with a specific career in mind. Then, after less than a year on the job, they decide to go in a different direction. Ouch! What a waste of time and money!

Finances

Yes, not choosing a career for early focus can be costly. Every time a student's career expectations oscillate, it usually translates into unnecessary expenditures. All the books purchased for other classes are essentially useless. Dropping classes may get some of the tuition returned, but it is rarely the full amount. Then, there is the expense of taking extra credits to satisfy another career choice. A student may actually take extra years worth of credits simply because he/she cannot make a decision regarding a future career.

Focus

Finally, we have come full circle back to the importance of choosing a career for early focus. Studies have proven that students with a clear focus for the future are more intrinsically motivated to succeed.

The translation is simple. Kids with a plan are likely to push themselves to achieve the best education possible. Grades will be higher, courses will be well-chosen to compliment the plan, and students will be less apt to get involved in drugs or other questionable activities. The kids are running a race toward a positive career choice, and the finish line is in full view.

What Influences Your Career Choice?

When we think about career choice, several things immediately come to mind – job description, training and education required, career outlook, and salary – but there are a number of other factors that may influence your decisions. Let's explore some of these factors as addressed by multiple career development theories. Theories can help us frame why and how things happen. In this case, career development theories help us explain why and how we choose to pursue specific career fields. There are a lot of theories to consider in the relatively new field of career development. As you read through the factors below, you'll see that many of the related theories address some of the same issues. No one theory explains everything, so it's good to consider these factors from multiple perspectives.

Influence Factors

Skills and Abilities – Considering your skills and abilities and how they may fit a particular occupation comes out of one of the earliest career development fields, Trait-Factor theories, and is still used today. These theories recommend creating occupational profiles for specific jobs as well as identifying individual differences, matching individuals to occupations based on these differences. You can identify activities you enjoy and those in which you have a level of competency though a formal assessment. There are many available online, including the Skills Provider at CareerOneStop.

Interest and Personality Type – Holland's Career Typology is a widely used to connect personality types and career fields. This theory establishes a classification system that matches personality characteristics and personal preferences to job characteristics. The Holland Codes are six personality/career types that help describe a wide range of occupations. You can find out your Holland Codes, and receive a list of related occupations, by completing a questionnaire such as the one provided by the U. S. Department of Labour's O*Net Interest Profiler. Life Roles – Being a worker is just one of your life roles, in addition to others such as, student, parent, and child. Super's

Lifespan theory directly addresses the fact that we each play multiple roles in our lives and that these roles change over the course of our lives. How we think about ourselves in these roles, their requirements of them, and the external forces that affect them, may influence how we look at careers in general and how we make choices for ourselves.

Previous Experiences – Krumboltz's Social Learning and Planned Happenstance theories address factors related to our experiences with others and in previous work situations. Having positive experiences and role models working in specific careers may influence the set of careers we consider as options for ourselves. One aspect of Social Cognitive Career Theory addresses the fact that we are likely to consider continuing a particular task if we have had a positive experience doing it. In this way, we focus on areas in which we have had proven success and achieved positive self-esteem.

Culture – Racial and ethnic background, as well as the culture of an individual's regional area, local community, and extended family, may impact career decisions. Our culture often shapes our values and expectations as they relate to many parts of our lives, including jobs and careers. Multicultural career counselling has emerged as a specialized field to take these influences into consideration when counselling clients and students. We can't attribute the predominant characteristics of a culture to any one of it's individuals, but having an awareness of the values and expectations of our culture may help us understand how we make our career choices.

Gender -– Both men and women have experienced career-related stereotypes. Gender is a factor included in multiple career development theories and approaches including, Social Learning and multicultural career counselling. How we view ourselves as individuals may influence both the opportunities and barriers we perceive as we make career decisions. Studies of gender and career development are ongoing as roles of men and women in the workforce, and in higher education, evolve.

Social and Economic Conditions – All of our career choices take place within the context of society and the economy. Several career theories, such as Social Cognitive Career Theory and Social Learning, address this context in addition to other factors. Events that take place in our lives may affect the choices available to us and even dictate our choices to a certain degree. Changes in the economy and resulting job market may also affect how our careers develop.

Childhood Fantasies – What do you want to be when you grow-up? You may remember this question from your childhood, and it may have helped shape how you thought about careers then, as well as later in life. Career counselling theories are expanding as programmes related to career choice are developed for all ages, including the very young. Ginzberg proposed a theory that describes three life stages related to career development. The first stage, fantasy, where early ideas about careers are formed, takes place up to age 11.

Work with Your Career Counsellor!

It's important to understand that career choice is not made based on any one factor. Our choices are subject to many influences – individual, cultural, social, and environmental. The combination and interaction of various influences on your decision-making are unique to you and your situation. There may also be multiple options, several "good-fits" for you, instead of a single, right choice. Keep in mind that as you change, learning and experiencing new things, and external factors change, such as the economy, you will continue to revise and fine-tune your career choices.

There is a lot to consider, but you don't have to figure it all out on your own. Work with a career services counsellor at your institution's career centre or your State Workforce agency. These professionals will be able to assist you with assessments and additional resources, and discuss how different theories may be applied to your career development process.

Job Analysis

Job analysis is the important process of identifying the content of a job in terms of activities involved and attributes needed to perform the work and identifies major job requirements. Job analysis was conceptualized by two of the founders of industrial/organizational psychology, Frederick Taylor and Lillian Moller Gilbreth in the early 20th century. Job analyses provide information to organizations which helps to determine which employees are best fit for specific jobs. Through job analysis, the analyst needs to understand what the important tasks of the job are, how they are carried out, and the necessary human qualities needed to complete the job successfully. Essentially, job analyses provide information to organizations which helps to determine which employees are best fit for specific jobs. The process of job analysis involves the analyst describing the duties of the incumbent, then the nature and conditions of work, and finally some basic qualifications. After this, the job analyst has completed a form called a job psychograph, which displays the mental requirements of the job. The measure of a sound job analysis is a valid task list. This list contains the functional or duty areas of a position, the related tasks, and the basic training recommendations. Subject matter experts (incumbents) and supervisors for the position being analyzed need to validate this final list in order to validate the job analysis. Job analysis is crucial for first, helping individuals develop their careers, and also for helping organizations develop their employees in order to maximize talent. The outcomes of job analysis are key influences in designing learning, developing performance interventions, and improving processes. The application of job analysis techniques makes the implicit assumption that information about a job as it presently exists may be used to develop programmes to recruit, select, train, and appraise people for the job as it will exist in the future.

Job analysts are typically industrial/organizational psychologists or human resource officers who have been trained by, and are acting under the supervision of an industrial/organizational psychologist. One of the first industrial-organizational psychologists to introduce job analysis was Morris Viteles. In 1922, he used job analysis in order to select employees for a trolley car company. Viteles' techniques could then be applied to any other area of employment using the same process. Job analysis was also conceptualized by two of the founders of Industrial-Organizational psychology, Frederick Taylor and Lillian Moller Gilbreth in the early 20th century. Since then, experts have presented many different systems to accomplish job analysis that have become increasingly detailed over the decades. However, evidence shows that the root purpose of job analysis, understanding the behavioural requirements of work, has not changed in over 85 years.

Purpose

One of the main purposes of conducting job analysis is to prepare job descriptions and job specifications which in turn helps hire the right quality of workforce into an organization. The general purpose of job analysis is to document the requirements of a job and the work performed. Job and task analysis is performed as a basis for later improvements, including: definition of a job domain; description of a job; development of performance appraisals, personnel selection, selection systems, promotion criteria, training needs assessment, legal defence of selection processes, and compensation plans. The human performance improvement industry uses job analysis to make sure training and development activities are focused and effective. In the fields of human resources (HR) and industrial psychology, job analysis is often used to gather information for use in personnel selection, training, classification, and/or compensation.

Industrial Psychologists use job analysis to determine the physical requirements of a job to determine whether an individual who has suffered some diminished capacity is capable of performing the job with, or without, some accommodation. Edwin Flieshman, Ph.D. is credited with determining the underlying factors of human physical fitness. Professionals developing certificationexams use job analysis (often called something slightly different, such as "task analysis" or "work analysis") to determine the elements of the domain which must be sampled in order to create a content valid exam. When a job analysis is conducted for the purpose of valuing the job (i.e., determining the appropriate compensation for incumbents) this is called "job evaluation."

Job analysis aims to answer questions such as:

- Why does the job exist?
- What physical and mental activities does the worker undertake?
- When is the job to be performed?
- Where is the job to be performed?
- How does the worker do the job?
- What qualifications are needed to perform the job?

Procedures

As stated before, the purpose of job analysis is to combine the task demands of a job with our knowledge of human attributes and produce a theory of behaviour for the job in question. There are two ways to approach building that theory, meaning there are two different approaches to job analysis.

Task-oriented

Task-oriented procedures focus on the actual activities involved in performing work. This procedure takes into consideration work duties, responsibilities, and functions. The job analyst then develops task statements which clearly state the tasks that are performed with great detail. After creating task statements, job analysts rate the tasks on scales indicating importance, difficulty, frequency, and consequences of error. Based on these ratings, a greater sense of understanding of a job can be attained.Task analysis, such as cognitively oriented task analysis (COTA), are techniques used to describe job expertise. For example, the job analysts may tour the job site and observe workers performing their jobs. During the tour the analyst may collect materials that directly or indirectly indicate required skills (duty statements, instructions, safety manuals, quality charts, etc.).

Functional job analysis (FJA) is a classic example of a task-oriented technique. Developed by Fine and Cronshaw in 1944, work elements are scored in terms of relatedness to data (0–6), people (0–8), and things (0–6), with lower scores representing greater complexity. Incumbents, considered subject matter experts (SMEs), are relied upon, usually in a panel, to report elements of their work to the job analyst. Using incumbent reports, the analyst uses Fine's terminology to compile statements reflecting the work being performed in terms of data, people, and things. The Dictionary of Occupational Titles uses elements of the FJA in defining jobs.

Worker-oriented

Worker-oriented procedures aim to examine the human attributes needed to perform the job successfully. These human attributes have been commonly classified into four categories: *knowledge, skills, abilities*, and *other characteristics* (KSAO). *Knowledge* is the information people need in order to perform the job. *Skills* are the proficiencies needed to perform each task. *Abilities* are the attributes that are relatively stable over time. *Other characteristics* are all other attributes, usually personality factors. The KSAOs required for a job are inferred from the most frequently-occurring, important tasks. In a worker-oriented job analysis, the skills are inferred from tasks and the skills are rated directly in terms of importance of frequency. This often results in data that immediately imply the important KSAOs. However, it can be hard for SMEs to rate skills directly.

The Fleishman Job Analysis System (F-JAS) developed by Edwin A. Fleishman represents a worker-oriented approach. Fleishman factor-analyzed large data sets to discover a common, minimum set of KSAOs across different jobs. His system of 73 specific scales measure three broad areas: Cognitive (Verbal Abilities; Idea Generation & Reasoning Abilities; Quantitative Abilities; Memory; Perceptual Abilities; Spatial Abilities; and Attentiveness), Psychomotor (Fine Manipulative Abilities; Control Movement Abilities; and Reaction

Time and Speed Abilities), and Physical (Physical Strength Abilities; Endurance; Flexibility, Balance, and Coordination; Visual Abilities; and Auditory and Speech Abilities). JobScan is a measurement instrument which defines the personality dynamics within a specific type of job. By collecting PDP ProScan Survey results of actual performers and results of job dynamics analysis surveys completed by knowledgeable people related to a specific job, JobScan provides a suggested ideal job model for that position. Although it does not evaluate the intellect or experience necessary to accomplish a task, it does deal with the personality of the type of work itself.

Example

For the job of a snow-cat operator at a ski slope, a work or task-oriented job analysis might include this statement: Operates Bombardier Sno-cat, usually at night, to smooth out snow rutted by skiers and snowboard riders and new snow that has fallen. On the other hand, a worker-oriented job analysis might include this statement: Evaluates terrain, snow depth, and snow condition and chooses the correct setting for the depth of the snow cat, as well as the number of passes necessary on a given ski slope.

Job analysis methods have evolved using both task-oriented and worker-oriented approaches. Since the end result of both approaches is a statement of KSAOs, neither can be considered the "correct" way to conduct job analysis. Because worker-oriented job analyses tend to provide more generalized human behaviour and behaviour patterns and are less tied to the technological parts of a job, they produce data more useful for developing training programmes and giving feed back to employees in the form of performance appraisal information. Also, the volatility that exists in the typical workplace of today can make specific task statements less valuable in isolation. For these reasons, employers are significantly more likely to use worker-oriented approaches to job analysis today than they were in the past.

KSAOs

Regardless of which approach to job analysis is taken, the next step in the process is to identify the attributes—the KSAOs that an incumbent needs for either performing the tasks at hand or executing the human behaviours described in the job analysis.

- Knowledge: "A collection of discrete but related facts and information about a particular domain...acquired through formal education or training, or accumulated through specific experiences."

- Skill: "A practiced act"
- Ability: "The stable capacity to engage in a specific behaviour"
- Other characteristics: "Personality variables, interests, training, and experiences"

Methods

Finally, once the appropriate KSAOs are identified, tests and other assessment techniques can be chosen to measure those KSAOs. Over the years, experts have presented several different systems and methods to accomplish job analysis. Many forms of systems are no longer in use, but those systems that still exist have become increasingly detailed over the decades with a greater concentration on tasks and less concentration on human attributes. That trend, however, has reversed in recent years for the better. Newer methods and systems have brought industrial-organizational psychology back to an examination of the *behavioural* aspects of work.

There are Several Ways to Conduct a job Analysis, Including: interviews with incumbents and supervisors, work sampling, the repertory grid technique, questionnaires (structured, open-ended, or both), observation, critical incident investigations, hierarchical task analysis, and gathering background information such as duty statements or classification specifications. In job analyses conducted by HR professionals, it is common to use more than one of these methods. Traditional job analysis methods of analysis can be labourious and time consuming, and there is always a tendency on the part of management to over analyze some jobs and under analyze some others. These traditional job analysis methods include: one-on-one interviewing; behavioural event interviews; phone interviews; surveys; work assessments; Developing a Curriculum (DACUM); job analysis worksheets; observations and procedural review. Job analysis at the speed of reality. Amherst, Mass.: HRD Press. All of these methods can be used to gather information for job analysis. The DACUM process developed in the late 1960s has been viewed as the fastest method used, but it can still can take two or three days to obtain a validated task list.

1. Observation: This was the first method of job analysis used by industrial-organizational psychologists. The process involves simply watching incumbents perform their jobs and taking notes. Sometimes they ask questions while watching, and commonly they even perform job tasks themselves. Near the

end of World War II, Morris Viteles studied the job of navigator on a submarine. He attempted to steer the submarine toward Bermuda. After multiple misses by over 100 miles in one direction or another, one officer suggested that Viteles raise the periscope, look for clouds, and steer toward them since clouds tend to form above or near land masses. The vessel reached Bermuda shortly after that suggestion. The more jobs one seriously observes, the better one's understanding becomes of both the jobs in question and work in general.

2. Interviews: It is essential to supplement observation by talking with incumbents. These interviews are most effective when structured with a specific set of questions based on observations, other analyses of the types of jobs in question, or prior discussions with human resources representatives, trainers, or managers knowledgeable about jobs.
3. Critical incidents and work diaries: The critical incident technique asks subject matter experts to identify critical aspects of behaviour or performance in a particular job that led to success or failure. For example, the supervisor of an electric utility repairman might report that in a very time-pressing project, the repairman failed to check a blueprint and as a result cut a line, causing a massive power loss. In fact, this is what happened in Los Angeles in September 2005 when half the city lost power over a period of 12 hours. The second method, a work diary, asks workers and/or supervisors to keep a log of activities over a prescribed period of time. They may be asked to simply write down what they were doing at 15 minutes after the hour for each hour of the work day. Or, they may list everything they have done up to a break.
4. Questionnaires and surveys: Expert incumbents or supervisors often respond to questionnaires or surveys as a part of job analysis. These questionnaires include task statements in the form of worker behaviours. Subject matter experts are asked to rate each statement form their experience on a number of different dimensions like importance to overall job success, frequency performance and whether the task must be performed on the first day of work or can be learned gradually on the job. Questionnaires also ask incumbents to rate the importance of KSAOs for performing tasks, and may ask the subject matter experts to rate work context. Unlike the results of observations

and interviews, the questionnaire responses can be statistically analyzed to provide a more objective record of the components of the job. To a greater and greater extent, these questionnaires and surveys are being administered online to incumbents.

5. The Position Analysis Questionnaire (PAQ) is a well-known job analysis instrument. Although it is labelled a questionnaire, the PAQ is actually designed to be completed by a trained job analyst who interviews the SMEs (e.g., job incumbents and their supervisors). The PAQ was designed to measure job component validity of attributes presented in aptitude tests. Job component validity is the relationship between test scores and skills required for good job performance. There are 195 behaviour-related statements in the PAQ divided into six major sections: information input, mental process, work output, relationships with others, job context, and other job characteristics.
6. Checklists are also used as a job analysis method, specifically with areas like the Air Force. In the checklist method, the incumbent checks the tasks he or she performs from a list of task statements that describe the job. The checklist is preceded by some sort of job analysis and is usually followed by the development of work activity compilations or job descriptions. The scope of task statements listed depends upon the judgement of the checklist constructor.

Six Steps of Job Analysis

1. Decide how to use the information since this will determine the data to collect and how to collect it. Some data collection techniques such as interviewing the employee and asking what the job entails are good for writing job descriptions and selecting employees for the job. Other techniques like the position analysis questionnaire do not provide qualitative information for job descriptions. Rather, they provide numerical ratings for each job and can be used to compare jobs for compensation purposes.
2. Review appropriate background information like organization charts, process charts, and job descriptions. Organization charts show the organization-wide work division, how the job in question relates to other jobs, and where the job fits in the overall organization. The chart should show the title of each position and, through connecting lines, show reports

to whom and with whome the job incumbent communicates. A process chart provides a more detailed picture of the work flow. In its simplest, most organic form, a process chart shows the flow of inputs to and outputs from the job being analyzed. Finally, the existing job description (if there is one) usually provides a starting point for building the revised job description.

3. Select representative positions. This is because there may be too many similar jobs to analyze. For example, it is usually unnecessary to analyze jobs of 200 assembly workers when a sample of 10 jobs will be sufficient.
4. Actually analyze the job by collecting data on job activities, necessary employee behaviours and actions, working conditions, and human traits and abilities required to perform the job. For this step, one or more than one methods of job analysis may be needed
5. Verify the job analysis information with the worker performing the job and with his or her immediate supervisor. This will help confirm that the information is factually correct and complete. This review can also help gain the employee's acceptance of the job analysis data and conclusions by giving that person a chance to review and modify descriptions of the job activities.
6. Develop a job description and job specification. These are two tangible products of the job analysis process. The job description is a written statement that describes the activities and responsibilities of the job as well as its important features such as working conditions and safety hazards. The job specification summarizes the personal qualities, traits, skills, and background required for completing a certain job. These two may be completely separate or in the same document.

Uses of Job Analysis Information

1. Recruitment and Selection: Job analysis provides information about what the job entails and what human characteristics are required in order to perform these activities. This information, in the form of job descriptions and specifications, helps management officials decide what sort of people they need to recruit and hire and select.
2. Compensation: Job analysis information is crucial for estimating the value of each job and its appropriate compensation.

Compensation (salary and bonus) usually depends on the job's required skill and education level, safety hazards, degree of responsibility, etc. — all factors which can be assessed through job analysis. Also, many employers group jobs into classes. Job analysis provides the information to determine the relative worth of each job and its appropriate class.

3. Performance Appraisal: A performance appraisal compares each employee's actual performance with his or her performance standards. Managers use job analysis to determine the job's specific activities and performance standards.
4. Training: The job description should show the activities and skills, and therefore training, that the job requires
5. Discovering Unassigned Duties: Job Analysis can also help reveal unassigned duties. For example, a company's production manager says an employee is responsible for ten duties, such as production scheduling and raw material purchasing. Missing, however, is any reference to managing raw material inventories. On further study, it is revealed that none of the other manufacturing employees are responsible for inventory management, either. From review of other jobs like these, it is clear that someone should be managing raw material inventories. Therefore, an essential unassigned duty has been revealed.
6. EEO Compliance: Job analysis plays a large role in EEO compliance. United States Federal Agencies' Uniform Guidelines on Employee Selection stipulate that job analysis is a necessary step in validating all major personnel activities. For example, employers must be able to show that their selection criteria and job performance are actually related. Doing this requires knowing what the job entails, which in turn requires job analysis.

JASR

The Job Analysis at the Speed of Reality (JASR) method for job analysis is a reliable, proven method to quickly create validated task lists. The end product, which can be used for many purposes, is the basis for many potential training opportunities. This method is a tested process that helps analysts complete a job analysis of a typical job with a group of subject matter experts and managers in two to three hours then deliver a validated task list.

1. Job incumbents should know their jobs better than anyone else. They can provide accurate, timely content information about the job.
2. JASR participants want to spend a minimum amount of time providing job data during a session and business leadership wants to minimize disruption to business operations.
3. Since JASR participants do not spend as much time thinking about training as training professionals do, they do not require much orientation to the process.
4. JASR uses the quickest methods and best possible technology to complete the job analysis.

Systems

For many years, the U.S. Department of labour published the Dictionary of Occupational Titles, which was a comprehensive description of over 20,000 jobs. However, the Department replaced the DOT with O NET online database, which includes all occupations from the DOT plus an additional 3,500. This makes O NET very useful for job analysis.

The O*Net (an online resource which has replaced the Dictionary of Occupational Titles (DOT)) lists job requirements for a variety of jobs and is often considered basic, generic, or initial job analysis data. Everyone can use this database at no cost and is continually updated by observing workers from each occupation. O*net also has a Career Exploration Tool which is an assessment to help workers and students who are searching for new careers.

Data available from O*Net includes physical requirements, educational level, and some mental requirements. Task-based statements describing the work performed are derived from the functional job analysis technique. O*Net also provides links to salary data at the US national, state and city level for each job.

O*NET was designed with several features in mind, including:

- The inclusion of multiple descriptors and content domains to capture the range of ways that work can be described
- The development of cross-job descriptors in order to enable comparisons between various jobs
- The use of a taxonomic approach to occupational classification to enable full coverage within a content domain

Using these principles, a content model was developed that identified 6 content domains and specific categories within each domain. These six domains and categories within them include:

1. Worker characteristics: enduring individual attributes that influence the capacities workers can develop
   - Abilities, occupational values and interests, and work styles
2. Worker requirements: general attributes developed through education and experience, thus are more amenable to change than worker characteristics
   - Knowledge skills and education
3. Occupational requirements: descriptors of the work itself rather than the worker
   - Generalized work activities, work context, and organizational context
4. Experience requirements: types and quantities of experience required for specific occupations
   - Worker experience in other jobs, related training, on-the-job training, and certification requirements
5. Individual occupation characteristics: reflects labour demand, supply, and other labour market information
6. Occupation-specific requirements: information unique to a particular job
   - Occupation-specific skills and knowledge, tasks and duties, and equipment used

Job Analysis in Modern United States

Over the past years, the concept of job analysis has been changing dramatically. One observer put it: "The modern world is on the verge of another huge leap in creativity and productivity, but the job is not going to be part of tomorrow's economic reality. There still is and will always be an enormous amount of work to do, but it is not going to be contained in the familiar envelopes we call jobs. In fact, many organizations are today well along the path toward being "de-jobbed."."

Jobs and job descriptions, until recently, tended to follow their prescriptions and to be fairly detailed and specific. By the mid-1900s writers were reacting to what they viewed as "dehumanizing" aspects of pigeonholing workings into highly repetitive and specialized jobs; many proposed solutions like job enlargement, job rotation, and job enrichment. Job enlargement means assigning workers additional same-level tasks, thus increasing the number of activities they perform. Job rotation means systematically moving workers from one job to another. Psychologist Frederick Herzberg argued that the best way to motivate workers is to build opportunities for challenge and achievement into their jobs through job enrichment. Job enrichment means re-designing jobs in a way that increases the opportunities for the worker to experience feelings of responsibility, achievement, growth and recognition.

Whether enriched, specialized or enlarged, workers still generally have specific jobs to do, and these jobs have required job descriptions. In many firms today, however, jobs are becoming more amorphous and difficult to define. In other words, the trend is toward dejobbing.

Dejobbing, broadening the responsibilities of the company's jobs, and encouraging employees to not limit themselves to what's on their job descriptions, is a result of the changes taking place in business today. Organizations need to grapple with trends like rapid product and technological changes, and a shift to a service economy. This has increased the need for firms to be responsive, flexible, and generally more competitive. In turn,the organizational methods managers use to accomplish this have helped weaken the meaning of JOB as a well-defined ad clearly delineated set of responsibilities. Here are some methods that have contributed to this weakening of JOB's meaning:

- Flatter organizations: Instead of traditional pyramid-shaped organizations with seven or more management layers, flat organizations with only three or four levels are becoming more prevalent
- Work teams: Managers increasingly organize tasks around teams and processes rather than around specialized functions. In an organization like this, employees' jobs change daily and there is an intentional effort to avoid having employees view their jobs as a specific set of responsibilities.
- The Boundaryless Organization: In a boundaryless organization, the widespread use of teams and similar structural mechanisms reduces and makes more permeable the boundaries that typically separate departments and hierarchical levels. These organizations foster responsiveness by encouraging employees to rid themselves of the 'its not my job' attitudes that typically create walls between one employee's area and another's. Instead,

the focus is on defining the project or task at hand in terms of the overall best interests of the organization, therefore further reducing the idea of a job as a clearly defined set of duties.

Most firms today continue to use job analysis and rely on jobs as traditionally defined. More firms are moving toward new organizational configurations built around jobs that are broad and could change daily. Also, modern job analysis and job design techniques could help companies implement high-performance strategies.

Employment Scenario in India

Employment generation is one of the major priorities drawing the attention of the governments and economic planners all over the world. India is no exception. The approach to tackling unemployment problem have varied from time to time. In the initial years of planning no attempt was made to define an independent employment strategy. The focus on economic growth was viewed as essential for improving the employment situation. Thus, in the Five Year Plans, the generation of employment was viewed as part of the process of development.

It was, however, observed that the rate of growth of employment was generally much lower than the GDP rate of growth of the economy. Seasons of severe drought and failure of monsoons exposed large sections of population to extensive deprivations and compounded the situation. Successive plan strategies, policies and programmes were, therefore, re-designed to bring about a special focus on employment generation as a specific objective. The seventies and eighties saw the emergence of special schemes like NREP, RLEGP to provide wage employment through public works programmes and schemes to promote self-employment and entrepreneurship to the unemployed and the poor. Employment levels expanded steadily during the seventies and eighties but the rate of growth of employment continued to lag behind that of the labour force. Unemployment among the educated showed a rising trend. In 1998-99, various poverty alleviation and employment generation programmes were re-grouped under two broad categories of self-employment schemes and wage employment schemes. Funding and organizational patterns were also rationalized for better results.

Workforce

India's labour force is growing at a rate of 2.5 percent annually, but employment is growing at only 2.3 per cent. Thus, the country is faced with the challenge of not only absorbing new entrants to the job market (estimated at seven million people every year), but also clearing the backlog. More than 90 per cent of the 37 crore strong labour force is employed in the "unorganised sector" and are largely bereft of social security and other benefits of employment available in the "organised sector".Sixty per cent of India's workforce is self-employed, many of them remain very poor. Nearly 30 per cent are casual workers who are only seasonally employed. In the rural areas, agricultural workers form the bulk of the unorganised sector.

Unorganised sector is also made up of jobs in which the Minimum Wage Act is either not, or only marginally, implemented. The absence of unions in the unorganized sector does not provide any opportunity for collective bargaining. The bane of India's labour force is that over 70 per cent of workers are either illiterate or educated below the primary level. With the opening of Indian economy and linking it to global economies, the rate of growth of employment declined sharply in 1990s as compared to 1980s. The decline in employment growth has been seen in conjunction with the decline in the labour force growth rate. There is also a wide variation in unemployment rates across the states. Measured on Current Daily Status basis, unemployment ranges from a low of around 3 percent in Himachal Pradesh and Rajasthan to a high of 21 percent in Kerala.

While there may be divergence of opinion on the extent of under employment and unemployment, there is convergence of views on the need to expand employment. In order to achieve this goal, the economists have emphasized that any programme for this purpose must focus on growth, labour productivity and relative price of labour and capital. They have further suggested that micro economic policy framework must be such as to facilitate accelerated growth rate of 9 percent on a sustained basis. According to the noted economist Dr. C. Rangarajan a sustained growth of 9 percent per annum will totally eliminate unemployment by 2012. Sector specific policies are required which would acclerate the growth of labour intensive sectors. These include among others agriculture, food processing and small-scale units in various sectors.

Nrega

One of the most significant interventions by the government to generate employment has been the launch of the National Rural Employment Guarantee Act (NREGA) in February 2006 in two hundred most backward districts of the country. Consequently, the scheme was extended to another 130 districts and from April 2008 it would be operative in all districts. For the current financial year, a budget provision of Rs.12, 000 crores was made for implementation of the Act. NREGA being demand driven, so far, nearly 2.12 crore house holds have been provided with employment. Under NREGA, 6.399.55 lakh person days works have been taken up for creating village assets that would in turn enrich rural and women has considerably gone up in this wage employment programme economy. The participation of weaker sections of the society, such as SC/STs

Skill Development

Skill development of labour force is fundamental both to employment generation and improving productivity of labour. India has one of the largest labour forces in the world but the least number of skilled workers constituting only 5 percent compared to South Korea's 95 percent. Almost 44 percent of labour force in 1999-2000 was illiterate and 33 percent had schooling up to secondary education level only. The other bane of our work force is that while their educational attainment is very low on the one hand, 61% of those educated up to secondary level and beyond, on the other hand, are without any professional skills. This is because our general education system is not oriented towards attaining vocational skills. The mid term appraisal of the 10th Plan points out, "our education system is not generating sufficient supply of trained people especially those trained in skills that are in demand." This has created a miss-match between the supply and demand of skills. Increasing pace of globalization and technological change provides both challenges and growing opportunities for economic expansion and job creation. "In a rapidly changing environment, new ways and means of ensuring that people who work, possess the necessary knowledge, skills and attitude are criteria for seizing the opportunities inherent in globalisation and technical progress while reducing their unwanted consequences", reports International Labour Organisation.

The Prime Minister Dr. Manmohan Singh addressing theIndian Labour Conference in early 2007 said that the country would have to meet the challenge of increasing the skilled work force from the present 5% to about 50%, which is the norm in developed countries. He said, "To make our working people employable, we must create adequate infrastructure for skill training and certification and for imparting training. Industrial Training Institutes must keep pace with the technological demands of modern industry and the expanding universe of technical knowledge".

Responding to meet the challenge of the present and future needs of skill development,the Ministry of Labour and Employment has initiated a massive skill development programme. It has embarked on an initiative to impart skills to country's half of the labour force within next five years. Under this initiative vocational training will be provided to one million persons in 5 years and subsequently to one million people each year in close collaboration with State Governments, Industries, Trade Associations and other training providers. A provision of Rs. 555 crore has been made so far for this purpose.

Modernisation of it is

The Ministry has also embarked on upgrading Industrial Training Institutes (ITIs) for meeting the emerging market needs. During the 10th Plan 500 ITIs have been taken up for upgradation through public-private partnership. In addition 1396 ITIs are being upgraded during the 11th Plan beginning with 300 ITIs each year from the current financial year. The upgraded ITIs to be known as 'Centres of Excellence' will produce workers with world-class skills to enable them to compete in the global labour markets. The important aspects of the modernizations are multi entry and multi exit options to workers to upgrade their skills through multi skilled courses and the public-private partnership, which is being ensured through greater involvement of industry in all aspects of training. One significant factor in the employment situation in the country is that the bulk of employment is in the unorganised sector. There has to be an endeavour to shift as much of labour force as possible from the unorganised to the organised sector. This would give workers a better deal in terms of wages. This is possible only if the rigidities in the labour market are relaxed and wage determination begins to reflect the resource endowment in the country. This would encourage establishments to adopt labour intensive technologies.

There has been a welcome and widespread social acceptance of the imperative need of the Indian economy to achieve higher growth rate of GDP in a sustained manner. The country recently achieved 9 percent GDP growth, which it not only plans to sustain but take it to a double-digit growth during the 11th plan. It may not be difficult to meet the formidable challenge of providing job opportunities to eight million people every year. For this the growth rate of economy has to be accelerated, special emphasis to be given to labour intensive sectors, improving labour skills and functioning of the labour market.

7

Employment Skills Training

Employment skills training is essential for anyone who wants a well paid job. It's a fact that any job where no skills training is required won't pay very much. There are plenty of unskilled people to fill that gap, but not so many to fill the gaps where employability expertise gained through a training course are required. Gaining skills for employment should be seen as an investment in your future, and not so much a means to an end.

Think of the long term and how a skills and employment strategy can give you, and those who depend on you, a better life. The first step is to take action. No amount of wishing will ever get you there, but wishing and taking action towards your goal, will. You won't be handed the career of your dreams on a silver platter, but seeing the challenge, facing it with ambition and determination will mean that the qualification you need to show a prospective employer that you have the employment skills they need, is well within your grasp.

Following an employment strategy is always a good idea to get you from where you are to where you want to be. It's a plan, if you like, a kind of blueprint you can follow and work through. Always be realistic in your ambitions. If you left school at 15 with no qualifications of any kind, then aiming to be a rocket scientist is probably not being very realistic.

However, identifying training courses that you feel you could get through, which in turn would place you in a position where you could then apply for a certain type of job requiring the competence level you have gained, is being realistic. The training gives you employability competence, which leaves you with just the actual job interview to pass. There are ways to present yourself at an interview that will enhance your chances of getting a job, and having those kinds of employment skills could be something you may wish to consider too.

There are many courses available for gaining certificates that will place you in a position whereby you can apply for jobs that require certain skill levels. National vocational qualifications, skills for life, key skills, technical certificates and apprenticeships are just a few examples. With these and with higher education there are many, many possibilities if you are determined enough to grasp the opportunities offered, progress and gain the right employment skills. Before you know it you will have changed your life for the better.

Self-employment

Self-employment is the act of generating one's income directly from a consumer as opposed to being an employee of a business (or person). Generally tax authorities will view a person as self-employed if the person (1) chooses to be recognized as such, or (2) is generating income such that the person is required to file a tax return under legislation that subsists in the relevant jurisdiction(s). In the real world the critical issue for the taxing authorities is not that the person is trading but is whether the person is profitable and hence potentially taxable. In other words the activity of trading is likely to be ignored if no profit is present. So, occasional and hobby- or enthusiast-based economic activity is generally ignored by authorities.

Self-employed people generally find their own work rather than being provided with work by an employer, earning income from a trade or business that they operate. In some countries governments (the US and UK, for example) are placing more emphasis on clarifying whether an individual is self-employed or engaged in disguised employment, often described as the pretense of a contractual intra-business relationship to hide what is otherwise a simple employer-employee relationship.

Self-employment in the United States

Although the common perception is that self-employment is concentrated in a few service sector industries, like real estate sales people and insurance agents, research by the Small Business Administration has shown that self-employment occurs across a wide segment of the US economy. Furthermore, industries that are not commonly associated as a natural fit for self-employment, such as manufacturing, have in fact been shown to have a large proportion of self-employed individuals and home based businesses. In the United States, any person is considered self-employed for tax purposes if that person is running a business as a sole proprietorship, independent contractor, as a member of a partnership, or as a member of a limited liability company that does not elect to be treated as a corporation. In addition to income taxes, these individuals must pay Social Security and Medicare taxes in the form of a SECA (Self-Employment Contributions Act) tax.

U.S. Taxation

The self-employment tax in the United States is typically set at 15.30% which is roughly the equivalent of the combined contributions of the employee and employer under the FICA tax. The rate consists of two parts: 12.4% for social security and 2.9% for Medicare. The social security portion of the self-employment tax only applies to the first $110,100 of income for the 2012 tax year. There is no limit to the amount that is taxable under the 2.9% Medicare portion of the self-employment tax. Generally, only 92.35% of the self-employment income is taxable at the above rates. Additionally, half of the self-employment tax, i.e., the employer-equivalent portion, is allowed as a deduction against income. The 2010 Tax Relief Act reduced the self-employment tax by 2% for self-employment income earned in calendar year 2011, for a total of 13.3%. This rate will continue for income earned in calendar year 2012, due to the Temporary Payroll Tax Cut Continuation Act of 2011.

Self-employed persons sometimes declare more deductions than an ordinary employee. Travel, uniforms, computer equipment, cell phones, etc., can be deducted as legitimate business expenses.

Self-employed persons report their business income or loss on Schedule C of IRS Form 1040 and calculate the self-employment tax on Schedule SE of IRS Form 1040. Estimated taxes must be paid quarterly using form 1040-ES if estimated tax liability exceeds $1,000.

401k Retirement Account

Self-employed workers cannot contribute to a company-run 401k plan of the type with which most people are familiar. However, there are various vehicles available to self-employed individuals to save for retirement. Many set up a Simplified Employee Pension Plan (SEP) IRA, which allows them to contribute up to 25% of their income, up to $51,000 (2013) per year. There is also a vehicle called the Self-

Employed 401k (or SE 401k) for self-employed people. The contribution limits vary slightly depending on how your business is organized but are generally higher than the other types of plans.

Effects on Income Growth

Research has shown that levels of self-employment in the United States are increasing, and that under certain circumstances this can have positive effects on per capita income and job creation. A 2011 study from the Federal Reserve Bank of Atlanta and Pennsylvania State University looked at U.S. self-employment levels from 1970 to 2000. According to data from the U.S. Bureau of Economic Analysis, the absolute number of people registered as non-farm proprietors (NFPs) or self-employed in metropolitan counties grew by 244% between 1969 and 2006, and by 93% in non-metropolitan counties. In relative terms, the share of self-employed within the labour force grew from 14% in 1969 to 21% in 2006 in metropolitan counties, and from 11% to 19% in non-metropolitan counties.

In non-metropolitan counties, the study found that increased levels of self-employment were associated with strong increases in per capita income and job creation and significant reductions in family poverty levels. In 1969, the average income of non-farm proprietors was $6,758 compared to $6,507 earned by salaried employees; by 2006 the difference in earnings widened to $12,041 in favour of salaried employees. The study notes that the gap could be due to underreporting of income by the self-employed. Alternatively, low-productivity workers could be losing their jobs and are forced to be self-employed. Further, some research shows that higher local unemployment rates lead workers to self-select into self-employment, as does past unemployment experience.

Self-employment in the United Kingdom

A self-employed person in the United Kingdom can operate as a sole trader or as a partner in a partnership (including a Limited Liability Partnership or "LLP") but not through an incorporated limited (or unlimited) liability company. It is also possible for someone to form a business that is run only part-time or concurrently while holding down a full-time job. This form of employment, while popular, does come with several legal responsibilities. When working from home clearance may sometimes be required from the local authority to use part of the home as business premises. Should the business hold records of customers or suppliers in any electronic form it is required to register with the Information Commissioner's Office. Other legal responsibilities include statutory public liability insurance cover, modifying premises to be disabled-friendly, and the proper recording and accounting of financial transactions. Free advice on the range of responsibilities is available from government operated Business Link centres.

Many people living with disabilities choose to be self-employed.

UK Taxation

A self-employed person doesn't pay tax in the UK until their turnover, after expenses reaches more than £9,440. In addition to both the employee and employer National Insurance contributions, there may be VAT, business rates and other taxes payable to central and local governments.

A Small Business - An Avenue of Self Employment

The economic condition of the people of Orissa is very poor as about 48 percent of the population resides below the poverty line. Despite being the state is endowed with plenty of natural resources, the people of Orissa are reeling under dire poverty. In rural areas unemployment prevails in disguise in agricultural sector. Rural people have poor resource base, low level of capacity, limited access to financial and other support services. They do not have enough opportunities around them to utilize their limited skill and resources. At this backdrop the encouragement of establishment of Micro-Enterprises is a very welcome step for the public sector as well as the NGOs. A small business is normally a single owner operated business, started with or without any employee with as little capital as possible. It also takes the name of Micro-Enterprise in the modern business terminology which means a term that refers to the countless tiny businesses begun by the poor in the cities, towns, and villages. Known by economists as the "informal economic sector", these micro enterprises play a major and crucial role in both rural and urban areas. The promoters of these micro - enterprises often work alone or with unpaid family members and cater to the needs of their neighbours and communities.

Objectives of the Study

The study involves the following main objectives

1. To make a study of the Government policies towards the Micro-Enterprises.
2. To make a study of the role of NGO's in the promotion of Micro-Enterprises.

3. To make a study of various problems of the micro-business in Orissa
4. To draw the conclusion on the basis of the study and to make some suggestions.

Government Policies Towards Micro-enterprises

All the self-employment programmes - Integrated Rural Development Programme (IRDP), Training of Rural Youth for Self Employment (TRYSEM), Development of Women & Children in Rural Areas (DWCRA), Supply of Improved Tool Kits to Rural Artisans (SITRA), Ganga Kalyan Yojana (GKY) and Million Wells Scheme (MWS) were merged into one self-employment programme - Swarna Jayanti Gram Swarojgar Yojana (SSGSY). The programme aims at establishing a large number of micro-enterprises in the rural areas to provide sustainable income to the rural poor. A new scheme - Credit-cum-Subsidy Scheme has come into operation w.e.f. April 1, 1999 to facilitate construction of houses for rural families with income up to Rs. 32,000 annually and who have some repayment capacity. Moreover, to encourage the use of cost-effective, environment friendly and scientifically tested and proven indigenous and modern designs, a scheme called Innovative Stream for Rural Housing and Habitat Development has been launched w.e.f. April 1, 1999. The programme of Kisan Credit Cards is progressing very well. Cooperative Banks, Regional Rural Banks and Commercial Banks together have so far issued more than 50 lakh cards and card-cum-pass books to the farmers.

The Role of NGO's in Micro-Enterprise Development

Orissa Organic Farming Network[1] : The NGO has undertaken few blocks of Orissa with the objectives of reducing food and livelihood insecurity in the state of Orissa, through sustainable farming methods focusing especially on drought and disaster prone regions, where the majority of indigenous people live. Major objectives of the institution is to assist small farmers/gardeners in forming mutual assistance groups to conduct trials on various crops, techniques and management approaches - to aware farmers and consumers about the hazards associated with use of pesticides, herbicides, fungicides etc and try out alternative paste management approaches - to promote gardening and tree planting among school children.

PRADAN[2](Professional Assistance for Development Action): It was established in 1983 with the mission of working in rural areas, with socio-economically disadvantaged communities, such as adivasis, scheduled castes, the landless and marginal and small cultivators. It undertakes small scale irrigation; better upland husbandry, the preparation of siali leaf plate and promotion of women's savings and credit groups in KBK districts, Boudh and Kandhamals in Orissa.

BISWA[3] (Bharat Integrated Social Welfare Agency): BISWA enjoys the credit in successfully providing self employment to more then 4500 entrepreneurs and employment to more then 500 wage earners along with creation of indirect employment opportunities for a population of more then 16000 in the rural sector with major focus on agri-horticulture, promotion of handicrafts, encouraging petty business. The support of the friends from USA, the Government of India and the Government of Orissa has made it possible along with the formal financial institutions that have extended credit facilities in pursuance of the income generating activities adopted by the entrepreneurs.

Vikash[4]

Vikash has promoted the use of bio-fertilizers on a large scale. It promotes Azolla which is an aquatic fern that multiplies asexually and is useful for paddy cultivation. It also reduces weed growth, improves soil texture, maintains moisture level and increases crop yield etc. Vikash is taking up many innovative initiatives for developing micro-enterprise schemes including research, training, consultancy, exposure visits and field guidance.

It has undertaken the construction of alternative cost-effective houses for the poor, production and marketing of organic fertilizer, promotion of Micro-Finance institution under the name "Krushak Nidhi" for the betterment of poor in the form of a federation of Self Help Groups.

Problems of Micro-Enterprises in Orissa

The Micro-Enterprise system suffers from the following problems in Orissa

* There is very low level of technology.
* There is very little coordination among the development actors.
* The Micro- Enterprise Network suffers from very low level of information communication among various stakeholders of development.
* The Micro-Entrepreneurs have very little knowledge about scope of the product marketing.

* Very little or non-existence of Small & Micro Enterprises (SME) poses hindrances in the way of development and growth of Micro-Enterprise.
* Small businesses have a little scope of getting industry association.

Summary and Conclusion of the Study

Credit and other enterprise development services can play a significant role in providing the basic necessities of life to the poor by strengthening their livelihood options. The NGOs and the Government of Orissa should extend their co-operation to make the dream a real one. On the basis of the study the following suggestions may be given

* Local institutions may be developed through promotion of SHGs to take care of the needy and poor people.
* Technology up gradation should be made through skill development of artisans.
* A Network of communication should be developed among artisans
* Above all there is the need of establishment and strengthening of Small & Micro Enterprises among Minority Communities.

The Purpose and Emerging Issues in the Development of

Self Help Group

India once named as the "golden bird" has gathered dust over the years and lost its golden shine. As Mahatma Gandhi said "India is made up of villages" so there should be a concerted effort to strengthen the rural masses. Development is said to have been complete only when it reaches the most remote place and the most neglected. Ironically there is no end to the road development but as we pass through the road, the places alongside should turn into green pastures of opportunity and prosperity for the people living there.

Even after 54 years if independence India still unable to untangle itself from the shackles of poverty. The magnitude of the problem of poverty faced by the country immense.

The expert group on "Estimation of proportion of number of poor" appointed by the planning commission has estimated in 1987 – 88, the percentage of persons below poverty line was 39.06 in rural area and 40.12 in urban areas. For the country as a whole, it was estimated to be 39.34 percent. The new estimates are higher than the earlier official estimates. A substantial decline has occurred since 1973 – 74 in the proportion of people below poverty line. Nevertheless, in terms of absolute numbers, people below the poverty line are very large and there has to be a multipronged approach to tackle the problem. Much of the objectives and strategies adopted towards alleviation of poverty in the various five year Plans remains in paper and never got implemented. The main challenge before a developing nation is to foster sustainable growth. The growth or its recovery, the nation's productive capacity has to be strengthened and expanded. An important issue relates to the problem of the provision and delivery of financial services and credit to the poor so that the poor emerge out of their poverty through meaningful productive activities. Creativity is within every individual, the only thing required is the will to explore the giant with in oneself. The rural people in spite of various constraints like improper education, improper technological information can still change the world around them.

A number of programmes were designed specifically to enlarge the flow of credit to the poor. The main thrust of these programmes was to provide financial assistance to poor by way of capital subsidy and bank credit so that they can improve their economic conditions. So a multiagency approach for rural credit delivery was adopted involving commercial banks, co-operative banks and regional rural banks. Beside several programmes were also designed for direct assault on poverty such as, the integrated rural development programme, the self employment programme for urban poor.

It's the women who are the most vulnerable to all the atrocities in the world. Building women into self reliant individuals is the first step towards development. Women should be made self reliant both economically and socially, As a maxim reveals explicitly that "Ideal Nation". Thus women beneficiaries were given special concession under the various government programmes. For example, under the IRDP, 40% of the beneficiaries were women.

In spite of such programmes being lined up to fight poverty much hasn't happened on the ground. The percentage of beneficiaries of the IRDP who might have crossed the poverty line is the only around 20% . The target oriented approach has also compromised the quality of the programmes. Broadly speaking, these efforts while impressive in quantitative terms have not brought desired results. The cumbersome lending procedures, inadequate supervision and at times the apathy of bank staff have resulted in delayed and untimely credit, which has been responsible for the large scale misutilisation and default of credit. The commercial banks suffer from two very basic weaknesses namely their high cost structure and their attitudinal character is basically urban oriented.the co-operative credit system is far from a healthy situation. The system suffers from a number of problems, such as excessive reliance on funds from a higher level structure, undue state control, poor deposit mobilization and poor recovery of loans. The problems associated with the Regional rural Banks are low interest rates, poor margins, high operating costs involved in handling of small loans and lending exclusively to the weaker sections in backward regions.

According to the price Water House study, 1995, 84% of the rural credit portfolio was met by informal means of credit such as trades, shopkeeper, moneylender, landlord and friends and relatives. 48% of the total respondents had never borrowed from bank. The money lenders charge as high as 120% interest rates and the poor get indebted to them for even life thus enabling them to break the vicious cycle of poverty. Given the fact the poor, both in rural and urban areas do not have the necessary capabilities to approach and negotiate with organized credit situations, the liking of formal credit situations with the rural and urban poor, through intermediaries such as non-governmental organization was thought as an alternative mechanism for meeting the credit needs of the poor.

India is placed in a unique situation, so a number of credit based poverty alleviation programmes are needed. Products should be created according to the customers needs and products should now be tailored with the rural poor in mind. The shortcomings of the rural poor will respect to availing of loans from the financial institutions are manifold, viz, inability to pay high interest rates on loans, lack of skills, unawareness of economic opportunities of the market, inability to overcome bureaucratic requirements, their needs for small consumption loans. As an alternative to this shortcoming a soothing role is played by the Nongovernmental organization and self help groups. The NGOs will be like that of a catalyst which would facilitate the project formulation by banks on the one hand and its effective implementation by the beneficiaries on the other. They help banks in the follow up and supervision of the projects and ensure that expected results are achieved. The establishment of self help groups can be traced to the existence of one or more common problems around which the consciousness of the rural poor is built. Such groups thus are normally a response to a perceived need, besides being centred around specific productive activities. These groups also promote savings among their members and use pooled resources to meet the needs of their constitutions.

Initiating and monitoring the credit programmes for the poor can be made more effective and less costly if banks attempts to organize the poor in self help groups hereby peer pressure can be used to ensure proper utilization of credit and prompt repayment of loans. Here loans are offered in a prompt and simpler manner, ensure need based loans and keep the loan size within the repaying capacity of the borrowers and more importantly the interest rate charges are as low as 2%

The main advantage to the banks of the link among them, the self help groups and the NGOs, would be the externalization of a part of the work items of the credit cycle viz., assessment of credit needs, appraisal, disbursal supervision and repayment, reduction in the formal paper work involved and a consequent reduction in the transaction cost.

The concept of people's participation has been tried by several developing countries the world over. Philippines, Indonesia and Bangladesh are some such countries. In Bangladesh, Prof.Mohammed Yunus seeded the concept of SHG which be named as Grameen Bank. The success of the Bangladesh Grameen Bank in providing financial assistance to the rural poor on reasonable terms for generating productive self employment has gained wide recognition. Here the loan proposals are entertained only on a group basis. The rate of interest is generally 16 to 16.5%. Its recovery performance was 98% in 1988 which was a world record. The Bangladesh Grameen Bank indeed provides several lessons in terms of mobilization of resources, lending policies and procedures and recoveries.

Self Help Groups

SHGs are self managed groups of poor men and women which primarily came into existence to mobilize financial resources through their own savings and lend the same amongst themselves to meet the credit needs of their members. SHGs usually consist of 15 to 20 poor men / women living in the same area. Each SHG has unique system of organizing and managing its own finance and operate on the principles of self help group, mutual trust and co-operation. Regular transactions like collecting savings, issuing loans and collection of repayment takes place at particular intervals where all members are present and can collectively take decisions. The SHGs also provides a forum for social interaction which serves as an alternate social structure for peer level interaction. During the initial stages, the own funds of SHGs are primarily used for meeting small time consumption and emergency needs.

Basic Purpose of Self Help Groups on Savings and Credit

SHGs are emerging as alternative system to provide financial services to the poor. The basic purposes for which these groups are promoted are

* To create a separate line of credit for consumption and emergencies, this would help the poor families to get out of the debt by trap bid by exploitative financial system.
* To create a habit of savings among the rural people, the concept of SHG has proved to be a boon
* To reduce the costs of lending for the formal banking systems, and the cost of borrowing for the rural poor.

SHGs as a Financial Institution

Each Self Help Group acts as a localized financial institution owned and managed by the poor – all the basic principles of financial management are applicable to the group.

Book Keeping and Accounting System: Maintaining of proper accounting and book keeping is an essential part of SHG system. The following books are usually maintained in each group.

* Minutes book
* Receipts
* Vouchers
* Cash book
* General ledger
* Members pass book and sub ledger for members

All the financial transactions are captured in these books. Individual pass books are given to each member while other books can be retained at a common place, normally in a box kept at the leader's house.

But some self Help Groups formed directly by Banks insist that the members pass books should be kept by the person concerned. This is a step to make them self reliant.

Each Self Help Group should have an accountant to maintain the books of accounts and the proceedings of the meetings. The accountant has to be appointed by the group.

Financial Transactions: The following transactions are undertaken during the regular meetings where all the members are present.

* Collection of savings
* Collection of loan repayment
* Collection of penalties, fee etc.
* Issues of loans
* Payment of expenses

Normally the meeting is conducted on a fixed date and continues for three to four hours and in most cases for one hour. All the financial transactions take e place during the regular meetings.

Sources and application of funds: SHGs can mobilize funds both for internal and external sources. The following table lists the major sources and application of funds.

Internal sources

* Regular savings by members
* Interest earned on loans
* Common fund of the group
* Loan repayment from the members
* Penalties, fees, etc

Applications:

Most of the funds available with the Self Help Group are issued as loans to its members . The major items on which the SHG funds are applied are listed below

* Loans to members
* Interest on savings by members
* Expenses for salary, stationary and travel
* Loans repayments from banks
* Deposits with banks and other agencies

The funds collected at each meeting is immediately disbursed in some cases but the money collected in the meeting is deposited in the bank the following day. Most of the times, the self help group has very little cash balances left unspent.

Profitability: Each SHG mobilises savings from all the members and lends the same as loan to the needy members. Normally, a self Help Group pays an interest of twelve percent per annum on the savings from members and lends at a rate of twenty four to thirty six percent per annum sleaving a spread of twelve percent. In addition the self help Group collects administrative fee, membership fee and penalities which adds on to the income. Self Help Group can leverage loans from bank at 12% and lends to members at 20% and lends to members at 24 to 36%. Self Help Groups can meet the cost of books, accountant salary, auditing fee and other meeting expenses from their income. The Profitability of the Self Help Group depends on the total volume of business. Each Self Help Group has to lay down clear cut norms for repayment and strict procedures for follow up. Poor performance can affect the profitability of the group.

Auditing: All the books of accounts of the groups have to be audited internally once in six months and externally by a Chartered Accountant once in a year. Sound accounting and financial practices can be ensured by the practice. As the groups are expected to establish a sustainable relationship with banks and act as a financial intermediary, auditing is essential.

Each Self Help Group has to conduct an Annual General Body meeting once a year where the audit report is shared and approved. Members can review the progress and achievements and prepare plans for the forthcoming year.

Role of Microfinance Institutions in Rural Development

More than subsidies poor need access to credit. Absence of formal employment make them non 'bankable'. This forces them to borrow from local moneylenders at exorbitant interest rates. Many innovative institutional mechanisms have been developed across the world to enhance credit to poor even in the absence of formal mortgage. The present paper discusses conceptual framework of a microfinance institution in India. The successes and failures of various microfinance institutions around the world have been evaluated and lessons learnt have been incorporated in a model microfinance institutional mechanism for India.

Micro-finance and Poverty Alleviation

Most poor people manage to mobilize resources to develop their enterprises and their dwellings slowly over time. Financial services could enable the poor to leverage their initiative, accelerating the process of building incomes, assets and economic security. However, conventional finance institutions seldom lend down-market to serve the needs of low-income families and women-headed households. They are very often denied access to credit for any purpose, making the discussion of the level of interest rate and other terms of finance irrelevant. Therefore the fundamental problem is not so much of unaffordable terms of loan as the lack of access to credit itself.

The lack of access to credit for the poor is attributable to practical difficulties arising from the discrepancy between the mode of operation followed by financial institutions and the economic characteristics and financing needs of low income households. For example, commercial lending institutions require that borrowers have a stable source of income out of which principal and interest can be paid back according to the agreed terms. However, the income of many self employed households is not stable, regardless of its size. A large number of small loans are needed to serve the poor, but lenders prefer dealing with large loans in small numbers to minimize administration costs. They also look for collateral with a clear title - which many low-income households do not have. In addition bankers tend to consider low income households a bad risk imposing exceedingly high information monitoring costs on operation.

Over the last ten years, however, successful experiences in providing finance to small entrepreneur and producers demonstrate that poor people, when given access to responsive and timely financial services at market rates, repay their loans and use the proceeds to increase their income and assets. This is not surprising since the only realistic alternative for them is to borrow from informal market at an interest much higher than market rates. Community banks, NGOs and grass root savings and credit groups around the world have shown that these micro enterprise loans can be profitable for borrowers and for the lenders, making microfinance one of the most effective poverty reducing strategies. To the extent that microfinance institutions become financially viable, self sustaining, and integral to the communities in which they operate, they have the potential to attract more resources and expand services to clients.

Despite the success of microfinance institutions, only about 2% of world's roughly 500 million small entrepreneurs is estimated to have access to financial services (Barry et al. 1996). Although there is demand for credit by poor and women at market interest rates, the volume of financial transaction of microfinance institution must reach a certain level before their financial operation becomes self sustaining. In other words, although microfinance offers a promising institutional structure to provide access to credit to the poor, the scale problem needs to be resolved so that it can reach the vast majority of potential customers who demand access to credit at market rates. The question then is how micro enterprise lending geared to providing short term capital to small businesses in the informal sector can be sustained as an integral part of the financial sector and how their financial services can be further expanded using the principles, standards and modalities that have proven to be effective. To be successful, financial intermediaries that provide services and generate domestic resources must have the capacity to meet high performance standards. They must achieve excellent repayments and provide access to clients.

And they must build toward operating and financial selfsufficiency and expanding client reach. In order to do so, microfinance institutions need to find ways to cut down on their administrative costs and also to broaden their resource base. Cost reductions can be achieved through simplified and decentralized loan application, approval and collection processes, for instance, through group loans which give borrowers responsibilities for much of the loan application process, allow the loan officers to handle many more clients and hence reduce costs (Otero et al. 1994).

Microfinance institutions can broaden their resource base by mobilizing savings, accessing capital markets, loan funds and effective institutional development support. A logical way to tap capital market is securitization through a corporation that purchases loans made by micro enterprise institutions with the funds raised through the bonds issuance on the capital market. There is at least one pilot attempt to securitize microfinance portfolio along these lines in Ecuador. As an alternative, BancoSol of Bolivia issued a certificate of deposit which are traded in Bolivian stock exchange. In 1994, it also issued certificates of deposit in the U.S. (Churchill 1996). The Foundation for Cooperation and Development of Paraguay issued bonds to raise capital for micro enterprise lending (Grameen Trust 1995).

Savings facilities make large scale lending operations possible. On the other hand, studies also show that the poor operating in the informal sector do save, although not in financial assets, and hence value access to client-friendly savings service at least as much access to credit. Savings mobilization also makes financial institutions accountable to local shareholders. Therefore, adequate savings facilities both serve the demand for financial services by the customers and fulfil an important requirement of financial sustainability to the lenders. Microfinance institutions can either provide savings services directly through deposit taking or make arrangements with other financial institutions to provide savings facilities to tap small savings in a flexible manner (Barry 1995).

Convenience of location, positive real rate of return, liquidity, and security of savings are essential ingredients of successful savings mobilization (Christen et al. 1994). Once microfinance institutions are engaged in deposit taking in order to mobilize household savings, they become financial intermediaries. Consequently, prudential financial regulations become necessary to ensure the solvency and financial soundness of the institution and to protect the depositors. However, excessive regulations that do not consider the nature of microfinance institution and their operation can hamper their viability. In view of small loan size, microfinance institutions should be subjected to a minimum capital requirement which is lower than that applicable to commercial banks. On the other hand, a more stringent capital adequacy rate (the ratio between capital and risk assets) should be maintained because microfinance institutions provide uncollateralized loans.

Governments should provide an enabling legal and regulatory framework which encourages the development of a range of institutions and allows them to operate as recognized financial intermediaries subject to simple supervisory and reporting requirements. Usury laws should be repelled or relaxed and microfinance institutions should be given freedom of setting interest rates and fees in order to cover operating and finance costs from interest revenues within a reasonable amount of time. Government could also facilitate the process of transition to a sustainable level of operation by providing support to the lending institutions in their early stage of development through credit enhancement mechanisms or subsidies.

One way of expanding the successful operation of microfinance institutions in the informal sector is through strengthened linkages with their formal sector counterparts. A mutually beneficial partnership should be based on comparative strengths of each sectors. Informal sector microfinance institutions have comparative advantage in terms of small transaction costs achieved through adaptability and flexibility of operations (Ghate et al. 1992). They are better equipped to deal with credit assessment of the urban poor and hence to absorb the transaction costs associated with loan processing. On the other hand, formal sector institutions have access to broader resource-base and high leverage through deposit mobilization (Christen et al. 1994).

Therefore, formal sector finance institutions could form a joint venture with informal sector institutions in which the former provide funds in the form of equity and the later extends savings and loan facilities to the urban poor. Another form of partenership can involve the formal sector institutions refinancing loans made by the informal sector lenders. Under these settings, the informal sector institutions are able to tap additional resources as well as having an incentive to exercise greater financial discipline in their management.

Microfinance institutions could also serve as intermediaries between borrowers and the formal financial sector and on-lend funds backed by a public sector guarantee (Phelps 1995). Business-like NGOs can offer commercial banks ways of funding micro entrepreneurs at low cost and risk, for example, through leveraged bank-NGO-client credit lines.

Under this arrangement, banks make one bulk loan to NGOs and the NGOs packages it into large number of small loans at market rates and recover them (Women's World Banking 1994). There are many on-going research on this line but context specific research is needed to identify the most appropriate model. With this in mind we discuss various possible alternatives of formal-informal sector linkages in India. In this context, following strategic, institutional and connectivity issues related to micro-finance arise.

Strategic Issues

* Is there a prevailing paradigm for micro-finance?
* Are there clearly visible pattern across the country?
* Is there a clearly defined foundation building blocks such as organizing principles, gender preferences and operational imperatives?
* What are methodological issues?

Institutional Issues

* Is there a need for a new institution?
* Should it operate all India or in a state?
* Where should it be located?
* Who can lead an institution of this sort?

* What will its contextual interconnections be?
* Who will be its beneficiaries?

Connectivity Issues

* How should the Corporate Financial Sector be involved?
* What is the role of donor agencies?
* How should communities be involved?
* Are there political issues that should be explicitly considered?
* Are there government policy issues?

The Formal Sector Institutions

Traditionally, the formal sector Banking Institutions in India have been serving only the needs of the commercial sector and providing loans for middle and upper income groups. Similarly, for housing the HFIs have generally not evolved a lending product to serve the needs of the Very LIG primarily because of the perceived risks of lending to this sector. Following risks are generally perceived by the formal sector financial institutions:

* Credit Risk;
* High transaction and service cost;
* Absence of land tenure for financing housing;
* Irregular flow of income due to seasonality;
* Lack of tangible proof for assessment of income;
* Unacceptable collaterals such as crops, utensils and jewellery.

As far as the formal financial institutions are concerned there are Commercial Banks, Housing Finance Institutions (HFIs), NABARD, Rural Development Banks (RDBs), Land Development Banks Land Development Banks and Cooperative Banks (CBs).

As regards the Co-operative Structures, the Urban Co.op Banks (UCB) or Urban Credit Co.op Societies (UCCS) are the two primary co-operative financial institutions operating in the urban areas. There are about 1400 UCBs with over 3400 branches in India having 14 million members, Their total lending outstanding in 1990-91 has been reported at over Rs 80 billion with deposits worth Rs 101 billion.

Similarly there exist about 32000 credit co.op societies with over 15 million members with their total outstanding lending in 1990-91 being Rs 20 billion with deposits of Rs 12 billion. Few of the UCCS also have external borrowings from the District Central Co.op Banks

(DCCBs) at 18-19%. The loans given by the UCBs or the UCCS are for short term and unsecured except for few which are secured by personal guarantees. The most effective security being the group or the peer pressure. The Government has taken several initiatives to strengthen the institutional rural credit system. The rural branch network of commercial banks have been expanded and certain policy prescriptions imposed in order to ensure greater flow of credit to agriculture and other preferred sectors. The commercial banks are required to ensure that 40% of total credit is provided to the priority sectors out of which 18% in the form of direct finance to agriculture and 25% to priority sector in favour of weaker sections besides maintaining a credit deposit ratio of 60% in rural and semiurban branches. Further the IRDP introduced in 1979 ensures supply of credit and subsidies to weaker section beneficiaries. Although these measures have helped in widening the access of rural households to institutional credit, vast majority of the rural poor have still not been covered. Also, such lending done under the poverty alleviation schemes suffered high repayment defaults and left little sustainable impact on the economic condition of the beneficiaries.

The Existing Informal Financial Sources

The informal financial sources generally include funds available from family sources or local money lenders. The local money lenders charge exorbitant rates, generally ranging from 36% to 60% interest due to their monopoly in the absence of any other source of credit for non conventional needs. Chit Funds and Bishis are other forms of credit system operated by groups of people for their mutual benefit which however have their own limitations.

Lately, few of the NGOs engaged in activities related to community mobilization for their socio-economic development have initiated savings and credit programmes for their target groups. These Community based financial systems (CBFS) can broadly be categorized into two models: Group Based Financial Intermediary and the NGO Linked Financial Intermediary. Most of the NGOs like SHARAN in Delhi, FEDERATION OF THRIFT AND CREDIT ASSOCIATION (FTCA) in Hyderabad or SPARC in Bombay have adopted the first model where they initiate the groups and provide the necessary management support. Others like SEWA in Ahmedabad or BARODA CITIZEN's COUNCIL in Baroda pertain to the second model. The experience of these informal intermediaries shows that although the savings of group members, small in nature do not attract high returns, it is still practiced due to security reasons and for getting loans at lower rates compared to that available from money lenders. These are short term loans meant for crisis, consumption and income generation needs of the members. The interest rates on such credit are not subsidized and generally range between 12 to 36%. Most of the loans are unsecured. In few cases personal or group guarantees or other collaterals like jewellery is offered as security.

While a census of NGOs in micro-finance is yet to be carried out, there are perhaps 250-300 NGOs, each with 50- 100 Self Help Groups (SHG). Few of them, not more than 20-30 NGOs have started forming SHG Federations. There are also agencies which provide bulk funds to the system through NGOs. Thus organizations engaged in micro finance activities in India may be categorized as Wholesalers, NGOs supporting SHG Federations and NGOs directly retailing credit borrowers or groups of borrower.

The Wholesalers will include agencies like NABARD, Rashtriya Mahila Kosh-New Delhi and the Friends of Women's World Banking in Ahmedabad. Few of the NGOs supporting SHG Federations include MYRADA in Bangalore, SEWA in Ahmedabad, PRADAN in Tamilnadu and Bihar, ADITHI in Patna, SPARC in Mumbai, ASSEFA in Madras etc. While few of the NGOs directly retailing credit to Borrowers are SHARE in Hyderabad, ASA in Trichy, RDO Loyalam Bank in Manipur.

Credit Mechanisms Adopted By Hdfc (India) For Funding The Low Income Group Beneficiaries

HDFC has been making continuous and sustained efforts to reach the lower income groups of society, especially the economically weaker sections, thus enabling them to realize their dreams of possessing a house of their own.

HDFCs' response to the need for better housing and living environment for the poor, both, in the urban and rural sectors materialized in its collaboration with Kreditanstalt fur Wiederaufbau (KfW), a German Development bank. KfW sanctioned DM 55 million to HDFC for low cost housing projects in India. HDFCs' approach to low-income lending has been extremely professional and developmental in nature. Negating the concept of dependence, HDFCs' low cost housing schemes are marked by the emphasis on peoples participation and usage of self-help approach wherein the beneficiaries contribute both in terms of cash and labour for construction of their houses. HDFC also ensures that the newly constructed houses are within the affordability of the beneficiaries, and thus promotes the usage of innovative low cost technologies and locally available materials for construction of the houses. For the purpose of actual implementation of the low cost housing projects, HDFC collaborates with organisations, both, Governmental and Non-Governmental. Such organisations act as co-ordinating agencies for the projects involving a collective of individuals belonging to the Economically Weaker Sections. The projects could be either in urban or rural areas. The security for the loan is generally the mortgage of the property being financed. The construction work is regularly monitored by the co-ordinating agencies and HDFC. The loans from HDFC are disbursed depending upon the stages of construction. To date, HDFC has experienced 100% recovery for the loans disbursed to various projects.

Strengths of Informal Sector

A synthesis that can be evolved out of the success of NGOs/ CBOs engaged in microfinance is based on certain preconditions, institutional and facilitating factors.

Preconditions to Success

Those NGOs/ CBOs have been successful that have istilled financial value/ discipline through savings and have demonstrated a matching value themselves before lending. A recovery system based on social intermediation and various options including non-financial mechanisms has proved to be effective. Another important feature has been the community governance. The communities in which households are direct stake holders have successfully demonstrated the success of programmes. A precondition for success is to involve community directly in the programme. Experience indicates that savings and credit are both critical for success and savings should precede credit. Chances of success more with women: Programmes designed with women are more successful.

Operating Indicators

The operating indicators show that programmes which are designed taking into account the localized and geographical differences have been successful. Effective and responsive accounting and monitoring mechanisms have been an important and critical ingradient for the success of programmes. The operational success has been more when interest rates are at or near market rates: The experience of NGOs/CBOs indicates that low income households are willing to pay market rates. The crucial problem is not the interest rates but access to finance. Eventually in absence of such programmes households end up paying much higher rates when borrowing from informal markets. Some NGOs have experimented where members of community decide on interest rates.

This is slightly different from Thailand experience where community decides on repayment terms and loan amount. A combination of the three i.e. interest rates, amount and repayment period if decided by community, the programme is most likely to succeed. A programme which is able to leverage maximum funds from formal market has been successful. Experience indicates that it is possible to leverage higher funds against deposits.

The spreads should be available to meet operational costs of NGOs. Most of the directed credit programme in India like Kfw have a ceiling on the maximum interest rate and the spread available to NGOs. A flexible rate of interest scheme would indicate a wider spread for NGOs.

Selected non-financial services, viz. business, marketing support services enhance success. Appropriate incentives for borrowing and proper graduation of credit has been essential component of success. A successful programme can not be generalized for all needs and geographical spread. The programmes which are simple and replicable in similar contexts have contributed to success.

Betterment in quality of life through better housing or better economic opportunities is a tangible indicator of success. The programmes which have been able to demonstrate on some measurable scale that the quality of life has improved have been successful. To be successful the programme productivity with outreach should match. The credit mechanism should be flexible meeting multiple credit needs: The programmes which have taken care of other needs such as consumption, marriage etc. besides the main shelter, infrastructure or economic needs are successful.

Facilitating Factor

Another factor that has contributed to the success is the broad environment. A facilitative environment and enabling regulatory regime contributes to the success. The NGOs/ CBOs which have been able to leverage funds from formal programmes have been successful. An essential factor for success is that all development programmes should converge across sectors.

Weaknesses of Existing Microfinance Models

One of the most successful models discussed around the world is the Grameen type. The bank has successfully served the rural poor in Bangladesh with no physical collateral relying on group responsibility to replace the collateral requirements. This model, however, has some weaknessed. It involves too much of external subsidy which is not replicable Grameen bank has not oriented itself towards mobilising peoples' resources. The repayment system of 50 weekly equal instalments is not practical because poor do not have a stable job and have to migrate to other places for jobs. If the communities are agrarian during lean seasons it becomes impossible for them to repay the loan. Pressure for high repayment drives members to money lenders. Credit alone cannot alleviate poverty and the Grameen model is based only on credit. Micro-finance is time taking process. Haste can lead to wrong selection of activities and beneficiaries.

Another model is Kerala model (Shreyas). The rules make it difficult to give adequate credit {only 40-50 percent of amount available for lending). In Nari Nidhi/Pradan system perhaps not reaching the very poor.

Most of the existing microfinance institutions are facing problems regarding skilled labour which is not available for local level accounting. Drop out of trained staff is very high.

One alternative is automation which is not looked at as yet. Most of the models do not lend for agriculture. Agriculture lending has not been experimented.

* Risk Management : yield risk and price risk;
* Insurance & Commodity Future Exchange could be explored.

All the models lack in appropriate legal and financial structure. There is a need to have a sub-group to brainstorm on statutory structure/ ownership control/ management/ taxation aspects/ financial sector prudential norms. A forum/ network of micro-financier (self regulating organization) is desired.

New Paradigm

A new paradigm that emerges is that it is very critical to link poor to formal financial system, whatever the mechanism may be, if the goal of poverty allieviation has to be achieved. NGOs and CBOs have been involved in community development for long and the experience shows that they have been able to improve the quality of life of poor, if this is an indicator of development. The strengths and weaknesses of existing NGOs/CBOs and microfinance institutions in India indicate that despite their best of efforts they have not been able to link themselves with formal systems. It is desired that an intermediary institution is required between formal financial markets and grassroot.

The intermediary should encompass the strengths of both formal financial systems and NGOs and CBOs and should be flexible to the needs of end users. There are, however, certain unresolved dilemmas regarding the nature of the intermediary institutions. There are arguments both for and against each structure. These dilemmas are very contextual and only strengthen the argument that no unique model is applicable for all situations. They have to be context specific.

Dilemmas

Community Based	*Investor Owned*
Community Managed	Professionally managed
Community (self) financed for on-lending	Accepting outside funds
Integrated (social & finance)	Minimalist (finance only)
Non profit / mutual benefit	For profit
Only for poor	For all under served clients
Self regulated'	Externally regulated

The four pillars of microfinance credit system are supply, demand for finance, intermediation and regulation. Whatever may the model of the intermediary institution, the end situation is accessibility of finance to poor. The following tables indicate the existing and desired situation for each component.

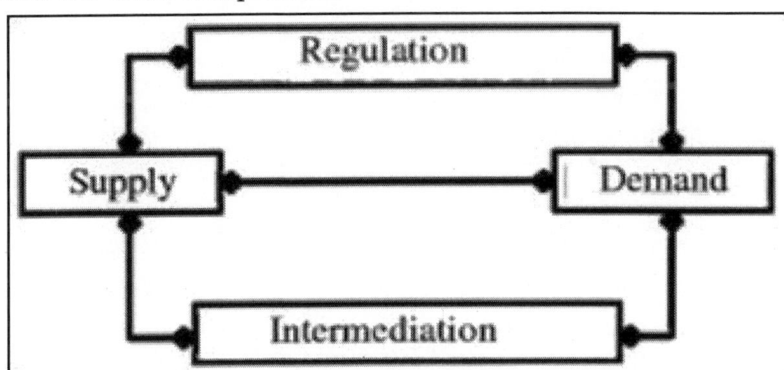

Demand

Existing Situation	*Desired Situation*
Fragmented	Professionally managed
Community Managed	Organized
Undifferentiated	Differentiated (for consumption, housing)
Addicted, corrupted by capital & subsidies	Deaddicted from capital & subsidies
Communities not aware of rights and responsibilities	Aware of rights and responsibilities

Supply

Existing Situation	*Desired Situation*
Grant based (Foreign/GOI)	Regular fund sources (borrowings/deposits)
Directed Credit - unwilling	Demand responsive and corrupt
Not linked with mainstream	Part of mainstream (banks/ FIs)
Mainly focussed for credit	Add savings and insurance
Dominated	Reduce dominance of informal, unregulated suppliers

Intermediation

Existing Situation	*Desired Situation*
Non specialized	Specialized in financial services
Not oriented to financial analysis	Thorough in financial analysis
Non profit capital	For profit
Not linked to mainstream FIs	Link up to FIs
Not organized	Self regulating

Regulation

Existing Situation	*Desired Situation*
Focused on formal service	include/informal recognize providers (informal not e.g. SHGs regulated)
regulating the wrong things	Regulate rules of game e.g. interest rates
Multiple and conflicting	Coherence and coordination (FCRA, RBI, IT, ROC, across regulators MOF/FIPB, ROS/ Commerce)
Negatively oriented	Enabling environment

Conclusion

Some valuable lessons can be drawn from the experience of successful Microfinance operation. First of all, the poor repay their loans and are willing to pay for higher interest rates than commercial banks provided that access to credit is provided. The solidarity group pressure and sequential lending provide strong repayment motivation and produce extremely low default rates. Secondly, the poor save and hence microfinance should provide both savings and loan facilities. These two findings imply that banking on the poor can be a profitable business. However, attaining financial viability and sustainability is the major institutional challenge. Deposit mobilization is the major means for microfinance institutions to expand outreach by leveraging equity (Sacay et al 1996). In order to be sustainable, microfinance lending should be grounded on market principles because large scale lending cannot be accomplished through subsidies.

A main conclusion of this paper is that microfinance can contribute to solving the problem of inadequate housing and urban services as an integral part of poverty alleviation programmes. The challenge lies in finding the level of flexibility in the credit instrument that could make it match the multiple credit requirements of the low income borrowers without imposing unbearably high cost of monitoring its end-use upon the lenders. A promising solution is to provide multi-purpose loans or composite credit for income generation, housing improvement and consumption support. Consumption loan is found to be especially important during the gestation period between commencing a new economic activity and deriving positive income. Careful research on demand for financing and savings behaviour of the potential borrowers and their participation in determining the mix of multipurpose loans are essential in making the concept work (tall 1996). Eventually it would be ideal to enhance the creditworthiness of the poor and to make them more “bankable” to financial institutions and enable them to qualify for long-term credit from the formal sector. Microfinance institutions have a lot to contribute to this by building financial discipline and educating borrowers about repayment requirements.

Women Enterpreneurship Development in India

Women entrepreneurship development is an essential part of human resource development. The development of women entrepreneurship is very low in India, especially in the rural areas.

Entrepreneurship amongst women has been a recent concern. Women have become aware of their existence their rights and their work situation. However, women of middle class are not too eager to alter their role in fear of social backlash. The progress is more visible among upper class families in urban cities. This paper focuses on women entrepreneur. Any understanding of Indian women, of their identity, and especially of their role taking and breaking new paths, will be incomplete without a walk down the corridors of Indian history where women have lived and internalized various role models. The paper talks about the status of women entrepreneurs and the problems faced by them when they ventured out to carve their own niche in the competitive world of business environment.

The Indian economy has been witnessing a drastic change since mid -1991, with new policies of economic liberalization, globalization and privatization initiated by the Indian government. India has great entrepreneurial potential. At present, women involvement in economic activities is marked by a low work participation rate, excessive concentration in the unorganized sector and employment in less skilled jobs. Any strategy aimed at economic development will be lop-sided without involving women who constitute half of the world population. Evidence has unequivocally established that entrepreneurial spirit is not a male prerogative. Women entrepreneurship has gained momentum in the last three decades with the increase in the number of women enterprises and their substantive contribution to economic growth. The industrial performance of Asia-Pacific region propelled by Foreign Direct Investment, technological innovations and manufactured exports has brought a wide range of economic and social opportunities to women entrepreneurs.

In this dynamic world, women entrepreneurs are an important part of the global quest for sustained economic development and social progress. In India, though women have played a key role in the society, their entrepreneurial ability has not been properly tapped due to the lower status of women in the society. It is only from the Fifth Five Year Plan (1974-78) onwards that their role has been explicitly recognized with a marked shift in the approach from women welfare to women development and empowerment. The development of women entrepreneurship has become an important aspect of our plan priorities. Several policies and programmes are being implemented for the development of women entrepreneurship in India. There is a need for changing the mindset towards women so as to give equal rights as enshrined in the constitution. The progress towards gender equality is slow and is partly due to the failure to attach money to policy commitments. In the words of president APJ Abdul Kalam "empowering women is a prerequisite for creating a good nation, when women are empowered, society with stability is assured. Empowerment of women is essential as their thoughts and their value systems lead to the development of a good family, good society and ultimately a good nation." When a woman is empowered it does not mean that another individual becomes powerless or is having less power. On the contrary, if a women is empowered her competencies towards decision- making will surely influence her family's behaviour.

In advanced countries, there is a phenomenon of increase in the number of self- employed women after the world war 11. In USA, women own 25% of all business, even though their sales on an average are less than two-fifths of those of other small business. In Canada, women own one-third of small business and in France it is one-fifth.

Concept of Entrepreneur- The word ' entrepreneur' derives from the French word "Entreprendre" (to undertake) .in the early 16th Century it was applied to persons engaged in military expeditions, and extend to cover construction and civil engineering activities in the 17th century, but during the 18th century , the word 'entrepreneur' was used to refer to economic activities. Many authors have defined 'entrepreneur' differently. Generally, an entrepreneur is a person who combines capital and labour for production. According to Cantillion "entrepreneur is the agent who buys means of production at certain prices, in order to sell at prices that are certain at the moment at which he commits himself to his cost". According to P.F Drucker " he is one who always (1) searches for change (2) responds to it (3) exploits it as an opportunity."

Concept of women Entrepreneur Enterprise-" A small scale industrial unit or industry –related service or business enterprise, managed by one or more women entrepreneurs in a concern, in which they will individually or jointly have a share capital of not less than 51% as shareholders of the private limited company, members of co-operative society".

Categories of Women Entrepreneurs

- Women in organized & unorganized sector
- Women in traditional & modern industries
- Women in urban & rural areas

- Women in large scale and small scale industries.
- Single women and joint venture.

Categories of Women Entrepreneurs in Practice in India

- First Category
  - Established in big cities
  - Having higher level technical & professional qualifications
  - Non traditional Items
  - Sound financial positions
- Second Category
  - Established in cities and towns
  - Having sufficient education
  - Both traditional and non traditional items
  - Undertaking women services-kindergarten, crèches, beauty parlors, health clinic etc
- Third Category
  - Illiterate women
  - Financially week
  - Involved in family business such as Agriculture, Horticulture, Animal Husbandry, Dairy, Fisheries, Agro Forestry, Handloom, Power loom etc.

Supportive Measures for Women's Economic Activities and Entrepreneurship

- Direct & indirect financial support
- Yojna schemes and programmes
- Technological training and awards
- Federations and associations

Direct & Indirect Financial Support

- Nationalized banks
- State finance corporation
- State industrial development corporation
- District industries centres
- Differential rate schemes
- Mahila Udyug Needhi scheme

- Small Industries Development Bank of India (SIDBI)
- State Small Industrial Development Corporations (SSIDCs)

Yojna Schemes and Programme

- Nehru Rojgar Yojna
- Jacamar Rojgar Yojna
- TRYSEM
- DWACRA

Technological Training and Awards

- Stree Shakti Package by SBI
- Entrepreneurship Development Institute of India
- Trade Related Entrepreneurship Assistance and Development (TREAD)
- National Institute of Small Business Extension Training (NSIBET)
- Women's University of Mumbai

Federations and Associations

- National Alliance of Young Entrepreneurs (NAYE)
- India Council of Women Entrepreneurs, New Delhi
- Self Employed Women's Association (SEWA)
- Association of Women Entrepreneurs of Karnataka (AWEK)
- World Association of Women Entrepreneurs (WAWE)
- Associated Country Women of the World (ACWW)

Table: *Women Entrepreneurship in India*

States	***No of Units Registered***	***No. of Women Entrepreneurs***	***Percentage***
Tamil Nadu	9618	2930	30.36
Uttar Pradesh	7980	3180	39.84
Kerala	5487	2135	38.91
Punjab	4791	1618	33.77
Maharastra	4339	1394	32.12
Gujrat	3872	1538	39.72
Karnatka	3822	1026	26.84
Madhya Pradesh	2967	842	28.38
Other States & UTS	14576	4185	28.71
Total	57,452	18,848	32.82

***Table:** Women Work Participation*

Country	*Percentage*
India (1970-1971)	14.2
India (1980-1981)	19.7
India (1990-1991)	22.3
India (2000-2001)	31.6
USA	45
UK	43
Indonesia	40
Sri Lanka	35
Brazil	35

Problems of Women Entrepreneurs in India

Women in India are faced many problems to get ahead their life in business. A few problems cane be detailed as;

1. The greatest deterrent to women entrepreneurs is that they are women. A kind of patriarchal – male dominant social order is the building block to them in their way towards business success. Male members think it a big risk financing the ventures run by women.
2. The financial institutions are skeptical about the entrepreneurial abilities of women. The bankers consider women loonies as higher risk than men loonies. The bankers put unrealistic and unreasonable securities to get loan to women entrepreneurs. According to a report by the United Nations Industrial Development Organization (UNIDO), "despite evidence that women's loan repayment rates are higher than men's, women still face more difficulties in obtaining credit," often due to discriminatory attitudes of banks and informal lending groups (UNIDO, 1995b).
3. Entrepreneurs usually require financial assistance of some kind to launch their ventures - be it a formal bank loan or money from a savings account. Women in developing nations have little access to funds, due to the fact that they are concentrated in poor rural communities with few opportunities to borrow money (Starcher, 1996; UNIDO, 1995a). The women entrepreneurs are suffering from inadequate financial resources and working capital. The women entrepreneurs lack access to

external funds due to their inability to provide tangible security. Very few women have the tangible property in hand.

4. Women's family obligations also bar them from becoming successful entrepreneurs in both developed and developing nations. "Having primary responsibility for children, home and older dependent family members, few women can devote all their time and energies to their business" (Starcher, 1996, p. .The financial institutions discourage women entrepreneurs on the belief that they can at any time leave their business and become housewives again. The result is that they are forced to rely on their own savings, and loan from relatives and family friends.
5. Indian women give more emphasis to family ties and relationships. Married women have to make a fine balance between business and home. More over the business success is depends on the support the family members extended to women in the business process and management. The interest of the family members is a determinant factor in the realization of women folk business aspirations.
6. Another argument is that women entrepreneurs have low-level management skills. They have to depend on office staffs and intermediaries, to get things done, especially, the marketing and sales side of business. Here there is more probability for business fallacies like the intermediaries take major part of the surplus or profit. Marketing means mobility and confidence in dealing with the external world, both of which women have been discouraged from developing by social conditioning. Even when they are otherwise in control of an enterprise, they often depend on males of the family in this area.
7. The male - female competition is another factor, which develop hurdles to women entrepreneurs in the business management process. Despite the fact that women entrepreneurs are good in keeping their service prompt and delivery in time, due to lack of organizational skills compared to male entrepreneurs women have to face constraints from competition. The confidence to travel across day and night and even different regions and states are less found in women compared to male entrepreneurs. This shows the low level freedom of expression and freedom of mobility of the women entrepreneurs.

8. Knowledge of alternative source of raw materials availability and high negotiation skills are the basic requirement to run a business. Getting the raw materials from different souse with discount prices is the factor that determines the profit margin. Lack of knowledge of availability of the raw materials and low-level negotiation and bargaining skills are the factors, which affect women entrepreneur's business adventures.
9. Knowledge of latest technological changes, know how, and education level of the person are significant factor that affect business. The literacy rate of women in India is found at low level compared to male population. Many women in developing nations lack the education needed to spur successful entrepreneurship. They are ignorant of new technologies or unskilled in their use, and often unable to do research and gain the necessary training (UNIDO, 1995b, p.1). Although great advances are being made in technology, many women's illiteracy, structural difficulties, and lack of access to technical training prevent the technology from being beneficial or even available to females ("Women Entrepreneurs in Poorest Countries," 2001). According to The Economist, this lack of knowledge and the continuing treatment of women as second-class citizens keep them in a pervasive cycle of poverty ("The Female Poverty Trap," 2001). The studies indicates that uneducated women don't have the knowledge of measurement and basic accounting.
10. Low-level risk taking attitude is another factor affecting women folk decision to get into business. Low-level education provides low-level self-confidence and self-reliance to the women folk to engage in business, which is continuous risk taking and strategic cession making profession. Investing money, maintaining the operations and ploughing back money for surplus generation requires high risk taking attitude, courage and confidence. Though the risk tolerance ability of the women folk in day-to-day life is high compared to male members, while in business it is found opposite to that.
11. Achievement motivation of the women folk found less compared to male members. The low level of education and confidence leads to low level achievement and advancement motivation among women folk to engage in business operations and running a business concern.

12. Finally high production cost of some business operations adversely affects the development of women entrepreneurs. The installation of new machineries during expansion of the productive capacity and like similar factors dissuades the women entrepreneurs from venturing into new areas.

How to Develop Women Entrepreneurs?

Right efforts on from all areas are required in the development of women entrepreneurs and their greater participation in the entrepreneurial activities. Following efforts can be taken into account for effective development of women entrepreneurs.

1. Consider women as specific target group for all developmental programmers.
2. Better educational facilities and schemes should be extended to women folk from government part.
3. Adequate training programme on management skills to be provided to women community.
4. Encourage women's participation in decision-making.
5. Vocational training to be extended to women community that enables them to understand the production process and production management.
6. Skill development to be done in women's polytechnics and industrial training institutes. Skills are put to work in training-cum-production workshops.
7. Training on professional competence and leadership skill to be extended to women entrepreneurs.
8. Training and counselling on a large scale of existing women entrepreneurs to remove psychological causes like lack of self-confidence and fear of success.
9. Counselling through the aid of committed NGOs, psychologists, managerial experts and technical personnel should be provided to existing and emerging women entrepreneurs.
10. Continuous monitoring and improvement of training programmers.
11. Activities in which women are trained should focus on their marketability and profitability.
12. Making provision of marketing and sales assistance from government part.

13. To encourage more passive women entrepreneurs the Women training programme should be organised that taught to recognize her own psychological needs and express them.
14. State finance corporations and financing institutions should permit by statute to extend purely trade related finance to women entrepreneurs.
15. Women's development corporations have to gain access to open-ended financing.
16. The financial institutions should provide more working capital assistance both for small scale venture and large scale ventures.
17. Making provision of micro credit system and enterprise credit system to the women entrepreneurs at local level.
18. Repeated gender sensitization programmers should be held to train financiers to treat women with dignity and respect as persons in their own right.
19. Infrastructure, in the form of industrial plots and sheds, to set up industries is to be provided by state run agencies.
20. Industrial estates could also provide marketing outlets for the display and sale of products made by women.
21. A Women Entrepreneur's Guidance Cell set up to handle the various problems of women entrepreneurs all over the state.
22. District Industries Centres and Single Window Agencies should make use of assisting women in their trade and business guidance.
23. Programmers for encouraging entrepreneurship among women are to be extended at local level.
24. Training in entrepreneurial attitudes should start at the high school level through well-designed courses, which build confidence through behavioural games.
25. More governmental schemes to motivate women entrepreneurs to engage in small scale and large-scale business ventures.
26. Involvement of Non Governmental Organizations in women entrepreneurial training programmes and counselling.

Conclusion - Entrepreneurship among women, no doubt improves the wealth of the nation in general and of the family in particular. Women today are more willing to take up activities that were once considered the preserve of men, and have proved that they are second to no one with respect to contribution to the growth of the economy. Women entrepreneurship must be moulded properly with entrepreneurial traits and skills to meet the changes in trends, challenges global markets and also be competent enough to sustain and strive for excellence in the entrepreneurial arena.

Characteristics of Entrepreneurs

The following list describes some common characteristics of an entrepreneur.

Works Hard: Self employment requires a great deal of time and effort. The entrepreneur must perform a wide variety of time consuming tasks. Seventy-seven percent of all entrepreneurs report working 50 hours or more per week, and 54 percent say that they work more than 60 hours per week. Such a time commitment requires that you have a high energy level.

Wants Financial Success: A primary reason that most entrepreneurs have for going into business is to achieve financial success. If you want to be an entrepreneur, you need to establish a reasonable financial goal that you want to achieve through self employment. This goal will help you measure how well you are doing in fulfilling your personal needs through an entrepreneurial career.

Has Family Support A successful entrepreneur needs family support. If you are married, your spouse must believe in your business because it will require that both of you sacrifice time and money. The stress may create disruptions in family relationships. If you have children, they will need encouragement in understanding your need to spend so much time away from the family. The more positive support you receive from your family, the more you can concentrate on making the business a success.

Is Energetic Self employment requires long work hours. You will frequently be unable to control the number of hours required to fulfill all the necessary tasks. The entrepreneur must have a high energy level to respond to the job's demands.

Has an Internal 'Locus of Control': Successful entrepreneurs have an internal locus of control or inner sense of responsibility for the outcome of a venture. To be an entrepreneur, you should have a strong sense of being a "victor" who is responsible for your actions. If, however, you often consider yourself a "victim" and blame other people, bad luck, or difficult circumstances for your failures, entrepreneurship might not be the right career move for you.

Takes Risks: Entrepreneurs are risk takers. They risk their careers, time and money in order to make a success of their businesses. To be successful in self employment, you should feel comfortable taking reasonable risks.

Sacrifices Employment Benefits: One of the major realities of self employment is that you won't receive a regular paycheck. You pay for your own fringe benefits. A nice office, secretarial assistance, equipment and other features of employment you have grown to expect are no longer available unless you provide them for yourself.

Has a Need to Achieve: Entrepreneurs have a strong need for achievement. They strive to excel and accomplish objectives that are quite high. You should be willing to set high goals for yourself and enjoy striving to achieve those goals.

Has Business Experience: An entrepreneur should have extensive business experience to be successful. General management experience is beneficial because an entrepreneur should know something about all types of management. Formal training and education in management also are helpful.

Is Independent

Entrepreneurs like to be independent and in control of situations. Many people who become self employed consider the opportunity to be their own boss as one of the major benefits of self-employment. Although being independent may not be a major concern for you, it is certainly an aspect of self employment that you need to feel comfortable with. If you cannot afford to hire other employees when you begin your business, you may at first be lonely as a self employed person.

Has a Self employed Parent as a Role Model: Research has shown that entrepreneurs are more likely to have a parent who is self employed. A parent's inspiration and knowledge about operating a business can contribute to an entrepreneur's success.

Has Self confidence: An important characteristic of entrepreneurs is self confidence. This factor is particularly important when you face major challenges and difficulties with your business. You need to believe in yourself. Your belief will help you overcome the problems that inevitably affect all self employed persons at some point in their careers.

Has Integrity: People often cite honesty and integrity as characteristics of entrepreneurs. Customers do not want to deal with business owners who are dishonest and unethical. You should feel positive about your ethical treatment of people and be committed to conducting your business with the utmost integrity.

Has Determination: One of the most important characteristics of entrepreneurs is determination. This trait is closely related to self confidence. The more you believe in yourself, the more likely you are to continue to struggle for success when faced with tremendous obstacles. You need determination in order to overcome the problems that beset every new venture.

Adapts to Change: A new business changes rapidly, so an entrepreneur must be able to adapt to change. Two primary skills are required for adaptation to change: the capacity to solve problems, and the ability to make quick decisions. Another skill is the ability to learn from your mistakes.

Has a Good Network of Professionals: An entrepreneur has a good network of professionals. This network provides access to those who can be consulted for advice, information, and referrals. You should have an extensive network of professionals to whom you can turn for assistance.

What are the Objectives of Guidance at Different Stages?

Guidance process is purposeful process. Without determining the objectives, this process cannot be completed or concluded. Due to the variations in the scope, guidance has a variety of objectives.

If we start guidance process without any objective it cannot be concluded because various sub-processes involved in the guidance cannot be given any direction and these activities ramain meaningless.

Objectives of guidance change at each level of education. Every stage of education enjoys different objective of guidance. For example, the functions and objectives of guidance at primary level will be different from those of middle stage.

Similar, objectives of guidance at high school or higher secondary stage will be different from those of middle stage:

Objectives of Guidance at Primary Stage: Every activity at primary stage includes guidance. At primary stage, there is need to pay special attention towards the health of the children. At this stage there is great need to coordinate the functions of a teacher, guidance worker, school, staff members of medical service and school social service workers.

All these persons help in learning properly essential skills for primary education, for acquiring basic knowledge, for adapting according to the social traditions and for developing proper attitude towards school activities. These too are the objectives of guidance at this stage. When a child leaves home and enters into the school environment, he has to make much coordination. School environment is very comprehensive for a child. In school, the child comes in contact with various types of persons, children and teachers. Also, he lacks security in the school and he becomes very fearful, hesitating and remains suppressed in the school. Those children are more in difficulty who are fully dependent on their parents. Primary stage ranges upto fifth class. During this period, children make their place in the school. Gradually they get themselves established in the school and they consider themselves an honourable member of the school.

When these children cross over from primary stage to higher stage, they feel suffocated. Behaviours of primary stage sometimes look like a joke. The traditions of new school, rules, administration, curriculum etc., are all new.

In such situations, the guidance worker plans the guidance programme in order to prepare the children of primary stage, for next higher school stage, such as arranging the visits of primary stage children to high schools, inviting high school teachers to primary schools, explaining the procedure for getting admission to high schools after leaving the primary schools, making them familiar with the curriculum of high schools etc.

In nut-shell we can say that the following are the objectives of guidance at the primary school stage:

1. To coordinate all the activities of all the workers such as a teacher, medical service staff members, school social- workers and the activities of a person providing guidance etc.
2. To assist developing higher attitude towards school activities,
3. To assist children adapting according to the school traditions and rules-regulations of the school.
4. To assist children in developing their physical and emotional stability.
5. Objective of finding out problems regarding adjustment in the school and to control them.
6. Objective of making children self-dependent.

7. Objective of creating the feeling of cooperation in the children.
8. Objectives of making children ready for crossing over from primary school to next higher stage.
9. Objective of supplying various informations to children regarding higher stage such as curriculum of next higher classes and distribution of booklets regarding various school functions among the children and their parents.

Objectives of Guidance at Secondary Stage: The child leaves primary stage and enters secondary stage. At this stage the scope of guidance becomes more comprehensive as compared to the scope of guidance at primary stage. At this stage, guidance becomes more important as a result of multiple reasons.

At this stage, teachers to teach according to the subjects. Therefore, all the children cannot contact all the teachers. At high and higher secondary schools, only subject specialists teach. At these stages, personal, social and vocational problems of the children come into light and solution of these problems is necessary. In order to achieve this objective, a comprehensive and organized guidance service is continuously required. In this way, we see the following are the objectives of guidance at secondary and higher secondary stages:

Objective of familiarizing with New School Life: A child is not familiar with the life of new school when he leaves the primary school and enters to a new higher school. He has to face a number of problems regarding admission. Also, it may become difficult for him to coordinate with new classmates and new friends. Hence, the objective of guidance service existing in the school should be to eliminate such problems of the pupils.

Objectives of Helping in Selecting the Subject: After reaching at this higher level, the selection of subject becomes necessary. In this task, the pupil may face difficulty. He is unable to understand in which subject he is competent and which subject he should not opt.

The selection of subjects has become very difficult task due to the variety of subjects. Hence, the objective of guidance mould is to understand this type of problem and the same should be solved.

Objective of Co-curricular Activities: Co-curricular activities are being considered very important for the physical development of the children, such as debates, sports, cultural activities, programmes of social service etc.

Hence, the important objective of guidance services is to guide the children for such activities so that their physical development may be given proper direction.

Objective of Fulfilling the Needs, Related to Students Health: The objectives of guidance service existing in the school is to take care of needs related to the health of the children and to inform timely the relevant persons regarding those health deficiencies so that the necessary action can be taken.

Objective of Maintaining the Records: In schools it is important to maintain the records regarding the development of the pupils, education, psychological development, cultural activities, because the entire guidance programme is to be conducted on the basis of these records. Hence, the objective of guidance programme workers should be to maintain such record so that the counsellor may feel convenience during counselling.

Objective of Emotional and Individual Needs: When an individual enters adolescence, an individual experiences emotional and personal needs. Therefore, the objective of guidance services should be to solve the problems related to such needs.

Objective of Cooperation: In solving the problems of the children, cooperation plays an important role. This cooperation is desirable in guidance at all levels. The objective of guidance services should be to create a feeling of cooperation among all the workers involved in this service. This cooperation acts as a substantial base for guidance at the next higher level.

Objective of Creating Environment: According to Crow and Crow, the creation of academic environment in accordance with the adolescent stage is very essential so that the pupils may be motivated in order to acquire higher education and they may be helped in selecting the subject according to abilities.

Objectives at College and University Stage: When a child enters the college he becomes a complete young man and his personality acquires has own pattern. Some of them have clear objectives. Some start feeling their responsibilities.

They are also very serious in their studies because they know the meaning of success and failure. But there are some persons who fail to understand what the college education means. They come to college without knowing what they can do. After securing admission to the college they face multiple difficulties. They consider their studies meaningless. That is why they go to college without any objective.

In such situations, the objective of college guidance programme is that the needs of such students should be looked into immediately who are unable to make progress in the college affairs and who can use their talent in their activities on providing proper educational facilities. In college, the objective of guidance service should also be to help the pupils in selecting the subject so that they can acquire specialization because such specializations help the pupils in their future vocational plans. Similarly other objectives of guidance service include organized programmes of tutorials and providing help to the pupils for making progress by studying the books existing in the library. It would be very meaningful if the students are made aware of objectives, nature and scope of college educations before its commencement in the college. According to other objectives of guidance service, the pupils should be informed regarding the various facilities existing in the college such as library facilities. If such is not informed, it would lead towards the wastage of pupil's time.

In this way, we see that there is no much difference between the functions and guidance objectives of high, higher secondary and college stage. Hence, the guidance objectives at college and university stage can also be presented in the following manner:

(i) To make available information's regarding admissions to college and university.

(ii) To provide information's regarding co-curricular activities in the college and university.

(iii) To help pupils selecting subjects so that they may achieve their future programme and objectives.

(iv) To provide vocational information's to the pupils so that they may take decision regarding their future.

(v) To arrange for testing the pupils.

(vi) The help the children eliminating their financial difficulties.

(vii) To make aware the pupils regarding the existing hostel facilities so that the problems of their boarding and lodging can be removed.

The objectives of guidance can also be expressed as follows:

(a) Objectives from pupils' point of view.

(b) From institution's point of view.

8

Behaviourist Theories

Behaviourists explain personality in terms of the effects external stimuli have on behaviour. The approaches used to analyze the behavioural aspect of personality are known as behavioural theories or learning-conditioning theories. These approaches were a radical shift away from Freudian philosophy. One of the major tenets of this concentration of personality psychology is a strong emphasis on scientific thinking and experimentation. This school of thought was developed by B. F. Skinner who put forth a model which emphasized the mutual interaction of the person or "the organism" with its environment. Skinner believed children do bad things because the behaviour obtains attention that serves as a reinforcer. For example: a child cries because the child's crying in the past has led to attention. These are the *response*, and *consequences*. The response is the child crying, and the attention that child gets is the reinforcing consequence. According to this theory, people's behaviour is formed by processes such as operant conditioning. Skinner put forward a "three term contingency model" which helped promote analysis of behaviour based on the "Stimulus - Response - Consequence Model" in which the critical question is: "Under which circumstances or antecedent 'stimuli' does the organism engage in a particular behaviour or 'response', which in turn produces a particular 'consequence'?"

Richard Herrnstein extended this theory by accounting for attitudes and traits. An attitude develops as the response strength (the tendency to respond) in the presences of a group of stimuli become stable. Rather than describing conditionable traits in non-behavioural language, response strength in a given situation accounts for the environmental portion. Herrstein also saw traits as having a large genetic or biological component as do most modern behaviourists. Ivan Pavlov is another notable influence. He is well known for his classical conditioning experiments involving dogs. These physiological studies led him to discover the foundation of behaviourism as well as classical conditioning.

Social Cognitive Theories

In cognitive theory, behaviour is explained as guided by cognitions (e.g. expectations) about the world, especially those about other people. Cognitive theories are theories of personality that emphasize cognitive processes, such as thinking and judging. Albert Bandura, a social learning theorist suggested the forces of memory and emotions worked in conjunction with environmental influences. Bandura was known mostly for his "Bobo Doll experiment". During these experiments, Bandura video taped a college student kicking and verbally abusing a bobo doll. He then showed this video to a class of kindergarten children who were getting ready to go out to play. When they entered the play room, they saw bobo dolls, and some hammers. The people observing these children at play saw a group of children beating the doll. He called this study and his findings observational learning, or modelling.

Early examples of approaches to cognitive style are listed by Baron (1982). These include Witkin's (1965) work on field dependency, Gardner's (1953) discovering people had consistent preference for the number of categories they used to categorise heterogeneous objects, and Block and Petersen's (1955) work on confidence in line discrimination judgements. Baron relates early development of cognitive approaches of personality to ego psychology. More central to this field have been:

- Attributional style theory dealing with different ways in which people explain events in their lives. This approach builds upon locus of control, but extends it by stating we also need to consider whether people attribute to stable causes or variable causes, and to global causes or specific causes.

Various scales have been developed to assess both attributional style and locus of control. Locus of control scales include those used by Rotter and later by Duttweiler, the Nowicki and Strickland (1973) Locus of Control Scale for Children and various locus of control scales specifically in the health domain, most famously that of Kenneth Wallston and his colleagues, The Multidimensional Health Locus of

Control Scale. Attributional style has been assessed by the Attributional Style Questionnaire, the Expanded Attributional Style Questionnaire, the Attributions Questionnaire, the Real Events Attributional Style Questionnaire and the Attributional Style Assessment Test.

- Achievement style theory focuses upon identification of an individual's Locus of Control tendency, such as by Rotter's evaluations, and was found by Cassandra Bolyard Whyte to provide valuable information for improving academic performance of students. Individuals with internal control tendencies are likely to persist to better academic performance levels, presenting an achievement personality, according to Cassandra B. Whyte

Recognition that the tendency to believe that hard work and persistence often results in attainment of life and academic goals has influenced formal educational and counselling efforts with students of various ages and in various settings since the 1970s research about achievement. Counselling aimed toward encouraging individuals to design ambitious goals and work toward them, with recognition that there are external factors that may impact, often results in the incorporation of a more positive achievement style by students and employees, whatever the setting, to include higher education, workplace, or justice programming. Walter Mischel (1999) has also defended a cognitive approach to personality. His work refers to "Cognitive Affective Units", and considers factors such as encoding of stimuli, affect, goal-setting, and self-regulatory beliefs. The term "Cognitive Affective Units" shows how his approach considers affect as well as cognition.

Cognitive-Experiential Self-Theory (CEST) is another cognitive personality theory. Developed by Seymour Epstein, CEST argues that humans operate by way of two independent information processing systems: experiential system and rational system. The experiential system is fast and emotion-driven. The rational system is slow and logic-driven. These two systems interact to determine our goals, thoughts, and behaviour. Personal construct psychology (PCP) is a theory of personality developed by the American psychologist George Kelly in the 1950s. Kelly's fundamental view of personality was that people are like naive scientists who see the world through a particular lens, based on their uniquely organized systems of construction, which they use to anticipate events. But because people are naive scientists, they sometimes employ systems for construing the world that are distorted by idiosyncratic experiences not applicable to their current social situation. A system of construction that chronically fails to characterize and/or predict events, and is not appropriately revised to comprehend and predict one's changing social world, is considered to underlie psychopathology (or mental illness.) From the theory, Kelly derived a psychotherapy approach and also a technique called *The Repertory Grid Interview* that helped his patients to uncover their own "constructs" with minimal intervention or interpretation by the therapist. The Repertory Grid was later adapted for various uses within organizations, including decision-making and interpretation of other people's world-views.

Humanistic Theories

Humanistic psychology emphasizes that people have free will and that this plays an active role in determining how they behave. Accordingly, humanistic psychology focuses on subjective experiences of persons as opposed to forced, definitive factors that determine behaviour. Abraham Maslow and Carl Rogers were proponents of this view, which is based on the "phenomenal field" theory of Combs and Snygg (1949). | Rogers and Maslow were among a group of psychologists that worked together for a decade to produce the *Journal of Humanistic Psychology*. This journal was primarily focused on viewing individuals as a whole, rather than focusing solely on separate traits and processes within the individual.

Robert W. White wrote the book *The Abnormal Personality* that became a standard text on abnormal psychology. He also investigated the human need to strive for positive goals like competence and influence, to counterbalance the emphasis of Freud on the pathological elements of personality development.

Maslow spent much of his time studying what he called "self-actualizing persons", those who are "fulfilling themselves and doing the best they are capable of doing". Maslow believes all who are interested in growth move towards self-actualizing (growth, happiness, satisfaction) views. Many of these people demonstrate a trend in dimensions of their personalities. Characteristics of self-actualizers according to Maslow include the four key dimensions:

1. Awareness - maintaining constant enjoyment and awe of life. These individuals often experienced a "peak experience". He defined a peak experience as an "intensification of any experience to the degree there is a loss or transcendence of

self". A peak experience is one in which an individual perceives an expansion of his or herself, and detects a unity and meaningfulness in life. Intense concentration on an activity one is involved in, such as running a marathon, may invoke a peak experience.

2. Reality and problem centred - having a tendency to be concerned with "problems" in surroundings.
3. Acceptance/Spontaneity - accepting surroundings and what cannot be changed.
4. Unhostile sense of humor/democratic - do not take kindly to joking about others, which can be viewed as offensive. They have friends of all backgrounds and religions and hold very close friendships.

Maslow and Rogers emphasized a view of the person as an active, creative, experiencing human being who lives in the present and subjectively responds to current perceptions, relationships, and encounters.

They disagree with the dark, pessimistic outlook of those in the Freudian psychoanalysis ranks, but rather view humanistic theories as positive and optimistic proposals which stress the tendency of the human personality toward growth and self-actualization. This progressing self will remain the centre of its constantly changing world; a world that will help mold the self but not necessarily confine it. Rather, the self has opportunity for maturation based on its encounters with this world.

This understanding attempts to reduce the acceptance of hopeless redundancy. Humanistic therapy typically relies on the client for information of the past and its effect on the present, therefore the client dictates the type of guidance the therapist may initiate. This allows for an individualized approach to therapy. Rogers found patients differ in how they respond to other people.

Rogers tried to model a particular approach to therapy- he stressed the reflective or empathetic response. This response type takes the client's viewpoint and reflects back his or her feeling and the context for it. An example of a reflective response would be, "It seems you are feeling anxious about your upcoming marriage". This response type seeks to clarify the therapist's understanding while also encouraging the client to think more deeply and seek to fully understand the feelings they have expressed.

Biopsychological Theories

Biology plays a very important role in the development of personality. The study of the biological level in personality psychology focuses primarily on identifying the role of genetic determinants and how they mold individual personalities. Some of the earliest thinking about possible biological bases of personality grew out of the case of Phineas Gage. In an 1848 accident, a large iron rod was driven through Gage's head, and his personality apparently changed as a result, although descriptions of these psychological changes are usually exaggerated.

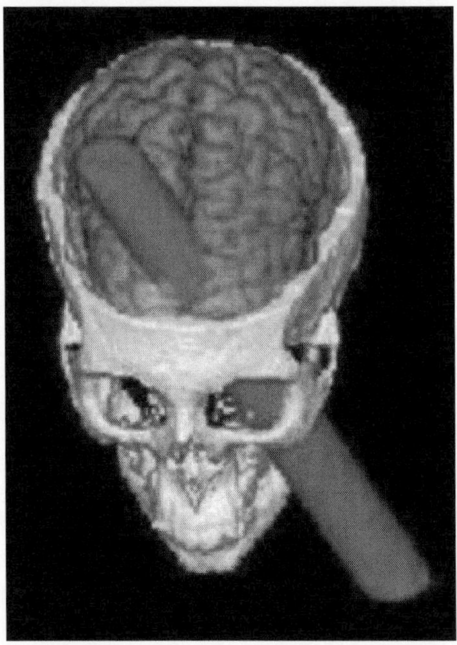

Figure: *Graphic by Damasio* et al. *showing how the tamping iron may have damaged both frontal lobes. (A 2004 study by Ratiu and colleagues suggests the damage was more limited.)*

In general, patients with brain damage have been difficult to find and study. In the 1990s, researchers began to use Electroencephalography (EEG), Positron Emission Tomography (PET) and more recently functional Magnetic Resonance Imaging (fMRI), which is now the most widely used imaging technique to help localize personality traits in the brain.

Genetic Bases of Personality

Ever since the Human Genome Project allowed for a much more in depth understanding of genetics, there has been an ongoing controversy involving heritability, personality traits, and environmental vs. genetic influence on personality. The human genome is known to play a role in the development of personality.

Previously, genetic personality studies focused on specific genes correlating to specific personality traits. Today's view of the gene-personality relationship focuses primarily on the activation and expression of genes related to personality. Genes provide numerous options for varying cells to be expressed, however, the environment determines which of these are activated. Many studies have noted this relationship in varying ways in which our bodies can develop, but the interaction between genes and the shaping of our minds and personality is also relevant to this biological relationship.

DNA-environment interactions are important in the development of personality because this relationship determines what part of the DNA code is actually made into proteins that will become part of an individual. It has been noted that while different choices are made available by the genome, in the end, the environment is the ultimate determinant of what becomes activated. Small changes in DNA in individuals are what lead to the uniqueness of every person as well as differences in looks, abilities, brain functioning, and all the factors that culminate to develop a cohesive personality.

Cattell and Eysenck have proposed that genetics have a strong influence on personality. A large part of the evidence collected linking genetics and the environment to personality have come from twin studies. This "twin method" compares levels of similarity in personality using genetically identical twins. One of the first of these twin studies measured 800 pairs of twins, studied numerous personality traits, and determined that identical twins are most similar in their general abilities. Personality similarities were found to be less related for self-concepts, goals, and interests.

Twin studies have also been important in the creation of the five factor personality model : neuroticism, extraversion, openness, agreeableness and conscientiousness. Neuroticism and extraversion are the two most widely studied traits. A person that may fall into the extrovert category can display characteristics such as impulsiveness, sociability, and activeness. A person falling into the neuroticism catergory may be more likely to be moody, anxious, or irritable. Identical twins however, have higher correlations in personality traits than fraternal twins. One studied measuring genetic influence on twins in five different countries found that the correlations for identical twins were .50, while for fraternal they were about .20. It is suggested that heredity and environment interact to determine one's personality.

Evolutionary Theory

Charles Darwin is the founder of the theory of the evolution of the species. The evolutionary approach to personality psychology is based on this theory. This theory examines how individual personality differences are based on natural selection. Through natural selection organisms change over time through adaptation and selection. Traits are developed and certain genes come into expression based on an organism's environment and how these traits aid in an organism's survival and reproduction. The theory of evolution has wide ranging implications on personality psychology. Personality viewed through the lens of evolutionary psychology places a great deal of emphasis on specific traits that are most likely to aid in survival and reproduction, such as conscientiousness, sociability, emotional stability, and dominance. The social aspects of personality can be seen through an evolutionary perspective. Specific character traits develop and are selected for because they play an important and complex role in the social hierarchy of organisms. Such characteristics of this social hierarchy include the sharing of important resources, family and mating interactions, and the harm or help organisms can bestow upon one another.

Mate competition within humans is theorized to play a very important role in the development of personality through evolution. Characteristics that are typically selected for through evolution are usually related to fertility and sexuality, as these traits will help ensure the continuation of the species. Some examples of this are traits that females seek in males related to features that will be helpful in a partner such as dominance, powerful status, and access to resources. Another such trait that can be explained by an evolutionary standpoint is sexual jealousy. Males are in competition to reproduce with the most fertile females and in order to prevent other weaker and less adept males from mating with their potential partners over time males evolved a predisposition to rage, aggression, and jealousy. It has also been speculated that violence and killing is much more common in young males because they need to eliminate their competition in order for successful mating and reproduction to occur. Consequently, the age in which killing occurs the most frequently in males is also the age in which mating is the highest.

One of the reasons in which men pursue romantic relationships can be explained by evolutionary theory. Sexual and romantic relationships increase the likelihood that an individual will be able to pass on his genetic material so men are predisposed to pursuing many women. Women have a different set of priorities because once they are pregnant they cannot reproduce during this time period and when they are rearing children they need to use the time they have available to nurture and protect them. Studies have supported this idea and found that in the area of romantic relationships and sexual behaviour men had felt much more regret looking back on the sexual experiences they did not have then did women.

Personality Tests

There are two major types of personality tests, projective and objective. *Projective tests* assume personality is primarily unconscious and assess individuals by how they respond to an ambiguous stimulus, such as an ink blot. Projective tests have been in use for about 60 years and continue to be used today. Examples of such tests include the Rorschach test and the Thematic Apperception Test.

The Rorschach Test involves showing an individual a series of note cards with ambiguous ink blots on them. The individual being tested is asked to provide interpretations of the blots on the cards by stating everything that the ink blot may resemble based on their personal interpretation. The therapist then analyzes their responses. Rules for scoring the test have been covered in manuals that cover a wide variety of characteristics such as content, originality of response, location of "perceived images" and several other factors. Using these specific scoring methods, the therapist will then attempt to relate test responses to attributes of the individual's personality and their unique characteristics. The idea is that unconscious needs will come out in the person's response, e.g. an aggressive person may see images of destruction.

The Thematic Apperception Test (also known as the TAT) involves presenting individuals with vague pictures/scenes and asking them to tell a story based on what they see. Common examples of these "scenes" include images that may suggest family relationships or specific situations, such as a father and son or a man and a woman in a bedroom. Responses are analyzed for common themes. Responses unique to an individual are theoretically meant to indicate underlying thoughts, processes, and potentially conflicts present within the individual. Responses are believed to be directly linked to unconscious motives. There is very little empirical evidence available to support these methods.

Objective tests assume personality is consciously accessible and that it can be measured by self-report questionnaires. Research on psychological assessment has generally found objective tests to be more valid and reliable than projective tests. Critics have pointed to the Forer effect to suggest some of these appear to be more accurate and discriminating than they really are. Issues with these tests include false reporting because there is no way to tell if an individual is answering a question honestly or accurately.

Inner Experience

Psychology has traditionally defined personality through its behavioural patterns, and more recently with neuroscientific studies of the brain. In recent years, some psychologists have turned to the study of inner experiences for insight into personality as well as individuality. Inner experiences are the thoughts and feelings to an immediate phenomenon. Another term used to define inner experiences is qualia. Being able to understand inner experiences assists in understanding how humans behave, act, and respond. Defining personality using inner experiences has been expanding due to the fact that solely relying on behavioural principles to explain one's character may seem incomplete. Behavioural methods allow the subject to be observed by an observer, whereas with inner experiences the subject is its own observer.

Methods Measuring Inner Experience

Descriptive experience sampling (DES), developed by psychologist Russel Hurlburt. This is an idiographic method that is used to help examine inner experiences. This method relies on an introspective technique that allows an individual's inner experiences and characteristics to be described and measured. A beep notifies the subject to record their experience at that exact moment and 24 hours later an interview is given based on all the experiences recorded. DES has been used in subjects that have been diagnosed with schizophrenia and depression. It has also been crucial to studying the inner experiences of those who have been diagnosed with common psychiatric diseases. Articulated thoughts in stimulated situations (ATSS): ATSS is a paradigm which was created as an alternative to the TA (think aloud) method. This method assumes that people have continuous internal dialogues that can be naturally attended to. ATSS also assesses a person's inner thoughts as they verbalize their cognitions. In this procedure, subjects listen to a scenario via a video or audio player and are asked to imagine that they are in that specific situation. Later, they are asked to articulate their thoughts as they occur in reaction to the playing scenario. This method is useful in studying emotional experience given that the scenarios used can influence specific emotions. Most importantly, the method has contributed to the study of personality. In a study conducted by Rayburn and Davison (2002), subjects' thoughts and empathy toward anti-gay hate crimes were evaluated. The researchers found that participants showed more aggressive intentions towards the offender in scenarios which mimicked hate crimes.

Experimental method: This method is an experimental paradigm used to study human experiences involved in the studies of sensation and perception, learning and memory, motivation, and biological psychology. The experimental psychologist usually deals with intact organisms although studies are often conducted with organisms modified by surgery, radiation, drug treatment, or long-standing deprivations of various kinds or with organisms that naturally present organic abnormalities or emotional disorders. Economists and psychologists have developed a variety of experimental methodologies to elicit and asses individual attitudes where each emotion differs for each individual. The results are then gathered and quantified to conclude if specific experiences have any common factors. This method is used to seek clarity of the experience and remove any biases to help understand the meaning behind the experience to see if it can be generalized.

Gray's Biopsychological Theory of Personality

One of the most widely accepted theories in terms of biological models in psychology is the biopsychological theory of personality proposed by Jeffrey Alan Gray in 1970. Gray hypothesized two systems controlling behavioural activity, the Behavioural Inhibition System (BIS) and the Behavioural Activation System (BAS). The BIS is thought to be related to sensitivity to punishment as well as avoidance motivation, while the BAS is thought to be related to sensitivity to reward as well as approach motivation. Using psychological test scales designed to correlate with the attributes of these hypothesized systems, neuroticism has been found to be positively correlated with the BIS scale, and negatively correlated with the BAS scale.

History

The Biopsychological Theory of Personality is similar to another one of Gray's theories, reinforcement sensitivity theory. The Biopsychological Theory of Personality was created after Gray disagreed with one of his colleague's theories. This colleague was Hans Eysenck, and his arousal theory dealt with biological personality traits. Eysenck looked at the ascending reticular activating system (ARAS) for answering questions about personality. The ARAS is part of the brain structure and has been proposed to deal with cortical arousal, hence the term arousal theory. Eysenck compared levels of arousal to a scale of introversion versus extraversion. The comparison of these two scales was then used to describe individual personalities and their corresponding behavioural patterns. Gray disagreed with Eysenck's theory because Gray believed that things such as personality traits could not be explained by just classical conditioning. Instead, Gray developed his theory which is based more heavily on physiological responses than Eysenck's theory.

Gray had a lot of support for his theories and experimented with animals to test his hypotheses. Using animal subjects allows researchers to test whether different areas of the brain are responsible for different learning mechanisms. Specifically, Gray's theory concentrated on understanding how reward or punishment related to anxiety and impulsivity measures. His research and further studies have found that reward and punishment are under the control of separate systems and as a result people can have different sensitivities to such rewarding or punishing stimuli.

Behavioural Inhibition System

The Behavioural Inhibition System (BIS), as proposed by Gray, is a neuropsychological system that predicts an individual's response to anxiety-relevant cues in a given environment. This system is activated in times of punishment, boring things, or negative events. By responding to cues such as negative stimuli or events that involve punishment or frustration, this system ultimately results in avoidance of such negative and unpleasant events. According to Gray's Theory, the BIS is related to sensitivity to punishment as well as avoidance motivation. It has also been proposed that the BIS is the causal basis of anxiety. High activity of the BIS means a heightened sensitivity to nonreward, punishment, and novel experience. This higher level of sensitivity to these cues results in a natural avoidance of such environments in order to prevent negative experiences such as fear, anxiety, frustration, and sadness. People with a highly active BIS have been shown to learn more effectively through use of punishment than by reward. The physiological mechanism behind the BIS is believed to be the septohippocampal system and its monoaminergic afferents from the brainstem.

Behavioural Activation System

The Behavioural Activation System (BAS), in contrast to the BIS, is based on a model of appetitive motivation - in this case, an individual's disposition to pursue and achieve goals. The BAS is aroused when it receives cues corresponding to rewards and controls actions that are not related to punishment, rather actions regulating approachment type behaviours. This system has an association with hope. According to Gray's theory, the BAS is sensitive to conditioned appealing stimuli, and helps curb impulsivity. It is also thought to be related to sensitivity to reward as well as approach motivation. The BAS is sensitive to nonpunishment and reward. Individuals with a highly active BAS show higher levels of positive emotions such as elation, happiness, and hope in response to environmental cues consistent with nonpunishment and reward, along with goal-achievement. In terms of personality, these individuals are also more likely to engage in goal-directed efforts and experience these positive emotions when exposed to impending reward. The physiological mechanism for BAS is not known as well as BIS, but is believed to be related to catecholaminergic and dopaminergic pathways in the brain. Dopamine is a neurotransmitter commonly linked with positive emotions, which could explain the susceptibility to elation and happiness upon achieving goals which has been observed. People with a highly active BAS have been shown to learn better by reward than by punishment, inverse to BIS as mentioned above.

Compare and Contrast

Together, the two systems work in an inverse relationship. In other words, when a specific situation occurs, an organism can approach the situation with one of the two systems. The systems will not be stimulated at the same time and which system is dominant depends on the situation in terms of punishment versus reward. This phenomenon of the differentiation between the two systems is thought to occur because of the distinct areas in the brain that becomes activated in response to different stimuli. This difference was noted years ago through electrical stimulation of the brain.

The behavioural activation system and behavioural inhibition system differ in their physiological pathways in the brain. The inhibition system has been shown to be linked to the septo-hippocampal system which appears to have a close correlation to a serotonergic pathway, with similarities in their innervations and stress responses. On the other hand, the activation, or reward system, is thought to be associated more with a mesolimbic dopaminergic system as opposed to the serotonerigic system.

The two systems proposed by Gray differ in their motivations and physiological responses. Gray also proposed that individuals can vary widely in their responsiveness of the behavioural inhibition system and the behavioural activation system. It has been found that someone who is sensitive to their BIS will be more receptive to the negative cues as compared to someone who is sensitive to their BAS and therefore responds more to cues in the environment that relate to that system, specifically positive or rewarding cues. Researchers besides Gray have shown interest in this theory and have created questionnaires that measure BIS and BAS sensitivity. Carver and White have been the primary researchers responsible for the questionnaire. Carver and White created a scale that has been shown to validly measure levels of individual scores of BIS and BAS. This measure focuses on the differences in incentive motivations and aversive motivations. As previously mentioned these motivations correlate to impulsivity and anxiety respectively.

Applications of the Biopsychological Model

Since the development of the BAS and BIS, tests have been created to see how individuals rate in each area. The questionnaire is called the Behavioural Inhibition System and Behavioural Activation System Questionnaire.

People can be tested based on their activation of either systems by using an EEG. These tests will conclude whether a person has a more active BIS or BAS. The two systems are independent of each other.

These tests can determine different things about a person's personality. They can determine if a person has more positive or negative moods. Using psychological test scales designed to correlate with the attributes of these hypothesized systems, neuroticism has been found to be positively correlated with the BIS scale, and negatively correlated with the BAS scale.

Now doctors and other professionals can determine if a person with bipolar disorder is on the brink of a manic or depressive episode based on how they rate on a scale of BAS and BIS sensitivity. If a person with bipolar disorder self-reports high sensitivity to BAS, it means that a manic episode could occur faster. Also, if a person with bipolar disorder reports high sensitivity to BIS it could indicate a depressive phase.

The BAS/BIS Questionnaire can also be used in the cases of criminal profiling. Previous research as reported by researchers MacAndrew and Steele in 1991 compared two groups on opposite spectrum levels of fear and the response of a variety of questions. The two groups in the study varied on levels of BIS, either high or low, and were selected by the researchers. One group was composed of women who had experienced anxiety attacks and together made up the high BIS group. The low BIS group was composed of convicted prostitutes who had been found to take part in illegal behaviour. Main findings showed that the responses to the questionnaires were distinctly different between the high BIS group and the low BIS group, with the convicted women scoring lower. Results from this study demonstrate that questionnaires can be used as a valid measurement to show differences in the behavioural inhibition systems of different types of people.

Future Research or Implications

As mentioned previously, psychological disorders have been analyzed in terms of the behavioural inhibition and activation systems. Understanding the differences between the systems may relate to an understanding of different types of disorders that involve anxiety and impulsivity. To date, there are many types of anxiety disorders that deal with avoidance theories and future research could show that the behavioural activation system plays a large role in such disorders and may have future implications for treatment of patients.

Hypostatic Model of Personality

The hypostatic model of personality is a view asserting that the human person presents herself in many different aspects or hypostases, depending on the internal and external realities she relates to, including different approaches to the study of personality. It is both a dimensional model and an aspect theory, in the sense of the concept of multiplicity. The model falls into the category of complex, biopsychosocial approaches to personality.

The term hypostasis can cover a wide range of personality-related entities usually known as type, stage, trait, system, approach. The history of the concept can be traced back to Peirce's hypostatic abstraction, or personification of traits. Different authors have described various *dimensions of the self* (or *selves*), personality dimensions and subpersonalities. Contemporary studies link different aspects of personality to specific biological, social, and environmental factors.

The work on subpersonalities was summarized by John Rowan in 1990. The term hypostatic model was used by Codrin Tapu in 2001. The model describes personality aspects and dimensions, as well as intra- and interpersonal relations. Not the person whole and alone, nor the relationship, but the relation between parts of person(s) is held as a central element that promotes both personal and social organization and disorganization.

Personality is viewed as both an agency and a construction, along with its development and psychopathology, as the model is accompanied by specific methods of assessment and therapy, addressing each of the personality dimensions. The hypostatic relations of the human mind also imply the existence of a hypostatic model of consciousness, representing the contents of consciousness as an identity of various aspects, different only with respect to each other, but tending to coincide in a certain aspect of their consideration.

Historical Background

Origins and terminology:

Charles Sanders Peirce introduced the concept of hypostatic abstraction, which is a formal operation that takes an element of information, such as might be expressed in a proposition of the form *"X is Y"*, and conceives its information to consist in the relation between a subject and another subject, such as expressed in a proposition of the form *"X has Y-ness"*.

In linguistics, Leonard Bloomfield introduced the concept of hypostasis to describe the personification of an object or state in sentences as *I'm tired of your buts and ifs*.

Aaron Rosanoff's theory of personality distinguishes seven dimensions (normal, hysteroid, manic, depressive, autistic, paranoid, and epileptoid), which can be epistatic or hypostatic dimensions, the manifestation of the latter being concealed or inhibited by the former.

Variants and evolution: selves and dimensions

In the philosophy of mind, double-aspect theory is the view that the mental and the physical are two aspects of the same substance.

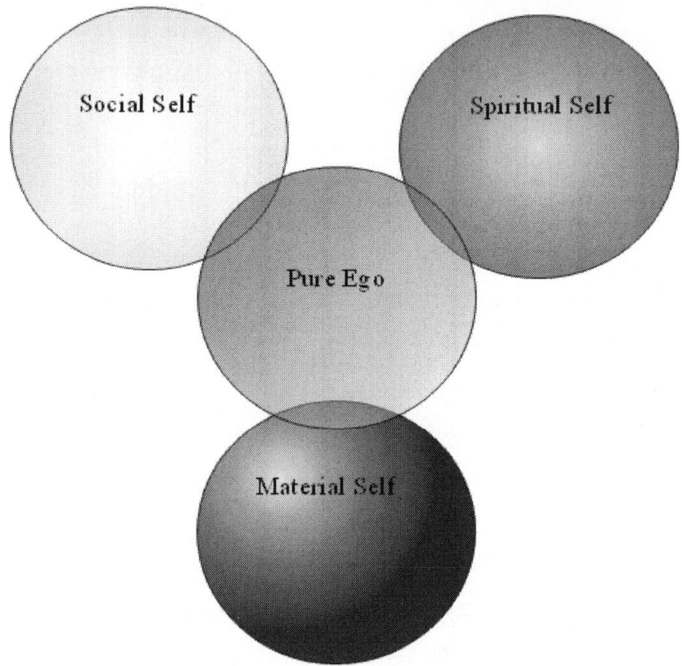

Figure: *Selves according to William James*

In his Principles of Psychology,William James describes four aspects of the self:

- material self (the body and the person's closest possessions and relatives, including the family);
- social self (the being-for-others);
- spiritual self (the person's inner and subjective being, her psychic faculties and dispositions, taken concretely);
- the "pure" ego (the bare principle of personal unity).

Using the same paradigm, cognitive psychologist Ulric Neisser describes five "selves":

- ecological self, as directly perceived with respect to the immediate physical environment;
- interpersonal self, also directly perceived, established by specific emotional communication;

- extended self, based on memory and anticipation;
- private self (our private conscious experiences);
- conceptual self, a system of socially-based assumptions and theories about human nature in general and ourselves in particular.

Carl Rogers distinguishes between the real self (the person as she is), and the ideal self (the person as the world told her she ought to be). Incongruence between these selves leads to feelings of anxiety.

Facet theory asserts that social-behavioural concepts are multivariate, and therefore they could be better described in terms of their "facets" and dimensions rather than as undifferentiated wholes; this can also be done using multidimensional scaling. Hans Eysenck's three factor model of personality contains the independent dimensions of extraversion, neuroticism, and psychoticism; these different dimensions are caused by the properties of the brain, which themselves are the result of genetic factors. The Minnesota Multiphasic Personality Inventory uses ten clinical scales measuring dimensions whose development and correlations in an individual determine her pathological tendencies. The Big Five model describes five personality dimensions that affect the whole behaviour, with each dimension having several facets. The Diagnostic and Statistical Manual of Mental Disorders uses a multiaxial system of diagnosis, taking into account five dimensions: mental state, global personality, physical condition, environment, and global functioning of the person.

Towards a Contemporary Integration

Differentiation between various mental states and behaviour patterns on the basis of their relation with brain and social environment became commonplace in contemporary psychology and sociology.

On the biopsychological side, functional MRI studies have shown that different behavioural and mental activities involve specific patterns of brain activation, corresponding to psychological states.C. Robert Cloninger defines three independent dimensions of personality, which are related to heritable variation in patterns of response to specific types of environmental stimuli; variation in each dimension is strongly correlated with activity in a specific central monoaminergic pathway:

- novelty seeking, with frequent exploratory activity and intense excitement in response to novel stimuli, and with low basal dopaminergic activity;

- harm avoidance, with intense responses to aversive stimuli and a tendency to learn to avoid punishment, novelty, and non-reward passively, and with high serotonergic activity;
- reward dependence, with intense responses to reward and succorance and a tendency to learn to maintain rewarded behaviour, and with low basal noradrenergic activity. These neurobiological dimensions interact to give rise to integrated patterns of differential responses to punishment, reward, and novelty.

On the social-environmental side, role theory defines the role as a set of connected behaviours, rights and obligations as conceptualized by actors in a social situation. Thus, roles can be:

- cultural roles: roles given by culture (e.g. priest);
- social differentiation: e.g. teacher, taxi driver;
- situation-specific roles: e.g. eye witness;
- bio-sociological roles: e.g. as human in a natural system;
- gender roles: as a man, woman, mother, father, etc.

Intersectionality is a methodology of studying "the relationships among multiple dimensions and modalities of social relationships and subject formations".

Roberto Assagioli uses the term "subpersonalities" for the social roles the person plays in different groups, roles that are mere "characters" played by the person, being different from her central inner Self.

As a core idea of his transactional analysis, Eric Berne asserts that there are at least three "persons" in each of us, calling them our "ego states": the Child (the emotional in us), the Adult (the rational in us), and the Parent (the authoritarian in us).

As functioning as a "society of mind", the self is populated by a multiplicity of "self-positions" that have the possibility to entertain dialogical relationships with each other.

Internal Family Systems Model combines systems thinking with the view that mind is made up of relatively discrete subpersonalities each with its own viewpoint and qualities.

Description

At a metatheoretical level, the hypostatic model argues that persons have several kinds of aspects, including, but not limited to:

- Adaptive aspects, pertaining to the internal organization of the person and the way she adapts to environment, including through actions and relations;
- Constitutive aspects - the ways in which personality is constituted within its relations with the organism and the external world;
- Temporal aspects, which represent the totality of forms that the person takes along the time line, short or long - including actions, states of consciousness, and developmental stages, as all these are only theoretically separated aspects of temporality;
- Referential aspects, which are the ways the person is perceived by herself or by the others (including personality scientists and theorists);
- Integrative aspects - various combinations of the previous, which can be (or have been) the object of numerous research projects in psychology and related fields.

Organization of personality

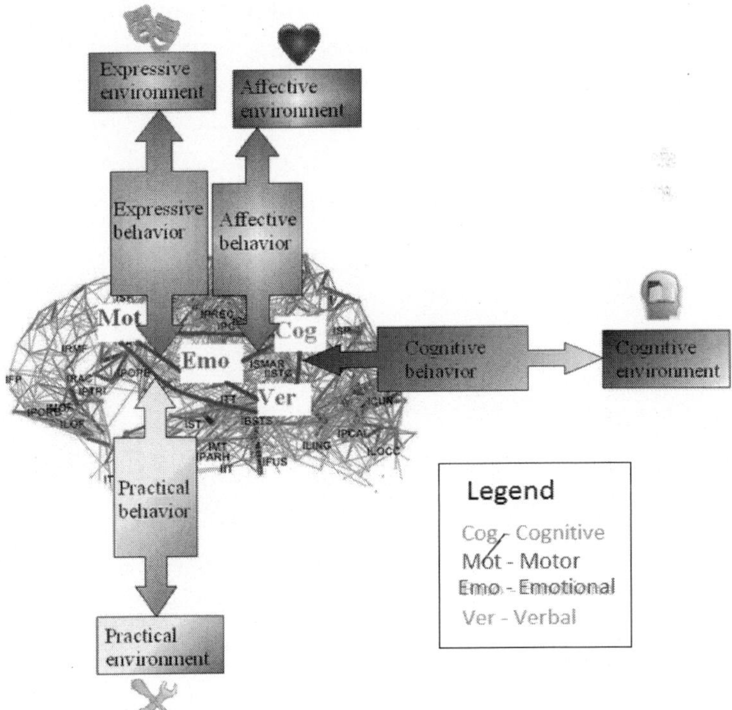

Figure: *Personality: brain, behaviour, environment.*

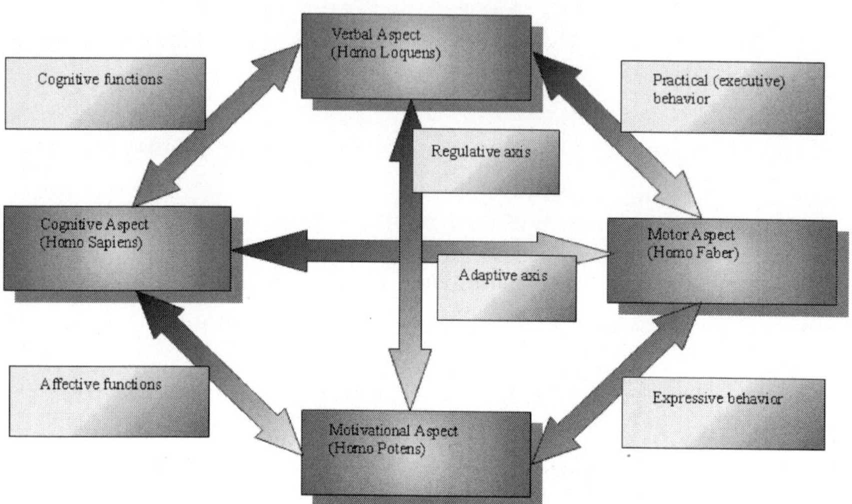

Figure: *Personality components*

Many schools of psychotherapy see subpersonalities as relatively enduring psychological structures or entities that influence how a person feels, perceives, behaves, and sees him- or herself.

According to the hypostatic model, human personality consists of four components or hypostases, which are patterns of traits pertaining to specific systems in the brain, and are conceptualized by virtually every culture as being characteristic and/or essential to humans:

- the basic cognitive component - "Homo Sapiens" (the intelligent person), which is in connection with sensory areas of the cerebral cortex;
- the verbal subsystem - "Homo Loquens" (the speaking, communicating, and [self-]controlling person), which is connected with the activities of association areas;
- the emotional and motivational subsystem - "Homo Potens" (the powerful and energetic person), which is correlated with the activity of the limbic system;
- the pragmatic (motor) component - "Homo Faber" (the productive and industrious person), which is linked to motor cortex activity.

One of these aspects can dominate the person, and lead to the development of - and adherence to - various philosophical views and schools:

- Cognitive-intuitive aspect focuses on concrete, immediate data, which are not subject of any kind of selection - it originated philosophical empiricism;
- Cognitive-intellectual aspect is only guided by reason; it leads to rationalism;
- Verbal aspect is dominated by all that is meaningful - it leads to philosophical nominalism;
- Emotional-hedonistic aspect views action as strictly limited to providing pleasure - it corresponds to philosophical hedonism;
- Emotional-idealistic aspect is dominated by superior motives of contributing to the world in accepted ways - it leads to stoicism;
- Pragmatic aspect values only things that facilitate practical action - it generates pragmatism.

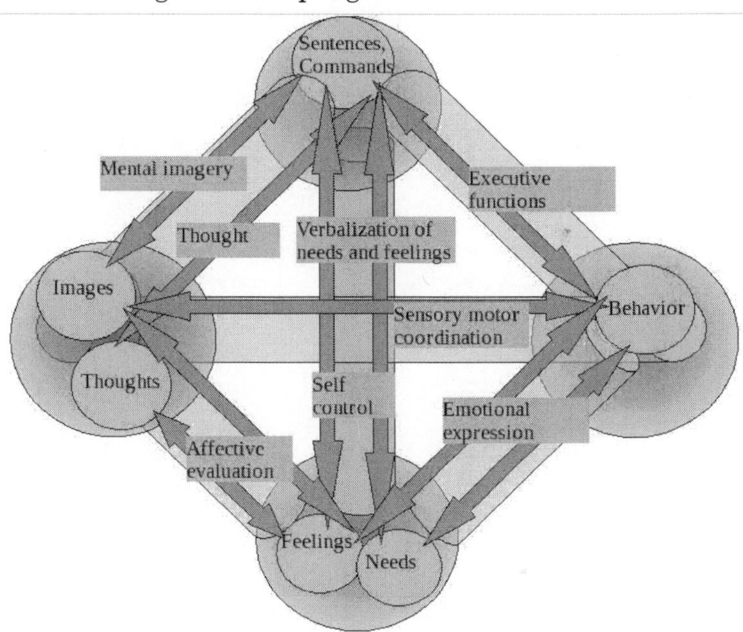

Figure: *Personality and mental operations*

Human behaviour is generated through the interaction and coupling of these human aspects, creating personality dimensions. The six behavioural, mental, and personality dimensions are:

- cognitive behaviour, generated by cognitive and verbal aspects;
- practical behaviour, produced by verbal and motor components;

- affective behaviour, conducted by cognitive and motivational components;
- expressive behaviour, "co-worked" by motivational and motor components;
- personality regulation, provided by verbal and motivational aspects, which form the regulative axis of personality;
- general perceptual-motor adaptation, performed by the cognitive component together with the motor component, which form the adaptive axis of personality.

These dimensions correspond to the following types of mental operations:

- cognitive operations - production and verbalization of images and thoughts;
- practical operations, pertaining to executive functions;
- affective operations - affective evaluation of the world and self;
- expressive operations (emotional expression);
- regulative operations - verbalization of needs, motives and feelings, and self-control;
- perceptual-motor adaptive operations (e.g., eye-hand coordination).

In every specific task of daily life, one of the first four dimensions (cognitive, practical, affective, or expressive) is dominant, being at the centre of the experience, whereas the other three are subordinated to it. Regulative and adaptive dimensions are constantly acting as a background throughout the behavioural process.

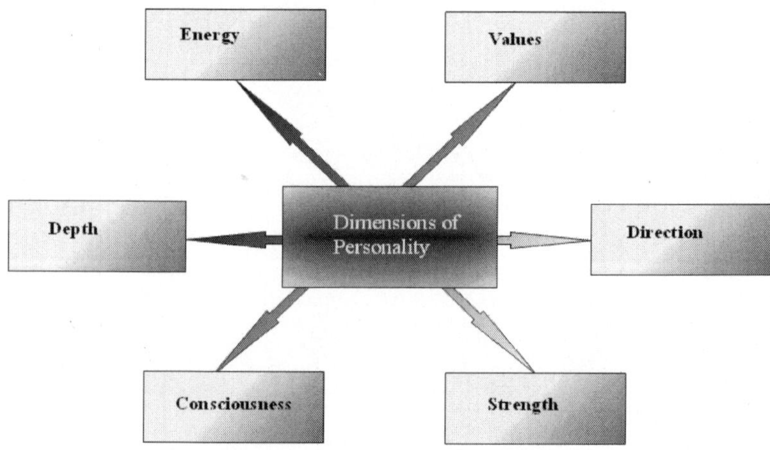

***Figure:** Personality dimensions*

Tessie J. Rodriguez describes personality dimensions as follows:

- Consciousness is the level of mental (cognitive) development;
- Strength is the overall capacity of the person to change or influence her surroundings, which is distinct from the vital or mental energy that she expresses;
- Values are what is most important or valuable to a person, and they imply evaluating what is good vs. what is bad;
- Energy is a subjective measure of the strength or intensity of personality (the vital or mental energy that it expresses through behaviour);
- Direction refers to the person's attitudes, motives, and intentions that regulate her behaviour;
- Depth refers to the levels of complexity of behaviour, ranging from simple reactions to complex adaptive patterns.

Rodriguez presents a composite view in which the six dimensions combine in complex ways to form "the web and woof of human personality". Within this view, the concrete, developing person may be represented as a point or a small three-dimensional object. Her trajectory for growth is to expand from that point in multiple dimensions to become a sphere, developing her four specific dimensions of knowledge, capacity, power, and enjoyment.

Cognitive and Affective "Paths": Brain Imaging Data

Research using functional magnetic resonance imaging of the brain suggests that cognitive and affective-expressive forms of communication and self-reflection have distinct neural bases. Clinical findings have long suggested that verbalizations are often very incoherent when the individual is trying to put into words something deeply emotional. Identification of words naming emotions (happy, neutral, sad) was found to be faster than identification of corresponding facial expressions. Recognition of face expressions was more difficult to suppress in favour of the recognition of words than vice versa, the two conditions presenting different patterns of brain activation. These experimental results suggest that reading and recognition of face expressions are stimulus-dependent and perhaps hierarchical behaviours, hence recruiting distinct regions of the medial prefrontal cortex. Research indicates that the representations of faces and objects in ventral temporal cortex are widely distributed and overlapping, face stimuli eliciting response patterns distinct from those elicited by object stimuli.

The phenomena that have been characterized clinically as "unconscious communication" may be defined systematically as emotional communication, which occurs both within and outside of awareness. Research suggested that the fundamental mechanism at the basis of the experiential understanding of others' actions is the activation of the mirror neuron system. A similar mechanism, but involving the activation of viscero-motor centres, underlies the experiential understanding of the emotions of others.

Activation of mirror neurons in a task relying on empathic abilities without explicit task-related motor components supports the view that mirror neurons are not only involved in motor cognition but also in emotional interpersonal cognition. Evidence suggests that there are at least two large-scale neural networks: frontoparietal mirror-neuron areas related to perceptual-motor interactions with others, and cortical midline structures that engage in processing information about the self and others in cognitive and evaluative terms.

Relations

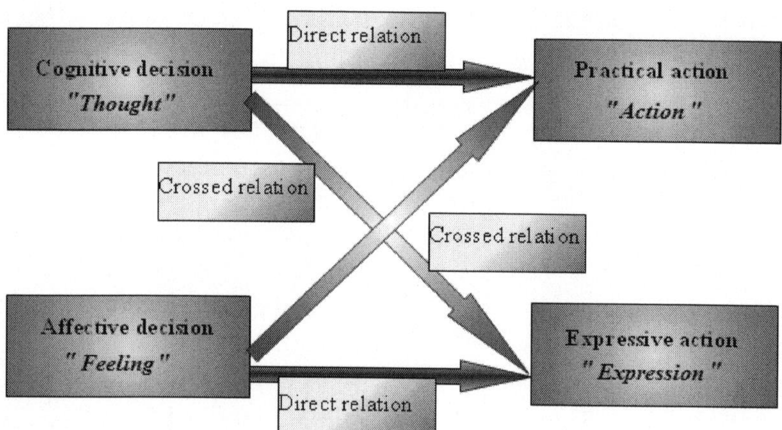

Figure: *Intrapersonal relations*

According to the model, intrapersonal relations can be:

- direct (adjusted) relations (cognitive decision followed by practical action: "I decided that's better for me to leave my boyfriend, and I told him that", or affective decision followed by expressive action: "I love my girlfriend, so I'm always gentle with her");
- crossed (unadjusted) relations (cognitive decision followed by expressive action: "Today I decided that it's better for me to

break up with my girlfriend, and I'll behave so that she will leave me", or affective decision followed by practical action: "We love each other; that's why we are moving in together").

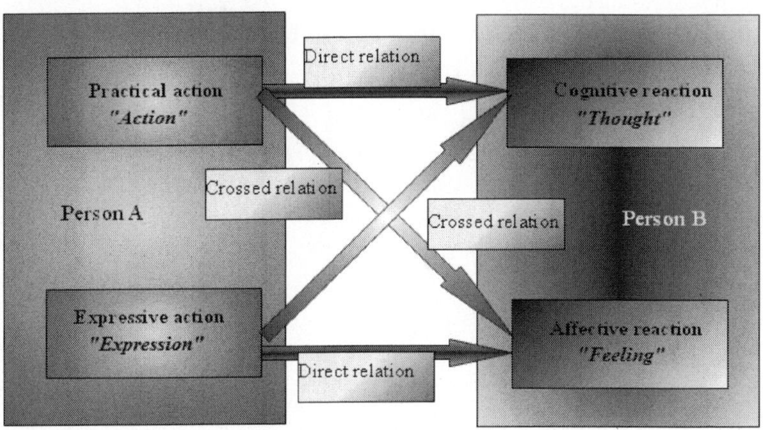

Figure: *Interpersonal relations*

Interpersonal relations can also be:

- direct (cognitive reaction to another persons's practical action: "My girlfriend wants to make up with me, and I agree, because that's better for both of us", or affective reaction to the other's expressive action: "She loves me, I can feel it in her eyes");
- crossed (affective reaction to other's practical action: "My partner wants to buy me a house, and therefore I assume he/ she loves me", or cognitive reaction to an expressive action of another person: "He is giving me a bitter look, and I'm wondering what is wrong?").

The locus of a relational disorder "is on the relationship rather than on any one individual in the relationship."

The Self

The self is the self-reflective dimension of mental life, which has long been considered as the central element and support of any experience, as the notion of "subject of experience" suggests. There is only one "me", but she is not always centre stage. Sometimes people are so focused on a task that they forget themselves altogether. The self is in fact at the centre of the experience only during self-evaluation. In cognitive, affective, practical, and expressive tasks, consistency of specific operations involved in accomplishing the tasks was found to be significantly higher than consistency of the results of self-assessment involved in the same tasks. Standard ways to tackle the self by considering self-evaluation do not target the self in its specificity. Instead, what is specific to the self is the subjective perspective, which is not intrinsically self-evaluative but rather relates any represented object to the representing subject.

We have no reason to believe that the self is permanently stuck into the heart of consciousness. I am not always as intensively aware of me as an agent, as I am of my actions. That results from the fact that I perform only part of my actions, the other part being conducted by my thought, expression, practical operations, and so on.

Unconscious Phenomena

As adaptive and regulative axes of personality provide integration of consciousness and personality, certain unconscious phenomena may result from the incomplete integration of one of these axes. For example, in subliminal perception, the adaptive, perceptual-motor axis is not properly integrated with other mental operations, and in dissociative disorders, the regulative axis is the one affected. If one of the axes does not function properly, both consciousness and performance in specific tasks are impaired.

Intelligence and Personality

Intelligence and personality are often seen as fundamentally different, a fact which ignores both the performance aspect of personality, and intelligence-related traits. Thus, cognitive and emotional instruments are artificially separated from their energetic and value contents. The concept of dimensional capacity is therefore proposed as a binder of behavioural performance and content.

Biological and Social Adaptation

The hypostatic model suggests that human behaviour is usually the result of the random interference of two separate behaviour systems: the "animal" system (biological adaptation) and the "human" system (social adaptation), both having the same biological underpinnings and partially sharing the same behavioural repertoire with different effects, not directly related. For example, while homosexual behaviour does not have biological (reproductive) effect, it has social adaptive value in cultures that permit it or, as in ancient Greece, require it. Also, heterosexual behaviour can have reproductive effect, but has no social adaptive value in monks or nuns. Cosmetic surgery has no biological value, but can be highly valued by society, while taking sleeping medication may have a biologically adaptive effect, but may not be socially adaptive in ascetic cultures. People can eat because they are hungry (biological adaptation), or because they like good food or want to enjoy the company of others (social adaptation). They can have sex to fulfill their sexual and reproductive needs (biological adaptation), or to fulfill their love, have children to bear their name, or simply have a good time together (social adaptation). People can use the same instinctual or learned behaviour to different adaptive purposes, biological or social.

In critical situations, biological and social fields of adaptation converge, forming an integrated, bio-social adaptation system: confronted with new and spreading disease and risk factors, modern medicine made people live longer, healthier, more productive lives, and that, in turn, set the ground for further progress of civilization. Nobel laureate Ralph M. Steinman prolonged his life with the help of his own scientific discoveries, and this allowed him to continue research in cancer immunotherapy.

Preliminary experiments needing extensive verification have suggested that in well-rested subjects, engaging in "biological" behaviour (eating, sex) does not lead to lowering of *mental* energy levels, as measured with a self-assessment scale, and engaging in "psychosocial" behaviour (cognitive tasks) does not lead to lowering of *physical* energy levels (measured with a similar scale). However, in subjects with exhaustion both results were positive (feeding-related and sexual activities lowered both physical *and* mental energy levels, and engaging in cognitive tasks did the same). These results have been interpreted as an indication that biological and social systems of adaptation are energetically independent in "normal" conditions, and become energetically integrated (create a common pool of energy) in exhausting, "heavy duty" situations.

In sum, do "human" and "animal" in us really struggle [with each other]? We say it isn't the case. Rather, there are times when Man is too busy being human to be much of an animal, and times when he is being too animal to be human enough.

Decision Making and Free Will

Subjects who had the possibility to choose freely between performing different cognitive, practical, affective, and expressive tasks reported that they chose each task because they either a) felt the need to do it, b) considered this was the task they could perform most efficiently in given circumstances, or c) for both previous reasons. No one of the three reasons above was statistically prevalent. This research suggested that human freedom can be scientifically interpreted in terms of an internal selection of environmental stimuli and internal variables, a selection which has a randomly variable, cognitive or affective locus. People with transient mental disorders, as well as people without disorders acted according to a probabilistic model, whereas those with chronic disorders showed a more deterministic pattern of behaviour.

Personality as an agency and as a construction

In addition to this "doing" dimension of personality, there is also a "being made" dimension, including the constitutive axes - each one formed of a mental content (which can be cognitive, verbal, motivational, or pragmatic, depending on the personality aspect), a mental and behavioural activity related to it (which can be cognitive, practical, affective, expressive, regulative, or adaptive), and their brain and environmental correlates, respectively. Each constitutive axis consists of two couples: one formed by a brain factor and the corresponding behaviour, shaping a psychological content (structuring a "trait"), and the other one formed by that psychological content and its environmental correlate, generating the specific behaviour (functioning). For example, assertive behaviour is determined by environmental factors and assertiveness, whereas assertiveness itself is the product of both brain predisposition and assertive behaviour. An obsessive-compulsive individual maintains his obsessions (*content*) if often left alone with his predisposing *brain* and ritualistic *behaviours*. A shy person (*trait*) displays less shy *behaviour* when in a familiar *environment*. This model provides a picture of the emergent relations between personality structuring, mental functioning (behaviour), environment, and biology.

Personality development

Development pertains to long term change versus stability of personality. According to the hypostatic view, the actual development of a person is the result of the opposition between stimulating and inhibiting factors of development, factors that are biological and environmental in nature. If stimulating factors are dominant, then developmental progress results (new acquisitions are made); if inhibiting factors are dominant, then the result is developmental regression (acquisitions are lost). If the two kind of factors are of relatively equal force, development is stagnant. Development can be accelerated, decelerated, or of uniform speed, depending on the dynamics of the relation between stimulating and inhibiting factors.

Type of factors	*Effect on personality development*	*Examples*
Biological	Stimulating	positive heredity, good nutrition
	Inhibiting	negative heredity, bad nutrition, trauma, disease
Environmental	Stimulating	good education, positive life events
	Inhibiting	bad education, negative life events

Childhood and Adolescence

Some of the characteristics of personality development during childhood and adolescence are summarized in the table below.

Age	*Regulation/adaptation strategies*	*Expressive behavior*	*Relational building*
0 to 12 months	Modulating reactivity	Expressive synchronization with others. Discriminating others' expressions.	Social play. Social referral.
12 to 24 months	Awareness of own emotional reaction	Self-evaluation generates expressive behavior	Anticipating different feelings towards different persons
2.5 to 5 years	Regulation of emotions. Awareness of own feelings.	"As if" expressive behavior in play	Understanding of relations and behavior expectancies
5 to 7 years	Regulation of shame	Fabricated expressions in the presence of peers	Coordinating affective and expressive scripts
7 to 10 years	Developing control strategies	Using expressive behavior to modulate relational dynamics	Multiple affective reactions towards the same person
10 to 13 years	Developing self-control in stressful situations	Differentiating genuine from controlled emotional expressions	Affective and expressive scripts related to social roles
13+ years	Awareness of personal emotional cycles	Self-presentation strategies	Increased awareness of reciprocal emotional communication[67]

Adulthood

During adulthood, the person is usually capable of creation and self-determination, and development can follow paths such as these:

- Evolutive–constructive–self-determined, which is characteristic to the free person who changes herself and the world she lives in according to her own projects;
- Stagnant–constructive–self-determined - the person who sacrifices her own evolution in order to invest her entire creative freedom in transforming the world (the "selfless creators");

- Evolutive–reactive–self-determined - the person who uses her freedom mainly to determine her own evolution (personal achievement);
- Evolutive–reactive–determined - the person affected by compelling biological factors or environmental events, positive or negative, that restrain her freedom (e.g. disease, war, winning the big pot);
- Stagnant–reactive–determined is the submissive, responsive, and complying person who lives in an non-stimulating environment (a "dull" existence).

Psychopathology

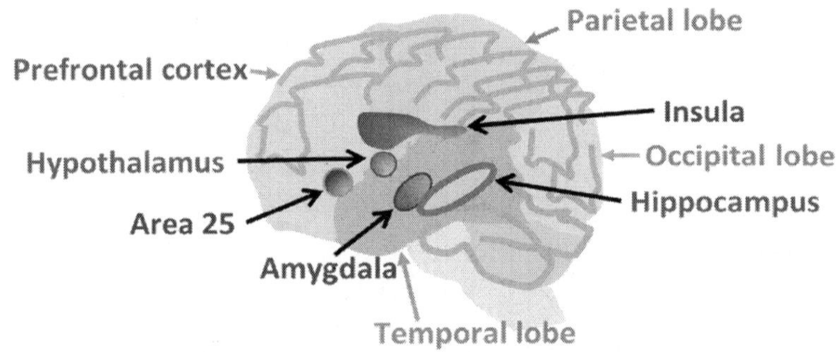

Figure: *Some areas of the brain implicated in psychopathology. Area 25 refers to Brodmann's area 25, related to depression.*

The unusual, the unnatural, and the counter-cultural in the area of mental life have been - in all ages - "subject of astonishment and reflection for individual reason, object of exclusion and confinement for social action", being met with "reserve or even repulsion by the public and with interest and even fascination by thinkers". In all cultures, aspects of internal disorganization*and* adaptive inefficiency of the person have generally been considered abnormal, whether they were referenced as "demonic possession", "madness", "mental illness", or "deviance" by different societies and theories. People displaying an efficient disorganization of personality and behaviour do their job in spite of the fact that they are not well organized, and are generally described as "strange" by others, while those presenting an inefficient organization are not successful in what they do, although their behaviour is consistent; they have a high rate of failure, caused by a low level of acquisitions and/or functioning. Efficient adaptive patterns are those in which specific adaptive behaviour is displayed only in situations that require it ("activating situations"), whereas inefficient adaptive patterns are those in which adaptive behaviour is inappropriate in the given situation. Inefficient adaptive patterns can be hyperadaptive, when adaptive operations are activated in both activating and non-activating situations (as in mania), or hypoadaptive, when adaptive operations remain inactive in both types of situations (as in depression).

People tend to neglect stimuli with low cognitive or affective significance to them, as well as forget excessively intense emotions and information that is too difficult for them to understand. Experiments performed on individuals which were given cognitive and affective (evaluative) tasks much above their current levels of cognitive and emotional competence led to difficulties in remembering the difficult tasks, associated with lowering of performance in previously mastered tasks. Improving performance in simple, repetitive tasks in anxious patients improves memory of failed tasks as anxiety symptoms decrease.

Broader Applications

The model of personality components and axes was extended to familial-organizational and societal levels. The model was also applied to the study of the historical evolution of human civilization in the process of globalization, as well as in the analysis of literary characters seen as novel creations "in humans' image" and part of the "neoverse" - the universe created by the author of a literary work.

Methods

Methodological Parameters: The hypostatic model uses several qualitative parameters for the assessment of personality investigation and intervention; these parameters can be applied to any scientific endeavour.

Parameters of Investigation Assessment

- Experimental productivity is the difference between the system of hypotheses and the system of experimental data resulting from the research; it measures the efficiency and precision of scientific prediction - a greater difference means a lower predictability of the experiment.
- Experimental progress is the difference between the hypothetical structure of the research and the structure of its conclusions ("theses"); it represents the contribution to knowledge of that particular research project. A greater

difference between hypotheses and conclusions means more new ideas suggested by the experimental outcome, thus a greater progress.

Parameters of Intervention Assessment

- Intervention amplitude is the difference between the current state of the person and her state projected as the outcome of the intervention - the "ambition" of the intervention;
- Intervention efficacy is the ratio of goal structure to outcome structure of the intervention;
- Interventional effect (transformation or change) is the difference between the person before and after intervention - it indicates the degree of modification of personality induced by the mental health professional or educator.

Nearest-neighbour Comparison

Nearest-neighbour comparison of two persons in a sample involves comparing a person A with the person B who has the closest match to A on one or more given criteria. It is also called the method of hypostatic definition, because of "defining" a person through her genus (in this case the nearest neighbour) by outlining her differentia. By comparing two very similar persons and trying to detect the differences between them, the researcher obtains a deeper knowledge of both persons.

The steps of the technique are:

- finding the nearest neighbour B of the person A;
- comparing the two persons (A and B) and finding as many differences as possible based on the methods used in data gathering;
- rebuilding a richer picture of each person (A and B), based on the differences that have been identified. For example, person B is almost as aggressive as person A (*nearest neighbour*). Through comparison it is found that while A is most aggressive at home, B is most aggressive at work (*difference*). Comprehensive data about concrete aspects of human personality gathered from many individuals all over the world can be digitized and stored in a "hypostatic library" with practically limitless growing potential, given the current developments in computing technology; data in this library could be used as reference in further research and practice.

Setting the Goals for Personality Change

In this kind of humanistic "psychological engineering", setting the goals for personality change is completely non-normative and non-judgemental. There is nothing wrong that must be remedied, no disease to cure, but an end state to be reached, like in the following goal formulations by the subjects and/or their families:

- "I want to be in a certain way, planned by me";
- "I want to be like I was before";
- "I want to be like other people";
- "I want to be the way that others want me to be";
- "I want to be different from how I am today".

Summary of Methods

The model uses the following methods of assessment and intervention:

- biological and ecological assessment through methods of dynamic analysis of development, investigating the complex interplay of stimulating and inhibiting factors of development and their effects on developmental speed (acceleration or deceleration), with prognostic implications;
- cognitive and affective techniques (method of prints of consciousness, based on self-coverage and self-report; human liberty test, using free-choice activities in order to study probability in an individual's behaviour);
- practical techniques (method of operational chains, a form of mental chronometry that ensured the identification of mental operations and allows the assessment of their speed and functionality);
- regulative techniques (task boosting techniques);
- perceptual-motor adaptation techniques (test of adaptive reactivity; method of adaptive therapy, based on non-specific perceptual-motor learning);
- psychopharmacological techniques, using drugs that act specifically on different constitutive axes of personality (cognitive, practical, affective, expressive);
- psycho-molecular method, influencing the activity of specific neurotransmitter systems through specific psychological tasks; the method is part of psycho-molecular medicine, which

integrates details of molecular structure into upper, psychosocial levels of the human organism.

- relational techniques, which aim to "set the things straight" by assessing relations and replacing crossed (indirect) relations with direct (straight) relations.

Psycho-molecular Therapy

The psycho-molecular method uses specific tasks in order to influence specific neurotransmitter systems. Through the control of the environment which is selectively enriched or deprived, some of the subject's brain areas can be stimulated or inhibited systematically, leading to changes in the seric levels of the metabolites of certain neurotransmitters, associated with clinical improvement in burnout individuals.

Behavioural approaches have a critical impact on molecular patterns of autoregulation, leading to the assumption of a bio-psycho-socio-molecular model of autoregulation, including stress and pain. Thus, molecules and behaviour may be seen as two sides of the same problem in pain and stress relief.

Psycho-molecular techniques can be stimulating or inhibiting. Stimulating techniques involve the presence of environmental materials that allow a single type of activity (cognitive, practical, affective, or expressive). For example, the subject sits in a room where he has nothing else to do except read.

Inhibiting techniques selectively exclude from the subject's environment materials that allow one specific type of activity, leaving all the other types available (for example, the subject can look at paintings, watch sports on TV, prepare his food, but has no books or other learning material in his room).

Stimulating techniques are:

- Practical technique, that involves living at a farm where the sole activity is food foraging and preparation;
- Expressive technique, that involves relational experiences in a room where the subject lives together with another person;
- Cognitive technique, that puts the subject in a room where books and other learning material are the only object of activity;
- Affective technique, that involves placing the subject in a room where there are only art works and audio and video hardware for listening music and watching movies.

Inhibiting techniques are:

- Cognitive technique, that excludes from the environment textbooks and other objects of cognitive behaviour;
- Affective technique, that excludes sources of affective and aesthetic evaluation;
- Practical technique, that excludes home appliances, cleaning activities, preparing food, and setting the table;
- Expressive technique, that places the subject in a room with all facilities, but where interactions with other persons are reduced at a minimum.

The control of the effects of these techniques is made through clinical scales and biochemical tests monitoring serum levels of metabolites of several stimulating and inhibiting neurotransmitters: dopamine (homovanillic acid), norepinephrine (3-methoxy-4-hydroxyphenylglycol), and serotonin (5-hydroxyindoleacetic acid). Although less spectacular than with psychopharmacological methods, the effect of psycho-molecular therapy is more complex and natural, and needs to be associated with psychopharmacological and psychotherapeutic treatments.

Relational Therapy

Relational (or direct relations) therapy (RT) is a method of psychotherapy aimed at changing the relations between the four dimensions of doing - thinking, acting, feeling, and expressing, both within the person and in her relationships.

Goals

The main goal of RT is improving client's communication and relationships through:

1. Replacing crossed intrapersonal relations with direct intrapersonal relations; instead of expressing what she thinks or acting out what she feels, the client should act the way she thinks and express what she feels. Characterological self-blame (through attributing affective and personal, relatively nonmodifiable sources to own actions) has been proved to be more depressogenic than behavioural self-blame (through attributing cognitive and impersonal, controllable sources to actions). For example, female victims of rape who said to themselves 'It was me, it was something I've done that provoked this' were more depressed than those who said 'The fact that I was walking through that part of the town caused the attack'.

2. Replacing crossed interpersonal relations with direct interpersonal relations; instead of feeling about others' acts or thinking about what others express, the client should think about others' acts and feel what others express. Many problems originate in acting to please or hurt others, and in being pleased or hurt by others' actions.

Being accepted and getting approval from others always will seem just out of reach. And, even if you succeed at pleasing others, you find that your fears of rejection, abandonment, or angry confrontation will not diminish or be alleviated. In fact, they grow stronger over time.

The Disease to Please creates a psychological blockade against both sending and receiving these negative emotions. For this reason, it cripples the very relationships you slave to satisfy and try so hard to protect.

Indications

The indications of RT consist of all kinds of relational problems that may arise in dating, family and work relationships, casual social encounters, as well as anxiety, depression, and other mental problems. In the case of problems in stable relationships, both partners should be assessed and participate in sessions, if needed.

Client-therapist Relationship

During therapy sessions, client and therapist promote direct relations between each other. For this they are required:

- to let their feelings for each other be expressed through their body language;
- to avoid verbalizing what they feel about each other;
- to freely and boldly verbalize what they think about one another;
- not to let their body language be the mean of communication of thoughts they do not dare utter;
- to try to feel each other's emotions as they are expressed through their body language;
- not to be emotionally moved by each other's actions, as in taking things personally;
- to reflect about the actions of each other;
- not to try to discover some meaning in each other's body language.

Relational therapy is in accord with other psychotherapeutic approaches in understanding the nature of human relationships and the therapeutic mechanisms: many forms of psychotherapy, such as psychoanalysis, person-centred therapy, and cognitive therapy, aim ultimately to create direct relations between thoughts and actions, and between feelings and expressions, so as the client's thoughts really get in touch with her feelings, and her expressions really support her actions.

We instruct the patient to put himself into a state of quiet, unreflecting self-observation, and to report to us whatever internal observations he is able to make not to exclude any of them, whether on the ground that it is too *disagreeable* or too *indiscreet* to say, or that it is too *unimportant* or *irrelevant*, or that it is *nonsensical* and need not be said.

— Sigmund Freud

Being genuine also involves the willingness to be and to express, in my words and my behaviour, the various feelings and attitudes which exist in me.

It is only by providing this genuine reality which is in me, that the other person can successfully seek for the reality in him.

— Carl Rogers

To help people achieve the three basic rational emotive behaviour therapy philosophies of unconditional self-acceptance, unconditional other-acceptance, and unconditional life-acceptance, cognitive, emotional, and behavioural methods are used.

— Albert Ellis

Initial Assessment

The initial assessment in RT has two main objectives:

- to establish what is the main problem that led the client to therapy;
- to identify crossed relations within the person, and between her and others.

Therapy Sessions and Techniques

A typical session of RT involves the following steps:

1. The client presents her crossed relations, as they occurred since the last session;

2. The therapist asks the client how she thinks the correct relation should sound like, and tells her that, if she could not say;
3. The therapist, along with the client, tries to identify crossed intrapersonal relations in people with whom the client interacts;
4. The therapist asks the client about what she thinks she could do to counteract those crossed relations, in order to improve communication relationships with those people, and makes suggestions to her, if she has no ideas.

Outcome Assessment

A final assessment through interview and questionnaire is made, to see:

1. If there are residual crossed relations in the client's life;
2. If she is able to prevent new crossed relations to occur;
3. If she is able to counteract crossed relations in others with whom she interacts, in order to maintain good communication relationships with those people;
4. To what extent the initial problems for which she addressed the therapist have been solved.

Treating Typical Problems

Interpersonal Problems: relationship management

Problem Definition: I decided that's better for me to leave my boyfriend, *and I tried to show him that* (expressing thoughts through behaviour).

Problem Solution: I decided that's better for me to leave my boyfriend, *and I told him that* (actively and explicitly communicating thoughts).

Problem Definition: My girlfriend wants to make up with me, *and I'm thrilled about that, because that means that she loves me* (feeling about the other's intended actions).

Problem solution: My girlfriend wants to make up with me, *and I think that's better for both of us* (thinking about the other's intended actions).

Problem definition: I love my girlfriend, *and I always make her gifts* (acting out feelings).

Problem solution: I love my girlfriend, *and I'm always gentle with her* (expressing feelings).

Problem definition: I can see in her eyes that *she thinks I'm smart* (thinking about other's expressions as indicating supposed thoughts).

Problem solution: I can see in her eyes that *she likes me* (feeling other's expressions).

An intrapersonal problem: fear of going to college

First, client and therapist identify crossed intrapersonal relations, through the following scenario:

- I plan to go to college [thought], but I can't do it [expression]. Thoughts not acted out give rise to pathological expressions (symptoms), because only feelings - and not thoughts - can be really expressed nonverbally. This is a crossed relation between thought and expression;
- I feel anxious and afraid [feeling], and I try to do something about that [action]. This is a crossed relation between feeling and action - the client tries to change his feelings through voluntary action but, as expected, he is unable to.

The first step of therapy consists of creating direct relations between feelings and expressions, and between thoughts and actions:

- I feel insecure [feeling], and that's why I can't go to college [expression]. The client interprets his inability to go to college as an *emotional expression of his insecurity*. This is a direct relation between feeling and expression;
- I plan to go to college [thought], and I try to do something about that [action], because I cannot simply command myself not to be afraid anymore (by means of rational decision). This is a direct relation between thought and action.

In the second step of therapy, the natural result of establishing direct relations is that the problem ceases to exist:

- I plan to go to college [thought], and I try to take concrete steps in that direction [action];
- I don't feel so anxious and afraid [the unwanted feeling is gone], and I feel I can go to college [the unwanted emotional expression is gone]. When I'm afraid about it [accepted feeling], I express my fears [accepted emotional expression].

Group Interventions

Relational therapy can be applied in families, organizations, and classrooms to change crossed relations and thus increase performance and satisfaction in work and learning. For example, confronted with a poor homework of a student, a teacher may think that by doing the homework that way, the student wants to defy him. If that is true, the problem is with the student - she tends to express her feelings indirectly, through her actions (feeling-action crossed intrapersonal relation). If that is not true, and the student was just lazy or incompetent, the problem is with the teacher - he tends to take personally and process emotionally the acts of others (action-feeling crossed interpersonal relation). Whatever the source of the problem, relations counsellor uses both individual and couple interventions, based on drawing a *relational matrix* of the group, which shows crossed relations. If, for some reason, one of the partners could not be changed, the other may be taught to compensate his crossed (distorted) relation through another crossed relation, the end result being an accurate communication at both rational and emotional levels. For example, if one of the partners is busy and does not have time to spend with the other, but does not dare to tell her that, and instead expresses that through his body language, the other learns to interpret this body language not as emotional indifference (what *it seems to be*), but as a sign of busyness (what *it actually is*), and thus she will not be hurt anymore.

Evaluation

Karl Jaspers criticized the hypostatic method as used in the study of personality, arguing that: Types, images, and theoretical systems are used by us purely as schemata of ideas to illuminate the path of our knowledge of particulars but they are not significant for knowledge in themselves. If now we objectify these schemata, images and theories and give them a being as if they were there as an object is there, then we 'hypostasise' an idea. This is the way in which ideas lose all their élan as a break-through movement of knowledge into the open and the knowledge we are left with is a sort of pseudo-knowledge which sooner or later will have to reveal itself as 'lacking in objectivity'.

— Karl Jaspers, *General Psychopathology*

Some presentations of the hypostatic model have been criticized for containing too many neologisms that make it difficult to understand, and for being "doomed to be incomplete".

The model was praised for being "original" and "provocative", and for inaugurating the field of "concrete-systemic" or "hypostatic" psychology. It alludes to understanding the affects of illicit substances and disease, as well as the underlying change in personality which likely ensues in relation. It shows that personality is believed to be static and relatively in-changeable, whereas ideology is more dynamic than personality. The model was quoted as one of the reference sources on the subjects of self, character, and personality.

Interpersonal Relationship

An interpersonal relationship is a strong, deep, or close association/ acquaintance between two or more people that may range in duration from brief to enduring. This association may be based on inference, love, solidarity, regular business interactions, or some other type of social commitment. Interpersonal relationships are formed in the context of social, cultural and other influences. The context can vary from family or kinship relations, friendship, marriage, relations with associates, work, clubs, neighbourhoods, and places of worship. They may be regulated by law, custom, or mutual agreement, and are the basis of social groups and society as a whole.

Field of Study

The study of interpersonal relationships involves several branches of the social sciences, including such disciplines as sociology, psychology, anthropology, and social work. Interpersonal skills are extremely vital when trying to develop a relationship with another person. The scientific study of relationships evolved during the 1990s and came to be referred to as 'relationship science', which distinguishes itself from anecdotal evidence or pseudo-experts by basing conclusions on data and objective analysis. Interpersonal ties are also a subject in mathematical sociology.

Development

Interpersonal relationships are dynamic systems that change continuously during their existence. Like living organisms, relationships have a beginning, a lifespan, and an end. They tend to grow and improve gradually, as people get to know each other and become closer emotionally, or they gradually deteriorate as people drift apart, move on with their lives and form new relationships with others. One of the most influential models of relationship development was proposed by psychologist George Levinger. This model was formulated to describe heterosexual, adult romantic relationships, but it has been applied to other kinds of interpersonal relations as well. According to the model, the natural development of a relationship follows five stages:

1. *Acquaintance and Acquaintanceship* – Becoming acquainted depends on previous relationships, physical proximity, first impressions, and a variety of other factors. If two people begin to like each other, continued interactions may lead to the next stage, but acquaintance can continue indefinitely. Another example is association.
2. *Buildup* – During this stage, people begin to trust and care about each other. The need for intimacy, compatibility and such filtering agents as common background and goals will influence whether or not interaction continues.
3. *Continuation* – This stage follows a mutual commitment to quite a strong and close long-term friendships, romantic relationship, or even marriage. It is generally a long, relative stable period. Nevertheless, continued growth and development will occur during this time. Mutual trust is important for sustaining the relationship.
4. *Deterioration* – Not all relationships deteriorate, but those that do tend to show signs of trouble. Boredom, resentment, and dissatisfaction may occur, and individuals may communicate less and avoid self-disclosure. Loss of trust and betrayals may take place as the downward spiral continues, eventually ending the relationship. (Alternately, the participants may find some way to resolve the problems and reestablish trust and belief in others.)
5. *Termination* – The final stage marks the end of the relationship, either by breakups, death, or by spatial separation for quite some time and severing all existing ties of either friendship or romantic love.

Friendships may involve some degree of transitivity. In other words, a person may become a friend of an existing friend's friend. However, if two people have a sexual relationship with the same person, they may become competitors rather than friends. Accordingly, sexual behaviour with the sexual partner of a friend may damage the friendship. Sexual activities between two friends tend to alter that relationship, either by "taking it to the next level" or by severing it.

A list of Interpersonal Skills includes:

- Verbal Communication - What we say and how we say it.
- Nonverbal Communication - What we communicate without words, body language is an example.

- Listening Skills - How we interpret both the verbal and non-verbal messages sent by others.
- Negotiation - Working with others to find a mutually agreeable outcome.
- Problem Solving - Working with others to identify, define and solve problems.
- Decision Making – Exploring and analysing options to make sound decisions.
- Assertiveness – Communicating our values, ideas, beliefs, opinions, needs and wants freely.

Flourishing, Budding, Blooming and Blossoming Relationships

Positive psychologists use the various terms "flourishing, budding, blooming, blossoming relationships" to describe interpersonal relationships that are not merely happy, but instead characterized by intimacy, growth, and resilience. Flourishing relationships also allow a dynamic balance between focus on the intimate relationships and focus on other social relationships.

Background

While traditional psychologists specializing in close relationships have focused on relationship dysfunction, positive psychology argues that relationship health is not merely the absence of relationship dysfunction. Healthy relationships are built on a foundation of secure attachment and are maintained with love and purposeful positive relationship behaviours. Additionally, healthy relationships can be made to "flourish." Positive psychologists are exploring what makes existing relationships flourish and what skills can be taught to partners to enhance their existing and future personal relationships. A social skills approach posits that individuals differ in their degree of communication skill, which has implications for their relationships. Relationships in which partners possess and enact relevant communication skills are more satisfying and stable than relationships in which partners lack appropriate communication skills.

Adult Attachment and Attachment Theory

Healthy relationships are built on a foundation of secure attachments. Adult attachment models represent an internal set of expectations and preferences regarding relationship intimacy that guide behaviour. Secure adult attachment, characterized by low attachment-related avoidance and anxiety, has numerous benefits.

Within the context of safe, secure attachments, people can pursue optimal human functioning and flourishing. This is because social acts that reinforce feelings of attachment also stimulate the release of neurotransmitters such as oxytocin and endorphin, which alleviate stress and create feelings of contentment. Attachment theory can also be used as a means of explaining adult relationships.

Romantic Love

The capacity for love gives depth to human relationships, brings people closer to each other physically and emotionally, and makes people think expansively about themselves and the world.

In his triangular theory of love, psychologist Robert Sternberg theorizes that love is a mix of three components: some (1) passion, or physical attraction; (2) intimacy, or feelings of closeness; and (3) commitment, involving the decision to initiate and sustain a relationship. The presence of all three components characterizes consummate love, the most durable type of love. In addition, the presence of intimacy and passion in marital relationships predicts marital satisfaction. Also, commitment is the best predictor of relationship satisfaction, especially in long-term relationships. Positive consequences of being in love include increased self-esteem and self-efficacy.

Referring to the emotion of love, Psychiatrist Daniel Casriel defined the "logic of love" as "the logic of pleasure and pain" in the concept of a "Relationship Road Map" that became the foundation of PAIRS'relationship education classes.

"We are drawn to what we anticipate will be a source of pleasure and will look to avoid what we anticipate will be a source of pain. The emotion of love comes from the anticipation of pleasure."

Based on Casriel's theory, sustaining feelings of love in an interpersonal relationship requires "effective communication, emotional understanding and healthy conflict resolution skills."

Theories and Empirical Research

Confucianism: Confucianism is a study and theory of relationships especially within hierarchies. Social harmony—the central goal of Confucianism—results in part from every individual knowing his or her place in the social order, and playing his or her part well. Particular duties arise from each person's particular situation in relation to others. The individual stands simultaneously in several different relationships with different people: as a junior in relation to parents and elders, and as a senior in relation to younger siblings, students, and others. Juniors are considered in Confucianism to owe their seniors reverence and seniors have duties of benevolence and concern toward juniors. A focus on mutuality is prevalent in East Asian cultures to this day.

Minding Relationships

The mindfulness theory of relationships shows how closeness in relationships may be enhanced. Minding is the "reciprocal knowing process involving the nonstop, interrelated thoughts, feelings, and behaviours of persons in a relationship." Five components of "minding" include:

1. Knowing and being known: seeking to understand the partner
2. Making relationship-enhancing attributions for behaviours: giving the benefit of the doubt
3. Accepting and respecting: empathy and social skills
4. Maintaining reciprocity: active participation in relationship enhancement
5. Continuity in minding: persisting in mindfulness

Culture of Appreciation

After studying married couples for many years, psychologist John Gottman has proposed the theory of the "magic ratio" for successful marriages. The theory says that for a marriage to be successful, couples must average a ratio of five positive interactions to one negative interaction. As the ratio moves to 1:1, divorce becomes more likely. Interpersonal interactions associated with negative relationships include criticism, contempt, defensiveness, and stonewalling. Over time, therapy aims to turn these interpersonal strategies into more positive ones, which include complaint, appreciation, acceptance of responsibility, and self-soothing. Similarly, partners in interpersonal relationships can incorporate positive components into difficult subjects in order to avoid emotional disconnection.

In addition, Martin Seligman proposes the concept of Active-Constructive Responding, which stresses the importance of practicing conscious attentive listening and feedback skills. In essence, practicing this technique aims to improve the quality of communication between members of the relationship, and in turn the gratitude expressed between said members.

Capitalizing on Positive Events

People can capitalize on positive events in an interpersonal context to work toward flourishing relationships. People often turn to others to share their good news (termed "capitalization"). Studies show that both the act of telling others about good events and the response of the person with whom the event was shared have personal and interpersonal consequences, including increased positive emotions, subjective well-being, and self-esteem, and relationship benefits including intimacy, commitment, trust, liking, closeness, and stability. Studies show that the act of communicating positive events was associated with increased positive affect and well-being (beyond the impact of the positive event itself a). Other studies have found that relationships in which partners responded to "good news" communication enthusiastically were associated with higher relationship well-being.

Other Perspectives

Neurobiology of Interpersonal Connections

There is an emerging body of research across multiple disciplines investigating the neurological basis of attachment and the prosocial emotions and behaviours that are the prerequisites for healthy adult relationships. The social environment, mediated by attachment, influences the maturation of structures in a child's brain. This might explain how infant attachment affects adult emotional health. Researchers are currently investigating the link between positive caregiver–child relationships and the development of hormone systems, such as the HPA axis.

Applications

Researchers are developing an approach to couples therapy that moves partners from patterns of repeated conflict to patterns of more positive, comfortable exchanges. Goals of therapy include development of social and interpersonal skills. Expressing gratitude and sharing appreciation for a partner is the primary means for creating a positive relationship. Positive marital counselling also emphasizes mindfulness. The further study of "flourishing relationships could shape the future of premarital and marital counselling as well."

Controversies

Some researchers criticize positive psychology for studying positive processes in isolation from negative processes. Positive psychologists argue that positive and negative processes in relationships may be better understood as functionally independent, not as opposites of each other.

Intrapersonal Communication

Intrapersonal communication is language use or thought internal to the communicator. It can be useful to envision intrapersonal communication occurring in the mind of the individual in a model which contains a sender, receiver, and feedback loop.

Definitions

Although successful communication is generally defined as being between two or more individuals, issues concerning the useful nature of intrapersonal communication made some argue that this definition is too narrow.

In Communication: *The Social Matrix of Psychiatry*, Jurgen Ruesch and Gregory Bateson argue that intrapersonal communication is indeed a special case of interpersonal communication, as "dialogue is the foundation for all discourse."

Intrapersonal communication can encompass:

- Speaking aloud (*talking to oneself*), reading aloud, repeating what one hears; the additional activities of speaking and hearing (in the third case of hearing again) what one thinks, reads or hears may increase concentration and retention. This is considered normal, and the extent to which it occurs varies from person to person. The time when there should be concern is when *talking to oneself* occurs outside of socially acceptable situations.
- Internal monologue, the semi-constant internal monologue one has with oneself at a conscious or semi-conscious level.
- Writing (by hand, or with a word processor, etc.) one's thoughts or observations: the additional activities, on top of thinking, of writing and reading back may again increase self-understanding ("How do I know what I mean until I see what I say?") and concentration. It aids ordering one's thoughts; in addition it produces a record that can be used later again. Copying text to aid memorizing, and note takeing also falls in this category.
    - o Writing need not be limited to words in a natural or even formal language. Doodling also falls into this category.

Children may be communicating intrapersonally when they doodle and adults sometimes argue that they do...

- Making gestures while thinking: the additional activity, on top of thinking, of body motions, may again increase concentration, assist in problem solving, and assist memory.
    - o Again, routinely observed in children, the equivalent of doodling without writing. Everyday images are transformed by gestures that form a new lens through which to view the images.
- Sense-making e.g. interpreting maps, texts, signs, and symbols
- Interpreting non-verbal communication e.g. gestures, eye contact
- Communication between body parts; e.g. "My stomach is telling me it's time for lunch."

Mechanisms

Our ability to talk to ourselves and think in words is a major part of the human experience of consciousness. From a young age, individuals are encouraged by society to introspect carefully, but also to communicate the results of that introspection. Simon Jones and Charles Fernyhough cite research suggesting that our ability to talk to ourselves is very similar to regular speech. This theory originates with the developmental psychologist Lev Vygotsky, who observed that children will often narrate their actions out loud before eventually replacing the habit with the adult equivalent: sub-vocal articulation. During sub-vocal articulation, no sound is made but the mouth still moves. Eventually, adults may learn to inhibit their mouth movements, although they still experience the words as "inner speech".

Jones and Fernyhough cite other evidence for this hypothesis that inner speech is essentially like any other action. They mention that schizophrenics suffering auditory verbal hallucinations (AVH) need only open their mouths in order to disrupt the voices in their heads. To try and explain more about how inner speech works, but also what goes wrong with AVH patients, Jones and Fernyhough adapt what is known as the "forward model" of motor control, which uses the idea of "efferent copies". In a forward model of motor control, the mind generates movement unconsciously. While information is sent to the necessary body parts, the mind basically faxes a copy of that same information to other areas of the brain. This "efferent" copy could then be used to make predictions about upcoming movements. If the actual sensations match predictions, we experience the feeling of agency. If there is a mismatch between the body and its predicted position, perhaps due to obstructions or other cognitive disruption, no feeling of agency occurs.

Jones and Fernyhough believe that the forward model might explain AVH and inner speech. Perhaps, if inner speech is a normal action, then the malfunction in schizophrenic patients is not the fact that actions (i.e. voices) are occurring at all. Instead, it may be that they are experiencing normal, inner speech, but the *generation of the predictive efferent copy* is malfunctioning. Without an efferent copy, motor commands are judged as alien (i.e. one does not feel like they caused the action). This could also explain why an open mouth stops the experience of alien voices: When the patient opens their mouth, the inner speech motor movements are not planned in the first place.

Evolved to Avoid People

Joseph Jordania suggested that talking to oneself can be used to avoid silence. According to him, the ancestors of humans, like many other social animals, used contact calls to maintain constant contact with the members of the group, and a signal of danger was communicated through becoming silent and freezing. Because of the human evolutionary history, prolonged silence is perceived as a sign of danger and triggers a feeling of uneasiness and fear. According to Jordania, talking to oneself is only one of the ways to fill in prolonged gaps of silence in humans. Other ways of filling in prolonged silence are humming, whistling, finger drumming, or having TV, radio or music on all the time.

Criticism of the Concept

In 1992, a chapter in *Communication Yearbook #15*, argued that "intrapersonal communication" is a flawed concept. The chapter first itemized the various definitions. Intrapersonal communication, it appears, arises from a series of logical and linguistic improprieties. The descriptor itself, 'intrapersonal communication' is ambiguous: many definitions appear to be circular since they borrow, apply and thereby distort conceptual features (e.g., sender, receiver, message, dialogue) drawn from normal inter-person communication; unknown entities or person-parts allegedly conduct the 'intrapersonal' exchange; in many cases, a very private language is posited which, upon analysis, turns out to be totally inaccessible and ultimately indefensible. In general, intrapersonal communication appears to arise from the tendency to interpret the inner mental processes that precede and accompany our communicative behaviours as if they too were yet another kind of communication process. The overall point is that this reconstruction of our inner mental processes in the language and idioms of everyday public conversation is highly questionable, tenuous at best.

Other Viewpoints

Dr. Sian Beilock, cognitive psychology professor at the University of Chicago, presents several techniques in her book *Choke*, that could offer help to anyone facing a challenging situation and struggling with mental chatter. It has been widely accepted that speaking in front of a crowd causes people considerable stress. Dr. Beilock suggests that practicing in front of family or friends does not help overcome this fear. She states that these so-called "friendly faces" can cause the person to become more self-conscious which can lead to the possibility of further choking. The elevated motivation to please parents or friends is what she theorizes causes brain functions to freeze. Since self talk is a form of self-regulation, parents or instructors could use this technique to help focus a young student's inner dialogue towards a process goal instead of an outcome based goal. When applied in an educational psychology classroom scenario, teachers can instruct students to focus on presentation material ignoring consequences, expectations, and/or the attempt to impress instructors or classmates.

9

Big Five Personality Traits

In psychology, the Big Five personality traits are five broad domains or dimensions of personality that are used to describe human personality. The theory based on the Big Five factors is called the Five Factor Model (FFM).The Big Five factors are openness, conscientiousness, extraversion, agreeableness, and neuroticism. Acronyms commonly used to refer to the five traits collectively are OCEAN, NEOAC, or CANOE. Beneath each factor, a cluster of correlated specific traits is found; for example, extraversion includes such related qualities as gregariousness, assertiveness, excitement seeking, warmth, activity, and positive emotions.

The Big Five has been preferably used rather than other models, because it is able to account for different traits in personality without overlapping. During studies, the Big Five personality traits show consistency in interviews, self-descriptions and observations. Moreover, this five-factor structure seems to be found across a wide range of participants of different ages and of different cultures.

The Five Factors

A summary of the factors of the Big Five and their constituent traits:

- Openness to experience: (*inventive/curious* vs. *consistent/cautious*). Appreciation for art, emotion, adventure, unusual ideas, curiosity, and variety of experience. Openness reflects the degree of intellectual curiosity, creativity and a preference for novelty and variety a person has. It is also described as the extent to which a person is imaginative or independent, and depicts a personal preference for a variety of activities over a strict routine. Some disagreement remains about how to interpret the openness factor, which is sometimes called "intellect" rather than openness to experience.

- Conscientiousness: (*efficient/organized* vs. *easy-going/careless*). A tendency to show self-discipline, act dutifully, and aim for achievement; planned rather than spontaneous behaviour; organized, and dependable.
- Extraversion: (*outgoing/energetic* vs. *solitary/reserved*). Energy, positive emotions, surgency, assertiveness, sociability and the tendency to seek stimulation in the company of others, and talkativeness.
- Agreeableness: (*friendly/compassionate* vs. *cold/unkind*). A tendency to be compassionate and cooperative rather than suspicious and antagonistic towards others. It is also a measure of ones' trusting and helpful nature, and whether a person is generally well tempered or not.
- Neuroticism: (*sensitive/nervous* vs. *secure/confident*). The tendency to experience unpleasant emotions easily, such as anger, anxiety, depression, or vulnerability. Neuroticism also refers to the degree of emotional stability and impulse control and is sometimes referred to by its low pole, "emotional stability".

The Big Five Model was discovered and defined by several independent sets of researchers. These researchers began by studying known personality traits and then factor-analyzing hundreds of measures of these traits (in self-report and questionnaire data, peer ratings, and objective measures from experimental settings) in order to find the underlying factors of personality. The Big five personality traits was the model to comprehend the relationship between personality and academic behaviours.

The initial model was advanced by Ernest Tupes and Raymond Christal in 1961 but failed to reach an academic audience until the 1980s. In 1990, J.M. Digman advanced his five factor model of personality, which Lewis Goldberg extended to the highest level of organization. These five overarching domains have been found to contain and subsume most known personality traits and are assumed to represent the basic structure behind all personality traits. These five factors provide a rich conceptual framework for integrating all the research findings and theory in personality psychology.

At least four sets of researchers have worked independently for decades on this problem and have identified generally the same Big Five factors: Tupes and Cristal were first, followed by Goldberg at the Oregon Research Institute, Cattell at the University of Illinois, and Costa and McCrae at the National Institutes of Health. These four sets of researchers used somewhat different methods in finding the five traits, and thus each set of five factors has somewhat different names and definitions. However, all have been found to be highly inter-correlated and factor-analytically aligned.

Because the Big Five traits are broad and comprehensive, they are not nearly as powerful in predicting and explaining actual behaviour as are the more numerous lower-level traits. Many studies have confirmed that in predicting actual behaviour the more numerous facet or primary level traits are far more effective (e.g., Mershon & Gorsuch, 1988; Paunonon & Ashton, 2001)

Each of the Big Five personality traits contains two separate, but correlated, aspects reflecting a level of personality below the broad domains but above the many facet scales that also comprise the Big Five. The aspects are labelled as follows: Volatility and Withdrawal for Neuroticism; Enthusiasm and Assertiveness for Extraversion; Intellect and Openness for Openness/Intellect; Industriousness and Orderliness for Conscientiousness; and Compassion and Politeness for Agreeableness.

Openness to Experience

Openness is a general appreciation for art, emotion, adventure, unusual ideas, imagination, curiosity, and variety of experience. People who are open to experience are intellectually curious, appreciative of art, and sensitive to beauty. They tend to be, when compared to closed people, more creative and more aware of their feelings. They are more likely to hold unconventional beliefs. On average, people who register high in openness are intellectually curious, open to emotion, interested in art, and willing to try new things. A particular individual, however, may have a high overall openness score and be interested in learning and exploring new cultures but have no great interest in art or poetry. There is a strong connection between liberal ethics and openness to experience such as support for policies endorsing racial tolerance. Another characteristic of the open cognitive style is a facility for thinking in symbols and abstractions far removed from concrete experience. People with low scores on openness tend to have more conventional, traditional interests. They prefer the plain, straightforward, and obvious over the complex, ambiguous, and subtle. They may regard the arts and sciences with suspicion or view these endeavours as uninteresting. Closed people prefer familiarity over novelty; they are conservative and resistant to change.

Sample Openness Items

- I have a rich vocabulary.
- I have a vivid imagination.
- I have excellent ideas.
- I am quick to understand things.
- I use difficult words.
- I spend time reflecting on things.
- I am full of ideas.
- I am not interested in abstractions. (*reversed*)
- I do not have a good imagination. (*reversed*)
- I have difficulty understanding abstract ideas. (*reversed*)

Conscientiousness

Conscientiousness is a tendency to show self-discipline, act dutifully, and aim for achievement against measures or outside expectations. It is related to the way in which people control, regulate, and direct their impulses. High scores on conscientiousness indicate a preference for planned rather than spontaneous behaviour. The average level of conscientiousness rises among young adults and then declines among older adults.

Sample Conscientiousness Items

- I am always prepared.
- I pay attention to details.
- I get chores done right away.
- I like order.
- I follow a schedule.
- I am exacting in my work.
- I leave my belongings around. (*reversed*)
- I make a mess of things. (*reversed*)
- I often forget to put things back in their proper place. (*reversed*)
- I shirk my duties. (*reversed*)

Extraversion

Extraversion is characterized by breadth of activities (as opposed to depth), surgency from external activity/situations, and energy creation from external means. The trait is marked by pronounced engagement with the external world. Extraverts enjoy interacting with people, and are often perceived as full of energy. They tend to be enthusiastic, action-oriented individuals. They possess high group visibility, like to talk, and assert themselves.

Introverts have lower social engagement and energy levels than extraverts. They tend to seem quiet, low-key, deliberate, and less involved in the social world. Their lack of social involvement should not be interpreted as shyness or depression; instead they are more independent of their social world than extraverts. Introverts need less stimulation than extraverts and more time alone. This does not mean that they are unfriendly or antisocial; rather, they are reserved in social situations.

Sample Extraversion Items

- I am the life of the party.
- I don't mind being the centre of attention.
- I feel comfortable around people.
- I start conversations.
- I talk to a lot of different people at parties.
- I don't talk a lot. (*reversed*)
- I keep in the background. (*reversed*)
- I think a lot before I speak or act. (*reversed*)
- I don't like to draw attention to myself. (*reversed*)
- I am quiet around strangers. (*reversed*)
- I have no intention of talking in large crowds. (*reversed*)

Agreeableness

Agreeableness is a tendency to be compassionate and cooperative rather than suspicious and antagonistic towards others. The trait reflects individual differences in general concern for social harmony. Agreeable individuals value getting along with others. They are generally considerate, friendly, generous, helpful, and willing to compromise their interests with others. Agreeable people also have an optimistic view of human nature.

Although agreeableness is positively correlated with good teamwork skills, it is negatively correlated with leadership skills. Those who voice out their opinion in a team environment tend to move up the corporate rankings, whereas the ones that do not remain in the same position, usually labelled as the followers of the team.

Disagreeable individuals place self-interest above getting along with others. They are generally unconcerned with others' well-being, and are less likely to extend themselves for other people. Sometimes their skepticism about others' motives causes them to be suspicious, unfriendly, and uncooperative.

Sample Agreeableness Items

- I am interested in people.
- I sympathize with others' feelings.
- I have a soft heart.
- I take time out for others.
- I feel others' emotions.
- I make people feel at ease.
- I am not really interested in others. (*reversed*)
- I insult people. (*reversed*)
- I am not interested in other people's problems. (*reversed*)
- I feel little concern for others. (*reversed*)

Neuroticism

Neuroticism is the tendency to experience negative emotions, such as anger, anxiety, or depression. It is sometimes called emotional instability, or is reversed and referred to as emotional stability. According to Eysenck's (1967) theory of personality, neuroticism is interlinked with low tolerance for stress or aversive stimuli. Those who score high in neuroticism are emotionally reactive and vulnerable to stress. They are more likely to interpret ordinary situations as threatening, and minor frustrations as hopelessly difficult. Their negative emotional reactions tend to persist for unusually long periods of time, which means they are often in a bad mood. For instance, neuroticism is connected to a pessimistic approach toward work, confidence that work impedes with personal relationships, and apparent anxiety linked with work. Furthermore, those who score high on neuroticism may display more skin conductance reactivity than those who score low on neuroticism. These problems in emotional regulation can diminish the ability of a person scoring high on neuroticism to think clearly, make decisions, and cope effectively with stress. Lacking contentment in one's life achievements can correlate with high neuroticism scores and increase one's likelihood of falling into clinical depression.

At the other end of the scale, individuals who score low in neuroticism are less easily upset and are less emotionally reactive. They tend to be calm, emotionally stable, and free from persistent negative feelings. Freedom from negative feelings does not mean that low scorers experience a lot of positive feelings.

Research suggests extraversion and neuroticism are negatively correlated.

Neuroticism is similar but not identical to being neurotic in the Freudian sense. Some psychologists prefer to call neuroticism by the term emotional stability to differentiate it from the term neurotic in a career test.

Sample Neuroticism Items

- I am easily disturbed.
- I change my mood a lot.
- I get irritated easily.
- I get stressed out easily.
- I get upset easily.
- I have frequent mood swings.
- I often feel blue.
- I worry about things.
- I am relaxed most of the time. (*reversed*)
- I seldom feel blue. (*reversed*)
- I am much more anxious than most people.

History

Early Trait Research: Sir Francis Galton made the first major enquiry into a hypothesis that by sampling language it is possible to derive a comprehensive taxonomy of human personality traits- the lexical hypothesis. In 1936 Gordon Allport and S.Odbert put Sir Francis Galton's hypothesis into practice by extracting 4,504 adjectives which they believed were descriptive of observable and relatively permanent traits from the dictionaries at that time. In 1940, Raymond

Cattell obtained the adjectives, and eliminated synonyms to reduce the total to 171. He constructed a personality test for the clusters of personality traits he found from the adjectives, called Sixteen Personality Factor Questionnaire. Then, in 1961, Ernest Tupes and Raymond Christal found five recurring factors from this 16PF Questionnaire. The recurring five factors were: "surgency", "agreeableness", "dependability", "emotional stability", and "culture". This work was replicated by Warren Norman, who also found that five major factors were sufficient to account for a large set of personality data. Norman named these factors surgency, agreeableness, conscientiousness, emotional stability, and culture; and these factors are through which Five Factor consensus has grown.

Hiatus in Research

For the next two decades, the changing zeitgeist made publication of personality research difficult. In his 1968 book *Personality and Assessment*, Walter Mischel asserted that personality tests could not predict behaviour with a correlation of more than 0.3. Social psychologists like Mischel argued that attitudes and behaviour were not stable, but varied with the situation. Predicting behaviour by personality tests was considered to be impossible.

Emerging methodologies challenged this point of view during the 1980s. Instead of trying to predict single instances of behaviour, which was unreliable, researchers found that they could predict patterns of behaviour by aggregating large numbers of observations. As a result correlations between personality and behaviour increased substantially, and it was clear that "personality" did in fact exist. Personality and social psychologists now generally agree that both personal and situational variables are needed to account for human behaviour. Trait theories became justified, and there was a resurgence of interest in this area. By 1980, the pioneering research by Tupes, Christal, and Norman had been largely forgotten by psychologists. Lewis Goldberg started his own lexical project, independently found the five factors once again, and gradually brought them back to the attention of psychologists. He later coined the term "Big Five" as a label for the factors.

Renewed Attention

In a 1980 symposium in Honolulu, four prominent researchers, Lewis Goldberg, Naomi Takemoto-Chock, Andrew Comrey, and John M. Digman, reviewed the available personality tests of the day. They concluded that the tests which held the most promise measured a subset of five common factors, just as Norman had discovered in 1963. This event was followed by widespread acceptance of the five factor model among personality researchers during the 1980s. Peter Saville and his team included the five-factor "Pentagon" model with the original OPQ in 1984. Pentagon was closely followed by the NEO five-factor personality inventory, published by Costa and McCrae in 1985.

Biological Factors

Heritability: Twin studies suggest that heritability and environmental factors equally influence all five factors to the same degree. Among four recent twin studies, the mean percentage for heritability was calculated for each personality and it was concluded that heritability influenced the five factors broadly. The self-report measures were as follows: openness to experience was estimated to have a 57% genetic influence, extraversion 54%, conscientiousness 49%, neuroticism 48%, and agreeableness 42%.

Age Differences

Many studies of longitudinal data, which correlate people's test scores over time, and cross-sectional data, which compare personality levels across different age groups, show a high degree of stability in personality traits during adulthood. It is shown that the personality stabilizes for working-age individuals within about 4 years after starting working. There is also little evidence that adverse life events can have any significant impact on the personality of individuals. More recent research and meta-analyses of previous studies, however, indicate that change occurs in all five traits at various points in the lifespan. The new research shows evidence for a maturation effect. On average, levels of agreeableness and conscientiousness typically increase with time, whereas extraversion, neuroticism, and openness tend to decrease. Research has also demonstrated that changes in Big Five personality traits depend on the individual's current stage of development. For example, levels of agreeableness and conscientiousness demonstrate a negative trend during childhood and early adolescence before trending upwards during late adolescence and into adulthood. In addition to these group effects, there are individual differences: different people demonstrate unique patterns of change at all stages of life.

Another area of investigation is the downward extension of Big Five theory into childhood. Studies have found Big Five personality traits to correlate with children's social and emotional adjustment and academic achievement. More recently, the Five Factor Personality

Inventory – Children was published extending assessment between the ages of 9 and 18. Perhaps the reason for this recent publication was the controversy over the application of the Five Factor Model to children. Studies by Oliver P. John et al. with adolescent boys brought two new factors to the table: "Irritability" and "Activity". In studies of Dutch children, those same two new factors also became apparent. These new additions "suggest that the structure of personality traits may be more differentiated in childhood than in adulthood", which would explain the recent research in this particular area. In addition, some research (Fleeson, 2001) suggests that the Big Five should not be conceived of as dichotomies (such as extraversion vs. introversion) but as continua. Each individual has the capacity to move along each dimension as circumstances (social or temporal) change. He is or she is therefore not simply on one end of each trait dichotomy but is a blend of both, exhibiting some characteristics more often than others:

Research regarding personality with growing age has suggested that as individuals enter their elder years (79–86), those with lower IQ see a raise in extraversion, but a decline in conscientiousness and physical well being. A research by Cobb-Clark and Schurer indicates that personality traits are generally stable among adult workers. The research done on personality also mirrors previous results on locus of control.

Brain Structures

Some research has been done to look into the structures of the brain and their connections to personality traits of the FFM. Two main studies were done by Sato et al. (2012) and DeYoung et al. (2009). Results of the two are as follows:

- Neuroticism: negatively correlated with ratio of brain volume to remainder of intracranial volume, reduced volume in dorsomedial PFC and a segment of left medial temporal lobe including posterior hippocampus, increased volume in the mid-cingulate gryus.
- Extraversion: positively correlated with orbitofrontal cortex metabolism, increased cerebral, volume of medial orbitofrontal cortex.
- Agreeableness: negatively correlated with left orbitofrontal lobe volume in frontotemporal dementia patients, reduced volume in posterior left superior temporal sulcus, increased volume in posterior cingulate cortex.

- Conscientiousness: volume of middle frontal gyrus in left lateral PFC.
- Openness to experience: No regions large enough to be significant, although parietal cortex may be involved.

Group Differences

Gender Differences: Cross-cultural research has shown some patterns of gender differences on responses to the NEO-PI-R and the Big Five Inventory. For example, women consistently report higher Neuroticism, Agreeableness, warmth (an extraversion facet) and openness to feelings, and men often report higher assertiveness (a facet of extraversion) and openness to ideas as assessed by the NEO-PI-R.

A study of gender differences in 55 nations using the Big Five Inventory found that women tended to be somewhat higher than men in neuroticism, extraversion, agreeableness, and conscientiousness. The difference in neuroticism was the most prominent and consistent, with significant differences found in 49 of the 55 nations surveyed. Gender differences in personality traits are largest in prosperous, healthy, and more gender-egalitarian cultures. Differences in the magnitude of sex differences between more or less developed world regions were due to differences between men, not women, in these respective regions. That is, men in highly developed world regions were less neurotic, extraverted, conscientious and agreeable compared to men in less developed world regions. Women, on the other hand tended not to differ in personality traits across regions.

The authors of this study speculated that resource-poor environments (that is, countries with low levels of development) may inhibit the development of gender differences, whereas resource-rich environments facilitate them. This may be because males require more resources than females in order to reach their full developmental potential. The authors also argued that due to different evolutionary pressures, men may have evolved to be more risk taking and socially dominant, whereas women evolved to be more cautious and nurturing. Ancient hunter-gatherer societies may have been more egalitarian than later agriculturally oriented societies. Hence, the development of gender inequalities may have acted to constrain the development of gender differences in personality that originally evolved in hunter-gatherer societies. As modern societies have become more egalitarian, again, it may be that innate sex differences are no longer constrained and hence manifest more fully than in less-developed cultures. Currently, this hypothesis remains untested, as gender differences in modern societies have not been compared with those in hunter-gatherer societies.

Birth-order Differences

Frank Sulloway argues that firstborns are more conscientious, more socially dominant, less agreeable, and less open to new ideas compared to laterborns. Large scale studies using random samples and self-report personality tests, however, have found milder effects than Sulloway claimed, or no significant effects of birth order on personality.

Cultural Differences

The Big Five have been replicated in a variety of languages and cultures, such as German, Chinese, Indian, etc. For example, Thompson has demonstrated the Big Five structure across several cultures using an international English language scale. Cheung, van de Vijver, and Leong (2011) suggest, however, that the Openness factor is particularly unsupported in Asian countries and that a different fifth factor is sometimes identified.

Recent work has found relationships between Geert Hofstede's cultural factors, Individualism, Power Distance, Masculinity, and Uncertainty Avoidance, with the average Big Five scores in a country. For instance, the degree to which a country values individualism correlates with its average extraversion, whereas people living in cultures which are accepting of large inequalities in their power structures tend to score somewhat higher on conscientiousness. Although this is an active area of research, the reasons for these differences are as yet unknown.

Attempts to replicate the Big Five in other countries with local dictionaries have succeeded in some countries but not in others. Apparently, for instance, Hungarians do not appear to have a single agreeableness factor. Other researchers have found evidence for agreeableness but not for other factors.

Relationships

Big Five and Personality Disorders: There is a rich literature concerning the FFM as a structural model for describing and understanding disorders of personality, including those within the Diagnostic and Statistical Manual of Mental Disorders.

As of 2002, there were over fifty published studies relating the FFM to personality disorders. Since that time, quite a number of additional studies have expanded on this research base and provided further empirical support for understanding the DSM personality disorders in terms of the FFM domains.

In her seminal review of the personality disorder literature published in 2007, Dr. Lee Anna Clark asserted that "the five-factor model of personality is widely accepted as representing the higher-order structure of both normal and abnormal personality traits".

The Five Factor Model has been shown to significantly predict all ten personality-disorder symptoms and outperform the MMPI in the prediction of borderline, avoidant, and dependent personality disorder symptoms.

Research results examining the relationships between the FFM and each of the ten DSM personality disorder diagnostic categories are widely available. For example, in a study published in 2003 titled "The five-factor model and personality disorder empirical literature: A meta-analytic review", the authors analyzed data from 15 other studies to determine how personality disorders are different and similar, respectively, with regard to underlying personality traits. In terms of how personality disorders differ, the results showed that each disorder displays a FFM profile that is meaningful and predictable given its unique diagnostic criteria. With regard to their similarities, the findings revealed that the most prominent and consistent personality dimensions underlying a large number of the personality disorders are positive associations with neuroticism and negative associations with agreeableness.

Big Five and Education

Academic Achievement: Personality plays an important role that effects academic achievement. A study conducted with 308 undergraduates who completed the Five Factor Inventory Processes and offered their GPA suggested that conscientiousness and agreeableness have a positive relationship with all types of learning styles (synthesis analysis, methodical study, fact retention, and elaborative processing), whereas neuroticism has an inverse relationship with them all. Moreover, extraversion and openness were proportional to elaborative processing. The Big Five personality traits accounted for 14% of the variance in GPA, suggesting that personality traits make great contributions to academic performance. Furthermore, reflective learning styles (synthesis-analysis and elaborative processing)were able to mediate the relationship between openness and GPA. These results indicate that intellectual curiousness has significant enhancement in academic performance if students can combine their scholarly interest with thoughtful information processing.

Studies conducted on college students have concluded that hope, which is linked to agreeableness has a positive effect of psychological well being. Individuals high in neurotic tendencies are less likely to display hopeful tendencies and are negatively associated with well-being. Personality can sometimes be flexible and measuring the big five personality for individuals as they enter certain stages of life may predict their educational identity. Recent studies have suggested the likelihood of an individual's personality affecting their educational identity.

Learning Styles

Learning styles have been described as "enduring ways of thinking and processing information."

Although there is no evidence that personality determines thinking styles, they may be intertwined in ways that link thinking styles to the Big Five personality traits. There is no general consensus on the number or specifications of particular learning styles, but there have been many different proposals.

Scientists have defined four types of learning styles:

- synthesis analysis
- methodical study
- fact retention
- elaborative processing

This model adopted from Smeck, Ribicj, and Ramanaih (1997) is often used because when all four facets are implicated within the classroom, they will each likely improve academic achievement. It asserts that students develop either agentic/shallow processing or reflective/deep processing. Deep processors are more often than not found to be more conscientious, intellectually open, and extraverted when compared to shallow processors. Deep processing is associated with appropriate study methods (methodical study) and a stronger ability to analyze information (synthesis analysis), whereas shallow processors prefer structured fact retention learning styles and are better suited for elaborative processing. The main functions of these four specific learning styles are as follow:

Name	***Function***
Synthesis analysis:	processing information, forming categories, and organizing them into hierarchies. This is the only one of the learning styles that has explained a significant impact on academic performance.
Methodical study:	methodical behaviour while completing academic assignments
Fact retention:	focusing on the actual result instead of understanding the logic behind something
Elaborative processing:	connecting and applying new ideas to existing knowledge

Openness has been linked to learning styles that often lead to academic success and higher grades like synthesis analysis and methodical study. Because conscientiousness and openness have been shown to predict all four learning styles, it suggests that individuals who possess characteristics like discipline, determination, and curiosity are more likely to engage in all of the above learning styles.

According to the research carried out by Komarraju, Karau, Schmeck & Avdic (2011), conscientiousness and agreeableness are positively related with all four learning styles, whereas neuroticism was negatively related with those four. Furthermore, extraversion and openness were only positively related to elaborative processing, and openness itself correlated with higher academic achievement.

Besides openness, all Big Five personality traits helped predict the educational identity of students. Based on these findings, scientists are beginning to see that there might be a large influence of the Big Five traits on academic motivation that then leads to predicting a student's academic performance

Recent studies suggest that Big Five personality traits combined with learning styles can help predict some variations in the academic performance and the academic motivation of an individual which can then influence their academic achievements. This may be seen because individual differences in personality represent stable approaches to information processing. For instance, conscientiousness has consistently emerged as a stable predictor of success in exam performance, largely because conscientious students experiences fewer study delays. The reason conscientiousness shows a positive association with the four learning styles is because students with high levels of conscientiousness develop focused learning strategies and appear to be more disciplined and achievement-oriented. However, the American Psychological Society recently commissioned a report whose conclusion indicates that no significant evidence exists to make the conclusion that learning-style assessments should be included in the education system. The APA also suggested in their report that all existing learning styles have not been exhausted and that there could exist learning styles that have the potential to be worthy of being included in educational practices. Thus, it is premature, at best, to conclude that the evidence linking the Big Five to "learning styles" or "learning styles" to learning itself is valid.

Big Five and Work Success

It is believed that the Big-Five traits are predictors of future performance outcomes. Job outcome measures include: job and training proficiency and personnel data. However, research demonstrating such prediction has been criticized, in part because of the apparently low correlation coefficients characterizing the relationship between personality and job performance. In a 2007 article co-authored by six current or former editors of psychological journals, Dr. Kevin Murphy, Professor of Psychology at Pennsylvania State University and Editor of the Journal of Applied Psychology (1996-2002), states:

The problem with personality tests is ... that the validity of personality measures as predictors of job performance is often disappointingly low.The argument for using personality tests to predict performance does not strike me as convincing in the first place. Such criticisms were put forward by Walter Mischel whose publication caused a two-decades' long crisis in personality psychometrics. However, later work demonstrated (1) that the correlations obtained by psychometric personality researchers were actually very respectable by comparative standards, and (2) that the economic value of even incremental increases in prediction accuracy was exceptionally large, given the vast difference in performance by those who occupy complex job positions. There have been studies that link national innovation to openness to experience and conscientiousness. Those who express these traits have showed leadership and beneficial ideas towards the country of origin.

Some businesses, organizations, and interviewers assess individuals based on the Big 5 personality traits. Research has suggested that individuals who are considered leaders typically exhibit lower amounts of neurotic traits, maintain higher levels of openness (envisioning success), balanced levels of conscientiousness (well-organized), and balanced levels of extraversion (outgoing, but not excessive). Further studies have linked professional burnout to neuroticism, and extraversion to enduring positive work experience. When it comes to making money, research has suggested that those who are high in agreeableness (especially men) are not as successful in accumulating income. It is possible that these individuals are too passive and do not aspire to obtain higher levels of income.

Measurements of the Big Five Personality Traits

Several measures of the Big Five exist:

- NEO-PI-R
- Self-descriptive sentence questionnaires
- Lexical questionnaires
- Self-report questionnaires
- Likert questionnaire
- Relative-scored Big 5 measure

The most frequently used measures of the Big Five comprise either items that are self-descriptive sentences or, in the case of lexical measures, items that are single adjectives. Due to the length of sentence-based and some lexical measures, short forms have been developed and validated for use in applied research settings where questionnaire space and respondent time are limited, such as the 40-item balanced *International English Big-Five Mini-Markers* or a very brief (10 item) measure of the Big Five domains. Research has suggested that some methodologies in administering personality tests are inadequate in length and provide insufficient detail to truly evaluate personality. Usually, longer, more detailed questions will give a more accurate portrayal of personality. The five factor structure has been replicated in peer reports. However, many of the substantive findings rely on self-reports.

Much of the evidence on the measures of the Big 5 rely on self-report questionnaires, which makes self-report bias and falsification of responses difficult to deal with and account for. It has been argued that the Big Five tests do not create an accurate personality profile because the responses given on these tests are not true in all cases. For example, questionnaires are answered by potential employees who might choose answers that paint them in the best light. This becomes especially important when considering why scores may differ between individuals or groups of people– differences in scores may represent genuine underlying personality differences, or they may simply be an artifact of the way the subjects answered the questions.

Research suggests that a relative-scored Big Five measure in which respondents had to make repeated choices between equally desirable personality descriptors may be a potential alternative to traditional Big Five measures in accurately assessing personality traits, especially when lying or biased responding is present. When compared with a traditional Big Five measure for its ability to predict GPA and creative achievement under both normal and "fake good"-bias response conditions, the relative-scored measure significantly and consistently predicted these outcomes under both conditions; however, the Likert questionnaire lost its predictive ability in the faking condition. Thus, the relative-scored measure proved to be less affected by biased responding than the Likert measure of the Big Five.

Criticisms

Much research has been conducted on the Big Five. This has resulted in criticism and support for the model. Critics argue that there are limitations to the scope of Big Five as an explanatory or predictive theory. It is argued that the Big Five does not explain all of human personality. The methodology used to identify the dimensional structure of personality traits, factor analysis, is often challenged for not having a universally-recognized basis for choosing among solutions with different numbers of factors. Another frequent criticism is that the Big Five is not theory-driven, it is merely a data-driven investigation of certain descriptors that tend to cluster together under factor analysis.

Limited Scope

One common criticism is that the Big Five does not explain all of human personality. Some psychologists have dissented from the model precisely because they feel it neglects other domains of personality, such as Religiosity, Manipulativeness/Machiavellianism, Honesty, sexiness/seductiveness, Thriftiness, Conservativeness, Masculinity/Femininity, Snobbishness/egotism, Sense of humour, and risk-taking/thrill-seeking. Dan P. McAdams has called the Big Five a "psychology of the stranger," because they refer to traits that are relatively easy to observe in a stranger; other aspects of personality that are more privately held or more context-dependent are excluded from the Big Five.

In many studies, the five factors are not fully orthogonal to one another; that is, the five factors are not independent. Orthogonality is viewed as desirable by some researchers because it minimizes redundancy between the dimensions. This is particularly important when the goal of a study is to provide a comprehensive description of personality with as few variables as possible.

Methodological Issues

The methodology used to identify the dimensional structure of personality traits, factor analysis, is often challenged for not having a universally recognized basis for choosing among solutions with different numbers of factors. That is, a five factor solution depends on some degree of interpretation by the analyst. A larger number of factors may, in fact, underlie these five factors. This has led to disputes about the "true" number of factors. Big Five proponents have responded that although other solutions may be viable in a single dataset, only the five factor structure consistently replicates across different studies.

Theoretical Status

A frequent criticism is that the Big Five is not based on any underlying theory; it is merely an empirical finding that certain descriptors cluster together under factor analysis. Although this does not mean that these five factors do not exist, the underlying causes behind them are unknown.

Jack Block's final published work before his death in January 2010 drew together his lifetime perspective on the five factor model.

He summarized his critique of the model in terms of:

- the atheoretical nature of the five-factors
- their "cloudy" measurement
- the model's inappropriateness for studying early childhood
- the use of factor analysis as the exclusive paradigm for conceptualizing personality
- the continuing non-consensual understandings of the five-factors
- the existence of unrecognized but successful efforts to specify aspects of character not subsumed by the five-factors

He went on to suggest that repeatedly observed higher order factors hierarchically above the proclaimed Big Five personality traits may promise deeper biological understanding of the origins and implications of these superfactors.

Applied Behaviour Analysis

Applied behaviour analysis (ABA), previously known as behaviour modification, is the application of behaviourism that modifies human behaviours, especially as part of a learning or treatment process. Behaviour analysts focus on the observable relationship of behaviour to the environment to the exclusion of what they call "hypothetical constructs". By functionally assessing the relationship between a targeted behaviour and the environment, the methods of ABA can be used to change that behaviour.

Methods in applied behaviour analysis range from validated intensive behavioural interventions—most notably utilized for children with an autism spectrum disorder (ASD)—to basic research which investigates the rules by which humans adapt and maintain behaviour. However, applied behaviour analysis contributes to a full range of areas including: AIDS prevention,business management, conservation of natural resources, education, gerontology, health and exercise, industrial safety, language acquisition, littering, medical procedures, parenting, psychotherapy, seatbelt use, severe mental disorders, sports,substance abuse, and zoo management and care of animals.

Definition

ABA is defined as the science in which the principles of the analysis of behaviour are applied systematically to improve socially significant behaviour, and in which experimentation is used to identify the variables responsible for change in behaviour. It is one of the three fields of behaviour analysis. The other two are conceptual analysis of behaviour, or the philosophy of the science; and experimental analysis of behaviour, or basic experimental research.

History

B.F. Skinner further revised the traditional theory of Behaviourism in the 1930s, and developed the modern form of it known as Behaviour Analysis.

Although deriving from the same philosophy, behaviour modification was one application of behaviourism that modified behaviour without addressing what was causing it. ABA *analyzes* what is prompting that behaviour (the antecedent) and develops consequential strategies to prevent such behaviours from reoccurring. The term "Applied Behaviour Analysis" (ABA) first came to widespread use after the 1968 introduction of *The Journal of Applied Behaviour*

Analysis which publishes research examining the application of behaviour analysis to socially-relevant behaviour. ABA is a science used in a wide range of fields to reinforce behaviour with various subtypes such as Organizational behaviour management (OBM), Positive behaviour support, (such as School-wide Positive Behavioural Interventions and Supports (SWPBIS)), and Clinical behaviour analysis (CBA, such as Contingency Management). Most of the time people use the subtype terms Early intensive behavioural intervention (EIBI, including the Lovaas/UCLA model and Pivotal response treatment (PRT)) interchangeably with ABA. However, the latter is a distinct psychological science of reinforcing behaviour.

Ole Ivar Lovaas is considered a grandfather of Applied Behaviour Analysis and developed standardized teaching interventions based on behavioural principals. Lovaas devoted nearly a half a century to groundbreaking research and practice aimed at improving the lives of children with autism and their families. In 1965, Lovaas published a series of articles that therapeutic approaches to autism. The first two articles presented his system for coding behaviours during direct observations and a pioneering investigation of antecedents and consequences that maintained a problem behaviour, a forerunner of what is now called experimental functional analysis. The subsequent articles built upon these methods and reported the first demonstration of an effective way to teach nonverbal children to speak, a study on establishing social (secondary) reinforcers, a procedure for teaching children to imitate, and several studies on interventions to reduce life-threatening self-injury and aggression.

Lovaas was cited in his early career to use low dosages of electroshock therapy to children with extreme self injurious behaviour. In 1973, Lovaas published a long-term follow-up for the behaviour modification intervention and was dismayed to find that most of the subjects had reverted to their pre-intervention behaviours. After these findings, Lovaas and his colleagues proposed several ways to improve outcomes such as starting intervention during the children's preschool years instead of later in childhood or adolescence, involving parents in the intervention, and implementing the intervention in the family's home rather than an institutional setting. Subsequent articles like the 1987 "Behavioural Treatment and Normal Educational and Intellectual Functioning in Young Autistic Children" reinforce this proposal of early and intensive intervention—without the use of aversives (such as electric shocks)—paired with continual therapy yields the most effective results for children with autism. Lovaas highly believed that the support and involvement in parents applying therapy at home contributed to a higher success rate. Lovaas dedicated his life to the study of autism and was a strong advocate for people with autism even co-founding what is today the Autism Society of America.

Characteristics

Baer, Wolf, and Risley's 1968 article is still used as the standard description of ABA. It describes the seven dimensions of ABA: application; a focus on behaviour; the use of analysis; and its technological, conceptually-systematic, effective, and general approach.

Applied

ABA focuses on areas that are of social significance. In doing this, behaviour scientists must take into consideration more than just the short-term behaviour change, but also look at how behaviour changes can affect the consumer, those who are close to the consumer, and how any change will affect the interactions between the two.

Behavioural

ABA must be behavioural, i.e.: behaviour itself must change, not just what the consumer *says* about the behaviour. It is not the goal of the behaviour scientists to get their consumers to stop complaining about behaviour problems, but rather to change the problem behaviour itself. In addition, behaviour must be objectively measured. A behaviour scientist cannot resort to the measurement of non-behavioural substitutes. (Obviously multidisciplinary work within behaviour and psychology may include, for example, analysis of cognition or demographics and exploration of the individual as well, where experimental standards are maintained.)

Analytic

ABA must be analytic, which means that the behaviour analyst can control the behaviour that is being changed by changing the control behaviour. In the lab, this has been easy as the researcher can start and stop the behaviour at will. However, in the applied situation, this is not always as easy, nor ethical, to do. According to Baer, Wolf, and Risley, this difficulty should not stop a science from upholding the strength of its principles. As such, they referred to two designs that are best used in applied settings to demonstrate control and maintain ethical standards. These are the reversal and multiple baseline designs. The reversal design is one in which the behaviour of choice is measured prior to any intervention. Once the pattern appears stable, an intervention is introduced, and behaviour is measured. If there is a change in behaviour, measurement continues until the new pattern of behaviour appears stable. Then, the intervention is removed, or reduced, and the behaviour is measured to see if it changes again. If the behaviour scientist truly has demonstrated control of the behaviour with the intervention, the behaviour of interest should change with intervention changes. Here control may be better called "effect" or "influence", of behaviour.

Technological

This means that if any other researcher were to read a description of the study, that researcher would be able to "replicate the application with the same results." This means that the description must be very detailed and clear. Ambiguous descriptions do not qualify. Cooper *et al.* describe a good check for the technological characteristic: "have a person trained in applied behaviour analysis carefully read the description and then act out the procedure in detail. If the person makes any mistakes, adds any operations, omits any steps, or has to ask any questions to clarify the written description then the description is not sufficiently technological and requires improvement." This is where the experiment is repeatable.

Conceptually Systematic

A defining characteristic is in regard to the interventions used; and thus research must be conceptually systematic by only using procedures and interpreting results of these procedures in terms of the principles from which they were derived.

Effective

ABA must be effective, which means that the application of these techniques changes the behaviour it seeks to change. Specifically, it is not a theoretical importance of the variable, but rather the practical importance (social importance) that is essential. If the application of behavioural techniques does not produce a large enough effects for practical value, then the application has failed.

Generality

ABA must be general, which means that it persists over time, in different environments, and spreads to other behaviours not directly treated by the intervention. In addition, continued change in specified behaviour after intervention for that behaviour has been withdrawn is also an example of generality. It is a goal to identify behaviour stimuli with long-lasting and general effect.

Proposed Additional Characteristics

In 2005, Heward, *et al.* added their belief that the following five characteristics should be added:

- Accountable: Direct and frequent measurement enables analysts to detect their success and failures to make changes in an effort to increase successes while decreasing failures. ABA is a scientific approach in which analysts may guess but then critically test ideas, rather than "guess and guess again." This constant revision of techniques, commitment to effectiveness and analysis of results leads to an accountable science.
- Public: Applied behaviour analysis is completely visible and public. This means that there are no explanations that cannot be observed, but of course these are each imposed. There are no mystical, metaphysical explanations, hidden treatment, or magic. Thus, ABA produces results whose explanations are available to all of the public.
- Doable: ABA has a pragmatic element in that implementors of interventions can consist of a variety of individuals, from teachers to the participants themselves. This does not mean that ABA requires one simply to learn a few procedures, but with the proper planning, it can effectively be implemented by almost everyone willing to invest the effort.
- Empowering: ABA provides tools to practitioners that allow them to effectively change behaviour. By constantly providing visual feedback to the practitioner on the results of the intervention, this feature of ABA allows clinicians to assess their skill level and builds confidence in their technology.
- Optimistic: According to several leading authors, practitioners skilled in behaviour analysis have genuine cause to be optimistic for the following reasons:
  - o Individual behaviour is largely determined by learning and cumulative effects of the environment, which itself is manipulable
  - o Direct and continuous measurements enable practitioners to detect small improvements in performance that might have otherwise been missed

- o As a practitioner uses behavioural techniques with positive outcomes, the more they will become optimistic about future success prospects
- o The literature provides many examples of success teaching individuals considered previously unteachable.

Concepts

Behaviour: Behaviour is the activity of living organisms. Human behaviour is the entire gamut of what people do including thinking and feeling. Behaviour can be determined by applying the Dead Man's test:

If a dead man can do it, it isn't behaviour. And if a dead man can't do it, then it is behaviour.

This is Obviously Only a Simple Rubric.

Behaviour is that portion of an organism's interaction with its environment that is characterized by detectable displacement in space through time of some part of the organism and that results in a measurable change in at least one aspect of the environment. Often, the term behaviour is used to reference a larger class of responses that share physical dimensions or function. In this instance, the term *response* indicates a single instance of that behaviour. If a group of responses have the same function, this group can be classified as a response class. Finally, when discussing a person's collection of behaviour, repertoire is used. It can either pertain specifically to a set of response classes that are relevant to a particular situation, or it can refer to every behaviour that a person can do.

Operant Conditioning

Operant behaviour is that which is selected by its consequences. The conditioning of operant behaviour is the result of reinforcement and punishment. Operant conditioning applies to so-called "voluntary" responses, which an organism emits and increase or decrease in frequency as a function of the consequences which follow. The term operant emphasizes this point: the organism's behaviour operates upon its environment to produce some type of desirable result. For example, operant conditioning is at work when we learn that toiling industriously can bring about a raise or that studying hard for a particular class will result in good grades, in positive reinforcement.

Respondent Conditioning

All organisms respond in predictable ways to certain stimuli. These stimulus–response relations are called reflexes. The response component of the reflex is called respondent behaviour. It is defined as behaviour which is elicited by antecedent stimuli. Respondent conditioning (also called classical conditioning) is learning in which new stimuli acquire the ability to elicit respondents. This is done through stimulus–stimulus pairing, for example, the stimulus (smell of food) can elicit a person's salivation. By pairing that stimulus (smell) with another stimulus (e.g., a light), the second stimulus can obtain the function of the first stimulus, given that the predictive relationship between the two stimuli is maintained. This is also known as "Pavlov's dog's bell".

Environment

The environment is the entire constellation of stimuli in which an organism exists. This includes events both inside and outside of an organism, but only real physical events are included. The environment consists of stimuli. A stimulus is an "energy change that affects an organism through its receptor cells."

A stimulus can be described:

- Topographically by its physical features.
- Temporally by when they occur in respect to the behaviour.
- Functionally by their effect on behaviour.

Reinforcement

Reinforcement is the most important principle of behaviour and a key element of most behaviour change programmes. It is the process by which behaviour is strengthened, if a behaviour is followed closely in time by a stimulus and this results in an increase in the future frequency of that behaviour. The addition of a stimulus following an event that serves as a reinforcer is termed positive reinforcement. If the removal of an event serves as a reinforcer, this is termed negative reinforcement. There are multiple schedules of reinforcement that affect the future probability of behaviour.

Punishment

Punishment is a process by which a consequence immediately follows a behaviour which decreases the future frequency of that behaviour. As with reinforcement, a stimulus can be added (positive punishment) or removed (negative punishment). Broadly, there are three types of punishment: presentation of aversive stimuli (e.g., pain), response cost (removal of desirable stimuli as in monetary fines, and restriction of freedom as in a 'time out'). Punishment in practice can often result in unwanted side effects. Some other potential unwanted effects include resentment over being punished, attempts to escape the punishment, expression of pain and negative emotions associated with it, and recognition by the punished individual between the punishment and the person delivering it.

Extinction

Extinction is the technical term to describe the procedure of withholding/discontinuing reinforcement of a previously reinforced behaviour, resulting in the decrease of that behaviour. The behaviour is then set to be extinguished (Cooper, *et al.*). Extinction procedures are often preferred over punishment procedures that are frequently deemed unethical and in many states prohibited. Nonetheless, extinction procedures must be implemented with utmost care by professionals, as they are generally associated with extinction bursts. An extinction burst is the temporary increase in the frequency, intensity, and/or duration of the behaviour targeted for extinction. Other characteristics of an extinction burst include a) extinction-produced aggression—the occurrence of an emotional response to an extinction procedure often manifested as aggression; and b) extinction-induced response variability—the occurrence of novel behaviours that did not typically occur prior to the extinction procedure. These novel behaviours are a core component of shaping procedures.

Discriminated Operant and Three-term Contingency

In addition to a relation being made between behaviour and its consequences, operant conditioning also establishes relations between antecedent conditions and behaviours. This differs from the S–R formulations (If-A-then-B), and replaces it with an AB-because-of-C formulation. In other words, the relation between a behaviour (B) and its context (A) is because of consequences (C), more specifically, this relationship between AB because of C indicates that the relationship is established by prior consequences that have occurred in similar contexts. This antecedent–behaviour–consequence contingency is termed the three-term contingency. A behaviour which occurs more frequently in the presence of an antecedent condition than in its absence is called a discriminated operant. The antecedent stimulus is called a discriminative stimulus (S^D). The fact that the discriminated operant occurs only in the presence of the discriminative stimulus is an illustration of stimulus control. More recently behaviour analysts have been focusing on conditions that occur prior to the circumstances for the current behaviour of concern that increased the likelihood of the behaviour occurring or not occurring. These conditions have been referred to variously as "Setting Event", "Establishing Operations", and "Motivating Operations" by various researchers in their publications.

Verbal behaviour

B.F. Skinner's classification system of behaviour analysis has been applied to treatment of a host of communication disorders. Skinner's system includes:

- Tact (psychology) – a verbal response evoked by a non-verbal antecedent and maintained by generalized conditioned reinforcement.
- Mand (psychology) – behaviour under control of motivating operations maintained by a characteristic reinforcer.
- Intraverbals – verbal behaviour for which the relevant antecedent stimulus was other verbal behaviour, but which does not share the response topography of that prior verbal stimulus (e.g., responding to another speaker's question).
- Autoclitic – secondary verbal behaviour which alters the effect of primary verbal behaviour on the listener. Examples involve quantification, grammar, and qualifying statements (e.g., the differential effects of "I think..." vs. "I know...")

For assessment of verbal behaviour from Skinner's system see Assessment of Basic Language and Learning Skills.

Measuring Behaviour

When measuring behaviour, there are both dimensions of behaviour and quantifiable measures of behaviour. In applied behaviour analysis, the quantifiable measures are a derivative of the dimensions. These dimensions are repeatability, temporal extent, and temporal locus.

Repeatability

Response classes occur repeatedly throughout time—i.e., how many times the behaviour occurs.

- Count is the number of occurrences in behaviour.
- Rate/frequency is the number of instances of behaviour per unit of time.
- Celeration is the measure of how the rate changes over time.

Temporal Extent

This dimension indicates that each instance of behaviour occupies some amount of time—i.e., how long the behaviour occurs.

- Duration is the amount of time in which the behaviour occurs.

Temporal Locus

Each instance of behaviour occurs at a specific point in time—i.e., when the behaviour occurs.

- Response latency is the measure of elapsed time between the onset of a stimulus and the initiation of the response.
- Interresponse time is the amount of time that occurs between two consecutive instances of a response class.

Derivative Measures

Derivative measures are unrelated to specific dimensions:

- Percentage is the ratio formed by combining the same dimensional quantities.
- Trials-to-criterion are the number of response opportunities needed to achieve a predetermined level of performance.

Analyzing Behaviour Change

Experimental Control: In applied behaviour analysis, all experiments should include the following:

- At least one participant
- At least one behaviour (dependent variable)
- At least one setting
- A system for measuring the behaviour and ongoing visual analysis of data
- At least one treatment or intervention condition
- Manipulations of the independent variable so that its effects on the dependent variable may be quantitatively or qualitatively analyzed
- An intervention that will benefit the participant in some way

Functional Analysis (Psychology)

Functional Behaviour Assessment (FBA): Functional assessment of behaviour provides hypotheses about the relationships between specific environmental events and behaviours. Decades of research have established that both desirable and undesirable behaviours are learned through interactions with the social and physical environment. FBA is used to identify the type and source of reinforcement for challenging behaviours as the basis for intervention efforts designed to decrease the occurrence of these behaviours.

Functions of Behaviour: The function of a behaviour can be thought of as the purpose a behaviour serves for a person.

Behaviour can serve the following common functions for an individual:

Access to Attention: e.g., Child throws toy because it characteristically results in mom's attention. (If this behaviour results in mom looking at child and giving him lots of attention—even if she's saying "NO"—he will be more likely to engage in the same behaviour in the future to get mom's attention.)

Escape/removal of a demand or aversive event e.g., Mom tells the child "Go clean up" and child runs to the kitchen because mom historically will not require him/her to complete the task when this behaviour occurs. Automatic reinforcement e.g., Child flaps (or other stereotypic, repetitive movement) because it produces perceptual stimulation/sensory consequences. This also includes pain attenuation via removal of unpleasant stimulation (e.g., toothache, stomach pain, fever) Access to tangibles (e.g., activities, toys, edibles) e.g., Child hits mom because s/he wants the toy mom is holding and mom typically delivers it following this behaviour. We can describe behaviours in various ways such as tantrums, noncompliance, inattention, aggression; however all behaviour can be classified as serving one or more of the functions above. Function is identified in an FBA by identifying the type and source of reinforcement for the behaviour of interest. Those reinforcers might be positive or negative social reinforcers provided by someone who interacts with the person, or automatic reinforcers produced directly by the behaviour itself.

- Positive reinforcement – social positive reinforcement (attention), tangible reinforcement, and automatic positive reinforcement.
- Negative reinforcement – social negative reinforcement (escape), automatic negative reinforcement.

Function Versus Topography

Behaviours may look different but can serve the same function and likewise behaviour that looks the same may serve multiple functions. What the behaviour looks like often reveals little useful information about the conditions that account for it. However, identifying the conditions that account for a behaviour, suggests what conditions need to be altered to change the behaviour. Therefore, assessment of function of a behaviour can yield useful information with respect to intervention strategies that are likely to be effective.

FBA Methods

FBA methods can be classified into three types:

- Functional (experimental) analysis
- Descriptive assessment
- Indirect assessment

Functional (Experimental) Analysis: A functional analysis is one in which antecedents and consequences are manipulated to indicate their separate effects on the behaviour of interest. This type of arrangement is often called synthetic because they are not conducted in a naturally occurring context. However, research is indicating that functional analysis done in a natural environment will yield similar or better results.

A standard functional analysis normally has four conditions (three test conditions and one control):

- Contingent attention
- Contingent escape
- Alone
- Control condition

While the above four conditions are the most widely used functional analysis experimental conditions, using the basic methodology of functional analysis (and experimental analysis in general) it is possible to arrange any combination of antecedents and consequences for behaviour to determine what effect, if any, they have on a behaviour.

- Advantages – it has the ability to yield a clear demonstration of the variable(s) that relate to the occurrence of a problem behaviour. It serves as the standard of scientific evidence by which other assessment alternatives are evaluated. It represents the method most often used in research on the assessment and treatment of problem behaviour.
- Limitations – assessment process may temporarily strengthen or increase the undesirable behaviour to gravely unacceptable levels or result in the behaviour acquiring new unpleasant

functions. Some behaviours may neither be amenable to functional analyses (e.g., those that, albeit serious, occur infrequently). Functional analyses conducted in contrived settings may not detect the variable that accounts for the occurrence in the natural environment.

Descriptive FBA

As with functional analysis, descriptive functional behaviour assessment utilizes direct observation of behaviour; unlike functional analysis, however, observations are made under naturally occurring conditions. Therefore, descriptive assessments involve observation of the problem behaviour in relation to events that are not arranged in a systematic manner.

There are Three Variations of Descriptive Assessment: There are several forms of Functional Behavioural Assessments they are generally divided into two categories 1)Informal Assessments: Descriptive Assessments 2) Formal Analyses: Analog Functional Analyses, Trial Based Functional Analyses, and single subject research designs.

Informal Assessments: This is a general term referring to both a procedure (directly observing the behaviour as it occurs in the natural environment), and the outcome (a statement or hypothesis of the variable(s) setting the occasion for and maintaining the occurrence of a particular behaviour. The primary elements of a descriptive analysis are the three (A-B-C) and sometimes four term contingency (when Motivational Operations are also considered). 2. A – The Antecedent Condition(s): 3. B - The Behaviour of interest (also known as the target behaviour) 4. C- The Consequence that follows the occurrence of the behaviour(any environmental change that occurs following

Observational data are collected (either on a continuous recording basis or using sampling procedures) on these elements and used to develop an hypothesis of function. This hypothesis can be used to develop an behaviour intervention plan or as a basis for a more formal analysis of function (i.e Trial based analysis,or analog analysis)

- Scatterplots – a procedure for recording the extent to which a target behaviour occurs more often at particular times than others.

Indirect FBA

This method uses structured interviews, checklists, rating scales, or questionnaires to obtain information from persons who are familiar with the person exhibiting the behaviour to identify possible conditions or events in the natural environment that correlate with the problem behaviour. They are called "indirect" because they do not involve direct observation of the behaviour, but rather solicit information based on others' recollections of the behaviour.

- Advantages – some can provide a useful source of information in guiding subsequent, more objective assessments, and contribute to the development of hypotheses about variables that might occasion or maintain the behaviours of concern.
- Limitations – informants may not have accurate and unbiased recall of behaviour and the conditions under which it occurred.

Conducting a FBA

Provided the strengths and limitations of the different FBA procedures, FBA can best be viewed as a four-step process:

1. The gathering of information via indirect and descriptive assessment.
2. Interpretation of information from indirect and descriptive assessment and formulation of a hypothesis about the purpose of problem behaviour.
3. Testing of a hypothesis using a functional analysis.
4. Developing intervention options based on the function of problem behaviour.

Technologies Discovered Through ABA Research

Task Analysis: Task analysis is a process in which a task is analyzed into its component parts so that those parts can be taught through the use of chaining: forward chaining, backward chaining and total task presentation. Task analysis has been used in organizational behaviour management, a behaviour analytic approach to changing organizations. Behavioural scripts often emerge from a task analysis. Bergan conducted a task analysis of the behavioural consultation relationship and Thomas Kratochwill developed a training programme based on teaching Bergan's skills. A similar approach was used for the development of microskills training for counsellors. Ivey would later call this "behaviourist" phase a very productive one and the skills-based approach came to dominate counsellor training during 1970–90. Task analysis was also used in determining the skills needed to access a career. In education, Englemann (1968) used task analysis as part of the methods to design the Direct Instruction curriculum.

Chaining

The skill to be learned is broken down into small units for easy learning. For example, a person learning to brush teeth independently may start with learning to unscrew the toothpaste cap. Once they have learned this, the next step may be squeezing the tube, etc.

For problem behaviour, chains can also be analyzed and the chain can be disrupted to prevent the problem behaviour. Some behaviour therapies, such as dialectical behaviour therapy, make extensive use of behaviour chain analysis.

Prompting

A prompt is a cue or assistance to encourage the desired response from an individual. Prompts are often categorized into a prompt hierarchy from most intrusive to least intrusive. There is some controversy about what is considered most intrusive: physically intrusive versus hardest prompt to fade (i.e., verbal). In a faultless learning approach, prompts are given in a most-to-least sequence and faded systematically to ensure the individual experiences a high level of success. There may be instances in which a least-to-most prompt method is preferred. Prompts are faded systematically and as quickly as possible to avoid prompt dependency. The goal of teaching using prompts would be to fade prompts towards independence, so that no prompts are needed for the individual to perform the desired behaviour.

Types of prompts:

- Vocal prompts: Utilizing a vocalization to indicate the desired response.
- Visual prompts: A visual cue or picture.
- Gestural prompts: Utilizing a physical gesture to indicate the desired response.
- Positional prompt: The target item is placed closer to the individual.
- Modelling: Modelling the desired response for the student. This type of prompt is best suited for individuals who learn through imitation and can attend to a model.
- Physical prompts: Physically manipulating the individual to produce the desired response. There are many degrees of physical prompts. The most intrusive being hand-over-hand, and the least intrusive being a slight tap to initiate movement.

This is not an exhaustive list of all possible prompts. When using prompts to systematically teach a skill, not all prompts need to be used in the hierarchy; prompts are chosen based on which ones are most effective for a particular individual.

Fading

The overall goal is for an individual to eventually not need prompts. As an individual gains mastery of a skill at a particular prompt level, the prompt is faded to a less intrusive prompt. This ensures that the individual does not become overly dependent on a particular prompt when learning a new behaviour or skill.

Thinning a Reinforcement Schedule

Thinning is often confused with fading. Fading refers to a prompt being removed, where thinning refers to the spacing of a reinforcement schedule getting larger. Some support exists that a 30% decrease in reinforcement can be an efficient way to thin. Schedule thinning is often an important and neglected issue in contingency management and token economy systems, especially when developed by unqualified practitioners.

Generalization

Generalization is the expansion of a student's performance ability beyond the initial conditions set for acquisition of a skill. Generalization can occur across people, places, and materials used for teaching. For example, once a skill is learned in one setting, with a particular instructor, and with specific materials, the skill is taught in more general settings with more variation from the initial acquisition phase. For example, if a student has successfully mastered learning colours at the table, the teacher may take the student around the house or his school and then *generalize* the skill in these more natural environments with other materials. Behaviour analysts have spent considerable amount of time studying factors that lead to generalization.

Shaping

Shaping involves gradually modifying the existing behaviour into the desired behaviour. If the student engages with a dog by hitting it, then he or she could have their behaviour shaped by reinforcing interactions in which he or she touches the dog more gently. Over many interactions, successful shaping would replace the hitting behaviour with patting or other gentler behaviour. Shaping is based on a behaviour analyst's thorough knowledge of operant conditioning principles and extinction. Recent efforts to teach shaping have used simulated computer tasks.

Video Modelling

One teaching technique found to be effective with some students, particularly children, is the use of video modelling (the use of taped sequences as exemplars of behaviour). It can be used by therapists to assist in the acquisition of both verbal and motor responses, in some cases for long chains of behaviour.

Interventions based on an FBA

Critical to behaviour analytic interventions is the concept of a systematic behavioural case formulation with a functional behavioural assessment or analysis at the core. This approach should apply a behaviour analytic theory of change. This formulation should include a thorough functional assessment, a skills assessment, a sequential analysis (behaviour chain analysis), an ecological assessment, a look at existing evidenced-based behavioural models for the problem behaviour (such as Fordyce's model of chronic pain) and then a treatment plan based on how environmental factors influence behaviour. Some argue that behaviour analytic case formulation can be improved with an assessment of rules and rule-governed behaviour. Some of the interventions that result from this type of conceptualization involve training specific communication skills to replace the problem behaviours as well as specific setting, antecedent, behaviour, and consequence strategies.

Efficacy in Autism

ABA-based techniques are often used to treat autism, so much so that ABA itself is often mistakenly considered to be synonymous with therapy for autism. ABA for autism may be limited by diagnostic severity and IQ. The most influential and widely cited review of the literature regarding efficacy of treatments for Autism is the National Research Council's book *Educating Children with Autism* (2001) which clearly concluded that ABA was the best research supported and most effective treatment for the main characteristics of Autism. Some critics claimed that the NRC's report was an inside job by behaviour analysts but there were no board certified behaviour analysts on the panel (which did include physicians, speech pathologists, educators, psychologists, and others). Recent reviews of the efficacy of ABA-based techniques in autism include:

- A 2007 clinical report of the American Academy of Pediatrics concluded that the benefit of ABA-based interventions in autism spectrum disorders (ASDs) "has been well documented" and that "children who receive early intensive behavioural treatment have been shown to make substantial, sustained gains in IQ, language, academic performance, and adaptive behaviour as well as some measures of social behaviour."
- Researchers from the MIND Institute published an evidence-based review of comprehensive treatment approaches in 2008. On the basis of "the strength of the findings from the four best-designed, controlled studies," they were of the opinion that one ABA-based approach (the Lovaas technique created by Ole Ivar Lovaas) is "well-established" for improving intellectual performance of young children with ASD.
- A 2009 review of psycho-educational interventions for children with autism whose mean age was six years or less at intake found that five high-quality ("Level 1" or "Level 2") studies assessed ABA-based treatments. On the basis of these and other studies, the author concluded that ABA is "well-established" and is "demonstrated effective in enhancing global functioning in pre-school children with autism when treatment is intensive and carried out by trained therapists."
- A 2009 paper included a descriptive analysis, an effect size analysis, and a meta-analysis of 13 reports published from 1987–2007 of early intensive behavioural intervention (EIBI, a form of ABA-based treatment with origins in the Lovaas technique) for autism. It determined that EIBI's effect sizes were "generally positive" for IQ, adaptive behaviour, expressive language, and receptive language. The paper did note limitations of its findings including the lack of published comparisons between EIBI and other "empirically validated treatment programmes."
- In a 2009 systematic review of 11 studies published from 1987–2007, the researchers wrote "there is strong evidence that EIBI is effective for some, but not all, children with autism spectrum disorders, and there is wide variability in response to treatment." Furthermore, any improvements are likely to be greatest in the first year of intervention.
- A 2009 meta-analysis of nine studies published from 1987–2007 concluded that EIBI has a "large" effect on full-scale

intelligence and a “moderate” effect on adaptive behaviour in autistic children.

- In 2011, investigators from Vanderbilt University under contract with the Agency for Healthcare Research and Quality performed a comprehensive review of the scientific literature on ABA-based and other therapies for autism spectrum disorders; the ABA-based therapies included the UCLA/Lovaas method and the Early Start Denver Model (the latter developed by Sally Rogers and Geraldine Dawson). They concluded that “both approaches were associated with ... improvements in cognitive performance, language skills, and adaptive behaviour skills.” However, they also concluded that “the strength of evidence ... is low,” “many children continue to display prominent areas of impairment,” “subgroups may account for a majority of the change,” there is “little evidence of practical effectiveness or feasibility beyond research studies,” and the published studies “used small samples, different treatment approaches and duration, and different outcome measurements.”

A 2009 systematic review and meta-analysis by Spreckley and Boyd of four 2000–2007 studies (involving a total of 76 children) came to different conclusions than the aforementioned reviews. Spreckley and Boyd reported that applied behaviour intervention (ABI), another name for EIBI, did not significantly improve outcomes compared with standard care of preschool children with ASD in the areas of cognitive outcome, expressive language, receptive language, and adaptive behaviour. In a letter to the editor, however, authors of the four studies meta-analyzed claimed that Spreckley and Boyd had misinterpreted one study comparing two forms of ABI with each other as a comparison of ABI with standard care, which erroneously decreased the observed efficacy of ABI. Furthermore, the four studies' authors raised the possibility that Spreckley and Boyd had excluded some other studies unnecessarily, and that including such studies could have led to a more favourable evaluation of ABI. Spreckley, Boyd, and the four studies' authors did agree that large multi-site randomized trials are needed to improve the understanding of ABA's efficacy in autism.

Bibliography

Alberta Education: *From Position to Program: Building a Comprehensive School Guidance and Counselling Program: Planning and Resource Guide,* Edmonton, Alberta, Canada, 1995.

Aluede, O. O., Adomeh, I. O. C., & Afen-Akpaida, J. E.: *Education,* Winter, 2004.

Betz, N.: *Handbook of Counseling Psychology,* Wiley, NY, 2008.

Brigman, G., & Early, B.: *Group Counseling for School Counselors: A Practical Guide,* Walch, Portland, ME, 2001.

Brooks-McNamara, V., & Torres, D.: *The Reflective School Counselor's Guide to Practitioner Research: Skills and Strategies for Successful Inquiry,* Corwin Press, Thousand Oaks, CA, 2008.

Campbell, C. A., & Dahir, C. A.: *Sharing the Vision: The National Standards for School Counseling Programs,* American School Counselor Association, Alexandria, VA, 1997.

Chen-Hayes, S. F., Miller, E. M., Bailey, D. F., Getch, Y. Q., & Erford, B. T.: *Transforming the School Counseling Profession,* Pearson, Boston, MA, 2011.

Chen-Hayes, S. F., Saud Maxwell, K., & Bailey, D. F.: *Equity-based school Counseling: Ensuring Career and College Readiness for Every Student.* Microtraining Associates, Hanover, MA, 2009.

Dimmitt, C., Carey, J. C., & Hatch, T.: *Evidence-based School Counseling: Making a Difference with Data-driven Practices,* Corwin Press, Thousand Oaks, CA, 2007.

Fitzpatrick, C., & Costantini, K.: *Counseling 21st Century Students for Optimal College and Career Readiness: A 9th-12th Grade Curriculum,* Routledge, New York, NY, 2011.

Goodnough, G. E., Perusse, R., & Erford, B. T.: *Transforming the School Counseling Profession,* Pearson, Boston, 2011.

Hart, P. J., & Jacobi, M.: *From Gatekeeper to Advocate: Transforming the Role of the School Counselor,* College Entrance Examination Board, New York, 1992

Henderson, D. A. & Thompson, C. L.: *Counseling Children,* Brooks/Cole/ Cengage, New York, 2010.

Heppner, P., Leong, F.T.L., Chiao, H.: *Handbook of Counseling Psychology.* John Wiley & Sons: New York, 2008.

Hosenshil, T. H., Amundson, N. E., & Niles, S. G.: *Counseling Around the World: An International Handbook,* American Counseling Association, Alexandria, VA, 2013.

Hossler, D., Schmidt, J., & Vesper, N.: *Going to College: How Social, Economic, and Educational Factors Influence the Decisions Students Make,* Johns Hopkins University Press, Baltimore, 1998.

Johnson, J., Rochkind, J., Ott, A., & DuPont, S.: *Can I get a Little Advice here? How an Overstretched High School Guidance System is Undermining Students' College Aspirations,* Public Agenda, San Francisco, 2010.

Johnson, R. S.: *Using Data to Close the Achievement Gap: How to Measure Equity in our Schools,* Corwin, Thousand Oaks, CA, 2002.

Perusse, R., & Goodnough, G. E.: *Leadership, Advocacy, and Direct Service Strategies for Professional School Counselors,* Brooks/Cole, Belmont, CA, 2004.

Schellenberg, R.: *The School Counselor's Study Guide for Credentialing Exams,* Routledge, New York, 2012.

Stone, C. B., & Dahir, C. A.: *School Counselor Accountability: A MEASURE of Student Success,* Pearson, Boston, MA, 2011.

Studer, J. R.: *The Professional School Counselor: An Advocate for Students,* Wadsworth, Belmont, CA, 2005.

Weinbaum, A. T., Allen, D., Blythe, T., Simon, K., Seidel, S., & Rubin, C.: *Teaching as Inquiry: Asking Hard Questions to Improve Student Achievement,* Teachers College Press, New York, 2004.

Whiston, S.C. and Rahardja, D.: *Handbook of Counseling Psychology,* Wiley, NY, 2008.

Winslade, J. M., & Monk G. D.: *Narrative Counseling in Schools: Powerful and Brief,* Corwin Press, Thousand Oaks, CA, 2007.

Index

H

I

L

M

P

R

S

T

V

W

❑❑❑